Lilian M. Heath

Platform Pearls for Temperance Workers and other Reformers

A Collection of Recitations and other Selections for Entertainments and Public Meetings

Lilian M. Heath

Platform Pearls for Temperance Workers and other Reformers
A Collection of Recitations and other Selections for Entertainments and Public Meetings

ISBN/EAN: 9783337296568

Printed in Europe, USA, Canada, Australia, Japan

Cover: Foto ©Suzi / pixelio.de

More available books at **www.hansebooks.com**

PLATFORM PEARLS

FOR

TEMPERANCE WORKERS AND OTHER REFORMERS

A Collection of Recitations and Other Selections for Entertainments and Public Meetings; especially adapted for Christian Endeavor Societies, Prohibition Clubs, Loyal Temperance Legions, Women's Christian Temperance Unions, etc., etc., etc.

COMPILED BY
LILIAN M. HEATH

NEW YORK
FUNK & WAGNALLS COMPANY
LONDON AND TORONTO
1896

PREFACE.

(OVERHEARD BY ACCIDENT.)

The Public: "Who comes here?"

Answer: "It is I, Platform Pearls, just arrived and looking for my friends. Can you direct me to them?"

The Public: "Perhaps, if you will give me their names."

Platform Pearls: "To save time, I'll give you their initials, for I am sure you must know them all: Y. P. S. C. E., W. C. T. U., Y. W. C. T. U., C. L. S. C., Y. M. C. A., Y. W. C. A., L. T. L., I. O. G. T., Proh—"

The Public (impatiently): "Hold on, hold on, that's enough for the present. Do you expect me to believe all that? Where did you come from?"

Platform Pearls: "From the North, the South, the East, the West; from Michigan, Indiana, Ohio, Illinois, Mississippi, Missouri, Pennsylvania, New York, Connecticut, Maine; from the mountains, the cities, and the islands of the sea; from foreign lands and from the Hub of the solar system; from every corner where there are pearls worth gathering."

The Public: "Well, well, you are quite a traveler. What brings you here, and what do you intend to do, having arrived?"

Platform Pearls: "I came because they said I was needed, and I intend to —"

The Public: "But who are 'they'?"

Platform Pearls: "Jessie A. Ackerman, Belle Kearney, Mattie McClellan Brown, Dr. Mary Wood Allen, Lou J. Beauchamp, Margaret B. Ellis, E. J. Wheeler, Clara C. Hoffman, and other national temperance workers; so many, indeed, that you would not have patience to hear me through the list. Now, as to my aims: First of all, I wish to create a channel through which the enthusiastic young people can help in the grandest reform of the age. Next, I would bring stirring words of truth to arouse the Christian Church to meet its glorious opportunity for progress. Then I would enlist every college on the side of right, and help students to convince others, through the words of our greatest orators and statesmen. past and present. I would place a ready weapon in the hands of temperance soldiers, by giving facts and figures showing that licensing sin does not pay. I would cultivate the gift of oratory, by making myself indispensable at medal contests. I would arouse the true spirit of patriotism. I have short, easy 'pieces' for the little ones, and carefully classified selections for the departments of the W. C. T. U., not forgetting the Departments of Mercy and of Peace and Arbitration. And in all this I would keep ever in view the value of time, and have therefore a special topical index, that each busy worker or student may readily find what is best adapted to the occasion. In such ways I would, with your kind permission, be helpful to those who are seeking to uplift the world."

The Public: "If you can do all this, you are indeed just what is needed. But how am I to know that what you say is true? And aren't you a little egotistical and over-ambitious — not to say conceited — for a new-comer?"

Platform Pearls: "If I seem so, it is because I have tried to answer your questions. The one who sent me would give me no introduction, but said I must speak for myself, and I have done so. Suppose you kindly read me through, and *then* judge." L. M. H.

TABLE OF CONTENTS.

(For List of Authors see page xi, and for Topical Index see page 241.)

	No.
"Abou Ben Adhem," *Caroline Spencer*	147
All the Rights She Wants, *Carl Spencer*	93
American Desert, *John G. Woolley*	16
Anti-Suffragist's Lament, *Hattie Horner Louthan*	25
Appeal for the Home, *Mrs. Jessie Brown Hilton*	132
Arsenal at Springfield, *H. W. Longfellow*	125
Baby Shoes, *Helen Josephine Baker*	15
Back to His Chrysalis, *Charlotte Perkins Stetson*	23
Battle Rally, *George A. Fish*	53
Big Four, *Sam Walter Foss*	140
Boundary Post, *Lelia B. Hewes*	57
Brand of Cain, *The Voice*	26
Calf Path, *Sam Walter Foss*	158
Case for Charity, *Hattie Horner Louthan*	99
Case of "Personal Liberty," *E. J. Wheeler*	28
Certainty of Progress, *Wendell Phillips*	20
Christian Endeavorer's Position, *John G. Woolley*	60
Columbia, *Fannie E. Ostrander*	29
Coming Era, *Leon Mead*	27
Compulsory Morality, *Horace Greeley*	119
Conscience Crystallized, *John G. Woolley*	153
Core of the Rum Question, *Horace Greeley*	86
Cost of a License, *Mrs. A. A. Rolfe*	13
Curtain Lecture, *Union Signal*	82
Cut Down the Tree, *Rev. Dr. Wm. H. Boole*	77
Dawn of Mercy, *Mary F. Lovell*	100
Deacon Beery's Protest, *Home Gazette*	72
Deacon's Match, *John P. St. John*	56
Decoration Day — 1882, *Thomas H. Burgess*	144
Difference, The, *Rev. J. C. Fernald*	103
Does it Pay? *T. V. Powderly*	94
Don't Sell Your Conscience, *Henry Ward Beecher*	10
"Dorlesky's Errents," *Josiah Allen's Wife*	74
Dreaming and Waking, *Lucy Larcom*	51
Drink, *Translated by H. G.*	63
Effect of Moral Cowardice, *Francis Wayland*	90
Eve's Recompense, *Mabel R. Winter*	73
Exactly of a Size, *Rev. P. J. Bull*	85
Expression, *M. McClellan Brown*	1
Faith and Liberty, *Rev. Joseph Cook*	37
Fanatic, A, *Maria L. Underhill*	61
Farmer and His Gun, *Tallie Morgan*	133
Father's Woe, A, *Helen M. Gougar*	155
"Feed My Sheep," *B. E. S.*	43
First Duty of Citizens, *Archbishop John Ireland*	40
First Reform, *John Lloyd Thomas*	83
Flower Mission, *Mary T. Lathrap*	104
Forces of Battle, *Rev. Dr. J. H. Ecob*	42
For God and Home, *E. H. Chace*	123
Four Million "Christian" Murderers, *E. J. Wheeler*	139
Fundamental Reform, *Bolton Hall*	98
Funeral To-Day, *Helen M. Gougar*	164
General Neal Dow, *Wm. Grant Brooks*	87
Getting at the Root, *Belle Kearney*	150
Give Them Justice, *John B. Finch*	88
Glorious Monument, *Prof. Chas. W. Sanders*	62
Gold of Right Habits, *Jessie F. Houser*	5

viii   TABLE OF CONTENTS.

	No.
Great Advance, *Rev. Dr. I. K. Funk*	166
Greatest Missionary Need, *A. Morehouse*	102
Great Problem, *Mrs. Nettie B. Fernald*	112
Ground Out by a Crank, *C. M., in The Voice*	134
House that Sam Built, *L. A. E. Stikeleather*	7
"If," *Wm. Howard*	75
Indictment, *John B. Finch*	39
"I've Got It!" *Lorin Ludlow*	65
Jug an' Me an' Jim, The, *Eleanor Mayfield*	17
Just the Same, *Every Day Church*	142
Land of Prohibition, *Mrs. Harrison Lee*	66
Lead the Boy	152
Letter Exercise, *Eva Jones*	148
Level of Civilization, *Wendell Phillips*	101
Liberty, *Mrs. L. E. Bailey*	145
Liquor and Wages, *C. De F. Hoxie*	96
Little Girl's Advice, *Union Signal*	149
Loyal Temperance Legion, *Mary T. Lathrap*	108
Mainspring of Triumph, *Chas. Sumner*	8
Master Calleth, The, *Frances E. Willard*	114
Merry Christmas, *The Voice*	97
Midnight Scenes, *Jessie A. Ackerman*	128
Moaning of the Bar, *E. J. Wheeler*	9
Moral Suasion, *Rev. Thos. Dixon*	58
Moral Warfare, *J. G. Whittier*	137
Mothers who Wear the Ribbon, *Harriet Francene Crocker*	151
Mussulman's View, *H. G. McKay*	6
Nation Exalted, *Lilian M. Heath*	172
Nectar of the Hills, *T. De Witt Talmage*	67
New Song of Sixpence, *Mrs. N. S. Kitchel*	110
Not a Mushroom Party, *J. J. Ashenhurst*	52
Not from My Bottle, *Hattie Horner*	3
On a Lehigh Valley Train, *Tallie Morgan*	157
On Certain Adjectives, *Amos Wells*	127
One Beauty of Civilization, *Rev. Chas. R. Kingsley*	129
Only Conclusion, *Archbishop John Ireland*	22
Our Beneficent License Laws, *Rufus C. Landon*	41
Our Watchword—Union! *Chas. Sumner*	14
Patriot's Ally, *Mary H. Hunt*	106
Peace Hymn of the Republic, *James Whitcomb Riley*	131
People's Voice, A, *J. G. Whittier*	154
"Personal Liberty" Cry, *Prof. Samuel Dickie*	80
Place in Heaven, *National W. C. T. U. Department of Mercy*	79
Politician's Wail, *Edna C. Jackson*	120
Power of Righteous Law, *Rev. Dr. E. H. Chapin*	111
Practise vs. Professions, *Erie Conference*	91
Prayer, *Rev. Dr. Chas. F. Deems*	113
Present Crisis, *James Russell Lowell*	81
Prohibition's Bugle Call, *Lide Meriwether*	78
Puzzled Santa Claus, *Alice M. Guernsey*	161
Queer, isn't it?, *Hattie Horner Louthan*	55
Question for Patriots, *E. J. Wheeler*	12
Quest Magnificent, *Lelia Belle Hewes*	21
Record of Non-Partisanship, *A. R. Heath*	160
Red Niagara, *Charles S. Morris*	32
Reformer, The, *J. G. Whittier*	43
Remedy within Reach, *Clara C. Hoffman*	130
Responsibility of Voters, *Henry Ward Beecher*	45
Run up the Flag, *Rev. Dr. Wm. H. Boole*	138
Sailor Lad, *Olive Harper*	122
Saint Monacella's Lambs, *Wm. C. A. Axon*	167
Same Old Swing, *Edna C. Jackson*	54
Self-Government, *John B. Finch*	85
Sense vs. License, *Horace Greeley*	18
Sermon in a Saw-mill, *Rev. D. R. Miller*	88
Shall Mothers Vote?, *Rollo Kirk Bryan*	126
Short Story, *Tallie Morgan*	141
Shovel Out, *Almon Trask Allis*	33
Silence in the Churches, *John G. Woolley*	171

Table of Contents.

	No.
Simon Grub's Dream, *Western Humane Journal*	146
Six Boys, *A. W. Hawks*	48
Song of Hope, *Mary A. Lathbury*	162
Song of Martyrdom, *O. F. B.*	76
Song of the Hour, *Fred. Lawrence Knowles*	2
Song of the Sot, *Henry W. Holloway*	11
Speechless, The, *Anna Drury*	70
Stamp it Out, *Petroleum V. Nasby*	4
Stand Firm, *Geo. Newell Lovejoy*	64
Supreme Curse, *B. O. Flower*	69
Temperance Army, *Mrs. Haycraft*	121
Temperance Education Law, *Hon. Byron M. Cutcheon*	107
Temperance Revolution, *Abraham Lincoln*	30
Terrors of Eviction, *Henry W. Grady*	109
That's the Question, *The Constitution*	135
Three Views of a Whisky Bottle, *Ingersoll, Buckley, and Heath*	34
To-morrow, *Gerald Massey*	95
Tower of Shame, *W. A. Greenwood*	124
Tramp's Views, A, *Lou J. Beauchamp*	31
Twisting and Turning, *Rev. P. J. Bull*	46
Unfortunate Trellis, *John G. Woolley*	44
Vessel in Danger, *Rev. Dr. Wm. H. Boole*	36
Victor, The, *M. A. Holt*	19
Voice of a Star, *Will Carleton*	168
Voice of Science, *Dr. B. W. Richardson*	118
Vot der Voomans haf Ton, *Jennie Fleming*	24
Voting vs. Resolving, *J. W. Rowe*	47
Wanted — A Boy, *Indiana Phalanx*	159
Wanted — True Men, *The Quest*	136
War God, The, *Alice May Douglas*	165
Warning, *Edmund Burke*	89
Weakness of Local Option, *Belle Kearney*	133
What Do You Care? *I. F. B. Tinling*	71
What is Faith? *John B. Gough*	105
What J. M. B. Thinks, *Katharine Lente Stevenson*	50
What will the Farmer Do? *The Voice*	116
Which are You? *Ella Wheeler Wilcox*	92
Whisky Deacon, *Rev. P. J. Bull*	84
White Heat, *Rev. J. C. Fernald*	169
White Ribbon Army, *Marian W. Hubbard*	117
White Ribbon Banner, *Kate Lunden*	156
Why? *Hattie Horner Louthan*	68
Woman's Answer, A, *Mary T. Lathrap*	143
Woman's Hour, *Mary T. Lathrap*	170
Word to the Y's, *Frances J. Barnes*	115
Worried About Katherine, *Will Carleton*	59

LIST OF AUTHORS.

Name	No.
Ackerman, Jessie A	128
Allis, Almon Trask	33
Ashenhurst, J. J	52
Axon, Wm. C. A	167
Bailey, Mrs L. E	145
Baker, Helen Josephine	15
Barnes, Frances J	115
Beauchamp, Lou J	31
Beecher, Henry Ward	10, 45
B. E. S.	49
Boole, Rev. Dr. Wm. H.	36, 77, 128
Brooks, Wm. Grant	57
Brown, Mattie McClellan	1
Bryan, Rollo Kirk	126
Buckley, Rev. Dr. J. M.	24
Bull, Rev. P. J.	35, 46, 84
Burgess, Thos. H.	144
Burke, Edmund	69
Carleton, Will	59, 108
Chace, E. H.	123
Chapin, Rev. Dr. E. H.	111
C. M.	134
Cook, Rev. Joseph	37
Crocker, Harriet Francene	151
Cutcheon, Hon. Byron M.	107
Deems, Rev. Dr. Chas. F.	113
Dickie, Prof. Samuel	80
Dixon, Rev. Thos.	58
Douglas, Alice May	105
Drury, Anna	70
Ecob, Rev. Dr. J. H.	42
Fernald, Mrs. Nettie B	112
Fernald, Rev. J. C	103, 169
Finch, John B.	39, 85, 88
Fish, George A	53
Fleming, Jennie	24
Flower, B. O.	69
Foss, Sam Walter	140, 158
Funk, Rev. Dr. I. K.	166
Gougar, Helen M	155, 164
Gough, John B.	105
Grady, Henry W	109
Greeley, Horace	18, 86, 119
Greenwood, W. A	124
Guernsey, Alice M.	161
Hall, Bolton	98
Harper, Olive	122
Hawks, A. W	48
Haycraft, Mrs.	121
Heath, A. R.	34, 160
Heath, Lillian M	172
Hewes, Leilia B.	21, 57
H. G.	63
Hilton, Mrs. Jessie Brown	132
Hoffman, Clara C	130
Holloway, Henry W	11
Holt, M. A.	19
Horner, Hattie	3
Houser, Jessie F	5
Howard, Wm	75
Hoxie, C. De F.	96
Hubbard, Marian W	117
Hunt, Mary H	106
Ingersoll, Robert G	34
Ireland, Archbishop John	22, 40
Jackson, Edna C	54, 120
Jones, Eva	148
"Josiah Allen's Wife"	74
Kearney, Belle	133, 150
Kingsley, Rev. Chas. R.	129
Kitchel, Mrs. N. S.	110
Knowles, Fred Lawrence	2
Landon, Rufus C	41
Larcom, Lucy	51
Lathbury, Mary A	162
Lathrap, Mary T.	104, 106, 143, 170
Lee, Mrs. Harrison	66
Lincoln, Abraham	80
Longfellow, H. W.	125
Louthan, Hattie Horner	25, 55, 68, 99
Lovejoy, Geo. Newell	64
Lovell, Mrs. Mary F	100
Lowell, James Russell	61
Ludlow, Lorin	65
Lunden, Kate	156
McKay, H. G.	6
Massey, Gerald	95
Mayfield, Eleanor	17
Mead, Leon	27
Meriwether, Lide	78
Miller, Rev. D. R.	38
Morehouse, A.	102
Morgan, Tallie	141, 157, 163
Morris, Charles S.	32
Nasby, Petroleum V	4
O. F. B.	76
Ostrander, Fannie E	20
Phillips, Wendell	20, 101
Powderly, T. V	94
Richardson, Dr. B. W.	118
Riley, James Whitcomb	131
Rolfe, Mrs. A. A.	13
Rowe, J. W.	47
St. John, John P	56
Sanders, Prof. Chas. W	62
Spencer, Carl	92
Spencer, Caroline	147
Stetson, Charlotte Perkins	23
Stevenson, Katherine Lente	50
Stikeleather, L. A. E.	7
Sumner, Chas	8, 14
Talmage, T. DeWitt	67
Thomas, John Lloyd	83
Tinling, I. F. B.	71
Underhill, Maria L.	61
Wayland, Francis	90
Wells, Amos	127
Wheeler, E. J.	9, 12, 28, 139
Whittier, J. G.	43, 137, 154
Wilcox, Ella Wheeler	92
Willard, Frances E	111
Winter, Mabel R	73
Woolley, John G.	16, 44, 60, 153, 172

PLATFORM PEARLS.

1. EXPRESSION.*

Great powers of thought can not be satisfied with crude forms of expression. The best workmanship, like the highest art, traces its incentives to the same potency. The supreme end of all genius as well as art, is expression. The inspiration of the poet, the infatuation of the scientist, the devotion of the sculptor, the thrill of the musician, the ardor of the architect, as well as the fervor and fire of the orator, are moved by the same inner relation to nature, to truth, and to God. All their passions are begotten of soul-germs, vitalizing energies of life. All great deeds are born of that imperative power which moves men and nations to creative expressions.

Some have found their prize in the painting of immortal pictures that hang on the soul-walls of time immemorial. Some in marbles, which like Angelo's Moses and David "speak" to the admiring art lovers of the centuries between. Some in architecture, like the Duomo at Milan which bespeaks a thousand indulgences to eternal life, for twenty years' gratuitous toil on its marvelous beauty. Some in poetry, like the sublime Milton, the majestic Shakespeare, and the sweet-toned Burns and Tennyson. Some in music, like Handel's Messiah, rushing "as a refiner's fire," leaping from the touch of a live coal from the inner altar of God.

Some find life's expression in the more material world, and Cyrus W. Field in the Atlantic cable was as truly passionate as was Rosa Bonheur in the portrayal of muscular animal force in the celebrated "Horse Fair." And what shall we say of the passion play of the naif Edison, as a virile human candlestick to the scientific world, a very comrade of the sun?

In all these, however, there is wanting that touch of divinity which attends the power of oratory. This form of expression is super-material in a sense which the others are not. It works its wonders on the sensitive nature of souls, in impressions which live in conduct, glow in character, and burn in

---
* From an address delivered at the presentation of a medal at an Independent Medal Contest, at Fairview, Ohio, Aug. 27, 1895.

spirit. It breaks all bars of the intellect. It liberates the spirit, by whatever heretofore bound. And the man is free. His step is ela·tic. His movement is firm and quick. He is all vital, "as if he stood on a mountain and was himself a hundred cubits high."

I am glad the youth of our country are so greatly helped in the acquisition of this power of expression. The time for its use draws nigh. The very energy of preparation in our country is a prophecy of the demand for the service of oratory. God speaks to His own through His own, by just such public inspirations. By this movement the country is prepared for a coming ordeal. Let it come. And let all be ready. The institutions of our country are rocking in the throes of a tremendous growth. Dormant principles struggle to be free. It is not every age that is called to the summits of progress to witness a test of Truth. God answers by fire. Truly the times are aglow with the dawn of His coming. Sentiment mounts to principle, principle to action. Presently character must leap from the volcanic hearts of patriots in spontaneous force of oratory. That day will set men free.

The inimitable Chatham once pictured to parliament the inviolable sanctity of the English home. "The poorest man," said he, "may in his cottage bid defiance to all the forces of the Crown. It may be frail — its roof may shake — the wind may blow through it — the storm may enter — but the King of England may not enter. All his forces dare not cross the threshhold of the ruined tenement."

The sanctity of American homes mourns, with flag at half mast, for want of such orators in Congress. The government's revenue partner, Rum, enters the sacred precincts of homes innumerable, without possible recourse for the victims. How long, oh, Lord, how long? Wake, ye voices of Pitt, of Mirabeau, of Brougham, of Clay, of Webster, of Choate, of Gough, of Finch. When such patriots rise to speak it shall be done. When they command, the law shall stand fast. For such oratory is the word of life to a nation. It is the assimilation of thought, action, and character. Its fruit is righteousness — right doing — the crown of life. And this glory shall come with the ripeness of this period of contests. The full, ripe time of God.

—*Mattie McClellan Brown.*

2. A SONG OF THE HOUR.

Men of might,
Once again for freedom fight !
  Children of the dusky race,
  Men of every rank and place,
Put the hostile hordes to flight !

Smite them low,
Midst the liquor's crimson flow !
  Back from every cursed shrine
  Hurl the votaries of wine ;
Let them feel they have a foe !

Struggle well,
In the teeth of shot and shell !
  In the fury of the storm
  Sound the war-cry of reform,
Shout defiance back to hell !

Wave on high
Banners bluer than the sky,
  Signals redder than the flood
  That is fed by martyr's blood ;
Let their folds triumphant fly !

*   *   *   *   *   *   *

God has come !
Tell it in the rolling drum ;
  See Him in his awful wrath
  Hunting on the bloody path ;
See Him strike His foemen dumb !

We shall win
O'er the ranks of crime and sin !
  Evil ever yields to right,
  Day has always followed night,
Vice has ne'er victorious been.

Far away
Gleam the first long lines of day !
  Darkness like a shroud is drawn
  Backward from the brow of dawn.
Gloria tibi Dominie !

       —*Fred Lawrence Knowles.*

3. NOT FROM MY BOTTLE.

"We must be polite," and "sometimes we must treat—"
    Not from *my* bottle, oh, no!
And some men "will have it" whenever they meet—
    Not from *my* bottle, oh, no!
The saloon may go on, and my vote may be lost,
My influence, too, may not count with the host,
And liquor be bought at whatever the cost—
    But not from *my* bottle, no, no!

"But all men are free, sir, to drink if they choose—"
    Not from *my* bottle, oh, no!
"'Twill be sold on the sly, and the license we'll lose—"
    But not from *my* bottle, oh, no!
The ladies may sip and the boys learn to drink,
And men stagger down unto Hell's awful brink,
And rum may flow on till all Christendom sink—
    Not from *my* bottle, no, no!

"It will always be drunk, tho a few may oppose—"
    Not from *my* bottle, oh, no!
"There is more sold than ever as each season goes—"
    Not from *my* bottle, oh, no!
"'Tis useless," they say, " you're a fraction so slight."
Perhaps. But the fraction at least will be right.
And God will reward him who all through the fight
    Cried: "*Not from* MY *bottle, oh, no!*
                              —*Hattie Horner.*

4. STAMP IT OUT.

    License throws no shield over the helpless wife, or the hungry child. It leaves the State with the regular burden of lunatics and paupers. The mill grinds on just the same, and the never-ending grist of fresh humanity, with capabilities for good, goes into the hopper, and out comes the horrible product of lunatics, paupers, and criminals, just the same.

    The wail of the worse than widow, the cry of the starved and suffering child goes to heaven, but human fatuity has interposed the shield of "regulation" and no answer comes—Regulation, forsooth! Can the vitiated appetite of the boy be "regulated"? Is there any way to regulate the man or boy who has implanted within himself an appetite which has taken from him every particle of will power? Can you save a man with a fever in any other way than to remove the cause of the fever? "Regulation?" Do you want to take a census to enumerate your children and say, "I will so regulate this evil that this child shall be mine and that one the saloon-keeper's?" In brief, do you want to perpetuate an evil, or do you want to kill it? If the rum power really owns the State and community, in God's name let it have its way in peace. If it does not, if humanity has any rights, if the State and the family have any claim to be considered, let the law assert itself, and stamp it out. —*Petroleum V. Nasby, in North American Review.*

5. THE GOLD OF RIGHT HABITS.

This bi-chloride treatment of gold, my dear boy,
   Of which in the papers we read,
Will doubtless bring joy into homes full of woe,
   And balm to some hearts which now bleed;
For many a man, who is traveling down
   The hill that most surely will lead
To death and destruction, will grasp at this gold,
   As drowning men grasp at a reed.

But gold can be taken in childhood, my boy,
   Which works in a far surer way;
The gold of right habits, pure thoughts and desires,—
   Bright bands, growing brighter each day;
The gold which is sent from the Father above,
   To shield from the tempter's hard sway,
Each boy, who will take up his stand for the right,
   And not for one moment delay.

So seek for this gold in your springtime, dear boy,
   This wisdom and strength from on high;
Then safely you'll walk through the years that will come,
   Though many a pitfall be nigh;
For God sends His angel to camp round that boy,
   Who dares to stand firm, tho he die,
And leads him through all of the dangers of youth,
   Up, up, to that home in the sky.

—*Jessie F. Houser.*

6. THE MUSSULMAN'S VIEW.

He was a converted Mussulman, and had come to America to complete studies prior to doing missionary work in his native country. Like all foreigners, he was inquisitive, and for some time had been keeping a prominent minister busy explaining the characteristics of this country.

Suddenly, one day he exclaimed: "What is the nature of this strong drink, alcohol, I hear so much about? In all Mohammedan countries it is practically unknown."

"Alcohol! Alcohol!" thundered the illustrious divine in reply. "It is a deadly poison, and is commonly used as a stimulant in this country; but with it alone 240,000 saloon-keepers annually kill over 60,000 people, and incite others to commit nine-tenths of the crime committed in this country."

"Then ought not these saloon-keepers, whom you style murderers, to be punished like other criminals?"

"Well, hardly. You see, by paying a certain sum they secure from the judges of our courts a legal right to poison their fellow men."

"Oh, then the judges are the responsible parties?"

"Not exactly. The judges are only the interpreters of the law, and are required to grant licenses to the proper applicants."

"I see. Then the prime instigators of all this crime are the legislators of the several States? But why do the people not only permit these murderers to remain in office, but, year after year, reelect them,— knowing, as they do, that permission will be given for the continuation of this damnable traffic?"

That is the question. Voters of this nation, think on these things!" —*H. G. McKay.*

---

7. THE HOUSE THAT SAM BUILT.

[A Government Distillery.]

This is the house that Sam built.

[The Distiller.]

This is the man
Who says that he can
Manage the house that Sam built.

[Whisky.]

This is the drink

(How sad to think!)
That is made by the man
Who swears that he can
Manage the house that Sam built.

[Legislators, Magistrates, Commissioners, etc.]

These are the law-makers,
Really law-breakers,
Who license the drink
(How sad to think!)
That is made by the man
Who swears that he can
Manage the house that Sam built.

[Democrats, Republicans, etc., many of them preachers, church members, and professing Christians.]

Then here are the people,
Some of whom worship
Under the church steeple!
And then cast their ballots
For these law-makers,
Really law-breakers,
That license the drink
(How sad to think!)
That is made by the man
Who swears that he can
Manage the house that Sam built.

[There are 700,000 drunkards in this country, made so by Uncle Sam's civilized (?) whisky.]

Alas! these are the drunkards,
Made so by the people,
Some of whom worship
Under the church steeple,
And then cast their ballots
For the law-makers,
Truly law-breakers,
That license the drink
(How sad to think!)
That is made by the man
That swears that he can
Manage the house that Sam built.

[Children, Mothers, Wives, etc.]

>Look at the children,
>Sad-eyed and dreary,
>The mothers and wives,
>Broken-hearted and weary,
>Of the men who are drunkards,
>Made so by the people ;
>Some of whom worship
>Under the steeple,
>And then cast their ballots
>For these law-makers,
>Really law-breakers,
>That license the drink
>(How sad to think !)
>That is made by the man
>Who swears that he can
>Manage the house that Sam built.
>
>—*L. A. E. Stikeleather.*

8. MAINSPRING OF TRIUMPH.[*]

I hear the old political saw, that "we must take the least of two evils." . . . For myself, if two evils are presented to me, I will take neither. There are occasions of political difference, I admit, when it may become expedient to vote for a candidate who does not completely represent our sentiments. There are matters legitimately within the range of expediency and compromise. The Tariff and the Currency are of this character. If a candidate differs from me on these more or less, I may yet vote for him. But the question before the country is of another character. This will not admit of compromise. It is not within the domain of expediency. To be wrong on this is to be wrong wholly. It is not merely expedient for us to defend Freedom when assailed, but our duty so to do, unreservedly, and careless of consequences. . . .

But it is said that we shall throw away our votes, and that our opposition shall fail. Fail, sir ! No honest, earnest effort in a good cause can fail. It may not be crowned with applause of men ; it may not seem to touch the goal of immediate worldly success, which is the end and aim of so much in life. But it is not lost. It helps to strengthen the weak with new

---

[*] From an address delivered June 28, 1848.

virtue—to arm the irresolute with proper energy—to animate all with devotion to duty, which in the end conquers all. Fail! Did the martyrs fail when with precious blood they sowed the seed of the church? Did the discomfited champions of Freedom fail, who have left those names in history that can never die? Did the three hundred Spartans fail, when in the narrow pass they did not fear to brave the innumerable Persian hosts, whose very arrows darkened the sun? Overborne by numbers, crushed to earth, they left an example greater far than any victory. And this is the least we can do. Our example will be the mainspring of triumph hereafter.

—*Charles Sumner.*

9. THE MOANING OF THE BAR.

Young 'Lijah was a likely lad,
  Upon a farm he grew;
He stood beside the bars at eve
  And watched the cows come through.

The farm became too slow for him,
  He sought the town afar;
And soon again, we grieve to say,
  Was standing by the bar.

There gathered round him "jolly friends,"
  As still such friends there are;
He soon assumed the next degree,
  "The prisoner at the bar."

He hears no more the low of kine,
  Nor sees the evening stars,
A sadder and a wiser youth,
  He stands behind the bars.

—*E. J. Wheeler.*

10. DON'T SELL YOUR CONSCIENCE.

Let us have firm courage, kindness of temper, willingness to make concessions in things of mere policy, but no concession of principles, no yielding of moral convictions, no paltering with our consciences. Thirty pieces of silver bought Christ and hung Judas. If you sell your convictions to Fear, you give yourself to a vagabond. If you sell your conscience to Interest, you traffic with a fiend. The fear of doing right is the grand treason in times of danger. When you consent to give up your convictions of justice, humanity, and liberty for the sake of tranquillity, you are like men who buy a treacherous truce of tyrants by giving up their weapons of war. Cowards are the food of despots.

When a storm is on the deep, and the ship labors, men throw over the deck-load; they cast forth the heavy freight, and ride easier as their merchandise grows less. But in our time men propose to throw overboard the compass, the charts, the chronometers and sextant, but to keep the freight!

For the sake of a principle our fathers dared to defy the proudest nation on the globe. They suffered. They conquered. We are never tired of praising them. But when we are called to stand firm for a principle, we tremble, we whine, we evade duty, we shuffle up a compromise by which we may sell our conscience and save our pocket.

—Henry Ward Beecher.

11. THE SONG OF THE SOT.

His clothes quite shabby and worn,
   And nose with blotches red,
A toper sat, with trembling hand,
   Supporting his dizzy head.
He drinks! drinks! drinks!
   And makes his life a blot;
His voice grows faint, and he more sad,
   Mumbling this "Song of the Sot."

"I drink! drink! drink!
   In the early hours of morn;
And drink! drink! drink!
   Till I feel so sad and lorn.
And why am I such a slave?
   Why make my life a curse?
Why drink so much, and brawl and rave,
   And go from bad to worse?

"I drink! drink! drink!
   Till my head begins to swim;
And drink! drink! drink!
   Till eyes are heavy and dim.
In sorrow, in want, in shame,

In shame and want and sorrow,
I drink and loaf the live-long day,
And do the same to-morrow.

"O men, with mothers fond !
O men, with sisters and wives !
You thus mar not merely your own,
But some other people's lives.
I drink ! drink ! drink !
In sorrow, want, and shame ;
I ruin myself, disgrace my kin,
And blast my name and fame.

"But why do I speak of fame,
When my life is blank and drear ?
Why talk so glibly of name,
Which I'd sell for a glass of beer ?
I might and should be a man,
But drink has marred my career ;
Has chilled my heart, benumbed my brain,
Till life is void of cheer.

"I drink ! drink ! drink !
But it does not slake my thirst ;
It burns my throat ; and oh ! my head :
It aches as if 'twould burst !
Look at my home ! which ought to glow
With bloom of health and cheer ;
Dear ones are sick, the stock is low ;
They're feeling want, I fear.

"I drink ! drink ! drink !
Till money and health are gone ;
And drink ! drink ! drink !
Till I'm lean and lank and wan.
My friends of yore, with haughty mien,
Pass by, with scarce a nod ;
They now regard my life, I ween,
As worth no more than a clod.

" If I had but one short hour,
A respite, e'en thus brief,
Would give some time for love and hope
To ease my load of grief.

> But my thirst for drink's so great —
> I yearn for the sparkling bowl —
> It must be quenched, in spite of fate,
> If I had to sell my soul."
>
> His clothes quite shabby and worn,
> And nose with blotches red,
> A toper sat, with trembling hand,
> Supporting his dizzy head.
> He drinks! drinks! drinks!
> And makes his life a blot;
> In a voice of gloom as drear as a pall
> He sang this "Song of the Sot."
>
> —*Henry W. Holloway.*

12. THE QUESTION FOR PATRIOTS.

Patriots of America, do you want this Government run by the gin-mills? That is the question of the present and of the future. All this prating about "personal liberty" is to avoid that thundering inquiry. The saloons are in control of every strategic point in politics. Find us, if you can, a leading politician in either old party that dares to stand out in the open air and tell the public that the saloon is a curse to our civilization. They know it is a curse and in their hearts they despise it; but they know too that it would break their political necks in a twinkling if they dared to make such an utterance. Every "boss" in American politics, from Tweed down, has been a "boss" by reason alone of his control over slum elements, and the statesmen who are guiding the destinies of America to-day are statesmen chosen for their inoffensiveness or positive friendliness to the liquor power. The 240,000 gin-mills of this land, if each controls but ten votes or is the medium through which ten votes are to be "influenced," would swing a vote of 2,400,000, and they can do it and will do it at any time for "boodle." The Prætorian Guard of Rome offering the emperorship of the world to the highest bidder hardly equaled the scene in this loved land in which the saloons, organized by counties, by States, and nationally, auction off political favors to the biggest "barrel."

Men say they don't think it hurts to drink a glass of beer once in a while. But does it hurt to have this country run by the gin-mills? That is the question. Any man who cares more for his occasional glass of wine or beer than he cares for decent government, is a man who is in imminent danger of spending to-morrow night in the gutter or the station house. Men say, "liquor doesn't hurt me"; but does it hurt them to have the government run by the gin-mills and to have gin-mill politicians decree legislation for the greatest Republic of all time?

The only way to get rid of saloon rule and saloon politics is by getting rid of the saloons. And the only way to get rid of the saloons is to vote into power the only party that says

The saloon must go!

—E. J. Wheeler.

13. THE COST OF A LICENSE.

Little Willie came in with a glowing face,
And his questioning eyes showed just a trace
Of excitement and, may be, of envy, too,
In their sunny depths so sweet and blue.
And he said, as his curls from his brow he tossed,
"Auntie! what is a license, and what does it cost?
Ned Baker's father, he told me at play,
Was going to buy a license to-day.
Papa's as rich as the Bakers, I know,
Why couldn't we have a license, too?"

O'er her soul there swept a cold, dread wave,
Such as we feel by a yawning grave—
A look of terror stole into her face;
She clasped the child in a close embrace,
As if she feared that he might be lost.
"I don't know just what licenses cost,
But the license that Baker will buy, I think,
Is a license to sell his neighbors drink.
Fifty dollars, I think, that Ephraim Stone
Paid for one in days that are gone.
I paid more, ten thousand times,
Tho 'twas not all in dollars and dimes.
My husband, your granduncle, Cyrus Jones,
Used to go over to Ephraim Stone's,
At first just to pass an hour away
And hear what others might have to say.
But, by and by, he began to drink;
Oh, my heart grows sick when I stop to think

How the dark storm gathered as time went by,
Till no light was left in my life's dull sky.
Slowly hope was crushed, for never more
Could I trust and believe as I did before.
  "But there were the children, Bessie and Jack,
And I hoped for a time they might win him back.
Sometimes remorse would o'er him sweep,
And he'd promise while I would pray and weep
That for the sake of those children and me
He would be the man that he used to be;
And that meant much — never prouder wife
Than I till that license wrecked my life.
But the promise was broken, and day by day
The darkness grew denser about my way.
His love seemed a thing of the long ago,
And at last one day he struck me a blow.
Years have passed since then; but on my brow
I seem to feel it burning now.
Joy and gladness were long since fled,
Hope in my heart lay crushed and dead,
And when he struck me that bitter blow
The last faint spark of love died, too.
He died very soon in a drunken spree;
I was almost glad, for it set me free.
My very life was wrapped up in Jack —
Sure he could not follow his father's track;
But, ere I knew it, my brave bright son
Was a slave to that license of Ephraim Stone.
Oh, Willie! my darling! I can not tell
How the night of horror over me fell,
And storm-clouds gathered thick and fast
O'er my helpless head, till they broke at last,
And my beautiful boy was brought home dead —
'Slain by a comrade's hand,' they said.
Over there in the shadows dark and deep
He lies, while I still live and weep.
  "And Bessie, you say: Well, there came to our place
A gay young man with a handsome face.
He was bright and pleasant and winning, too —
Such as girls are apt to fancy, you know.
I begged and pleaded; for it was known
He liked the tavern of Ephraim Stone.

'Twas all in vain — these tears will start;
She married him — and — he broke her heart.
Scarce two years and she lay at rest,
With my only grandchild on her breast.
"I'm childless and hopeless and all alone —
All for that license of Ephraim Stone.
All alone I live, and I sit and wonder
If, when I search the home over yonder,
I shall find even there all I've loved and lost —
God only knows what that license cost!"
— *Mrs. A. A. Rolfe.*

14. OUR WATCHWORD — UNION.*

Thus far the friends of freedom have been divided. Union, then, must be our watchword — union among men of all parties. By such union we consolidate an opposition which must prevail.

Let me call upon you, then, men of all parties, Whigs and Democrats, or however named, to come forward and join in a common cause. Let us all leave the old organizations and come together. In the crisis before us, it becomes us to forget past differences and those names which have been the signal of strife, only remembering our duties. When the fire-bell rings at midnight, we ask not if it be Whigs or Democrats who join us to extinguish the flames; nor do we make any such inquiry in selecting our leader then. To the strongest arm and the most generous soul we defer at once. To him we commit the direction of the engine. His hand grasps the pipe to pour the water upon the raging conflagration. So must we do now. Our leader must be the man who is the ablest and surest representative of the principles to which we are pledged.

Let Massachusetts, nurse of the men and principles that made our earliest revolution, vow herself anew to her early faith . . . the whole comprehended in that sublime relation of Christianity, the Brotherhood of Man.

In the contemplation of these great interests, the intrigues of party, the machinations of politicians, the combinations of office-seekers, all pass from sight. Politics and morals, no longer divorced from each other, become one and inseparable in the holy wedlock of Christian sentiment. Such a union ele-

* From an address delivered at Worcester, June 28, 1848.

vates politics, while it gives a new sphere to morals. Political discussions have a grandeur which they never before assumed. Released from topics which concern only the selfish squabble for gain, and are often independent of morals, they come home to the heart and conscience. A novel force passes into the contests of party, breathing into them the breath of a new life — of Hope, Progress, Justice. Humanity. —*Charles Sumner.*

---

15. THE BABY SHOES.

'Twas last month in camp; us fellers
   Had been haulin' logs fer days,
When there came a roarin' blizzard —
   Not with 'commodatin' ways —
But a regular ole timer.
   'Twarn't no use to try to haul,
So we settled down an' figured
   On a program we called " tall."
So that night as darkness gathered,
   We drew up around the fire ;
" Gracious," Tom said, " hear it blowin'!
   Can't ye pile the logs up higher ?"
And we did, then watched it blowin',
   Toastin' our bestockin'ed feet,
Then tossed pennies to determine
   Who should tell a story   Pete
Got heads. "Come on, ole feller,
   Tell us somethin' pretty bright,
Fer the kerosene's clean petered
   An' this fire don't give much light."
But he said he couldn't. Gracious !
   When us fellers spot a man
He has got to make a showin'
   Whether he jes' can't or can !
" Well," said he, " I've just one story,
   And that isn't funny, pards ;
But if you are bound to have it,
   I can talk without regards
To the fine points of a story.
   'Twas last winter, boys, and somehow
   Times was pretty hard with me —
Couldn't get a thing to work at,

With a family of three.
Well, you mind that camp up-river?
  I got work up there at last;
Tell ye, fellers, I was happy,
  'Fer,' says I, 'hard times is past.'
Came the day we got our silver;
  Not a moment would I lose
Fer it was the baby's birthday,
  And I'd made some little shoes
Out o' some soft buckskin leather.
  Oh, I'd seen those baby eyes
Lightin' up for months — in fancy —
  She had eyes jes' like the skies
When there isn't any blizzard,
  But the blue is all ye see.
Boys, I thought we'd have a party,
  Jes' with wife and babe and me.
Came the day we got our silver
  And I started home — well, boys,
I got off fer miles up-country
  So't I wouldn't hear the noise
Of them fellers when they landed
  Where the winehouse stands close by,
For when logmen get their silver
  They do carry things so high.
So I went in on a cross street
  Just to 'scape their jolly hold.
'Twas a stormy night like this one—
  Never saw a night so cold.
Suddenly — or was I dreaming?—
  Came that well-remembered smell
Of the wine that draws and chains one
  While it leads him on to hell!
Came the rattling, clicking, spinning
  Of the cue upon the balls —
Then the wild notes of a fiddle —
  Now the music rises, falls.
Tempted, overcome with passion —
  For I ceased to be a man —
I rushed in; think of the horror
  Of that action if you can.
When I sobered down next mornin' —

Or next night it might have been —
I had spent my last log silver,
  Started out for home again.
Yes, 'twas night, now I remember;
  Just the cold light of the moon
Lighted up our little kitchen.
  Oh, how cold it made the room!
And it fell upon the brown hair
  Of my wife, and her white face,
And the little frozen baby
  She had tried to keep in place
At her frozen breast. I'm sure, boys,
  If I'd got there when I tried,
Life would still be worth the livin';
  Wife and baby had not died.
Here's one shoe; the other's somewhere —
  Lost — and this is very cold;
Tried it on my baby: some way
  It's so chilly now to hold.
Of that freezin' winter evenin'
  Often do I think, ye see,
For it was the baby's birthday,
  And my wife expected me."
No one spoke as Pete had finished;
  Just the snow against the pane
Tapped and moaned; the embers brightened
  And then died away again.
Night was setting darkly earthward,
  It was late: but no one knew.
Just one picture filled our fancy —
  'Twas that little baby shoe.

                  —*Helen Josephine Baker.*

16. AN AMERICAN DESERT.

There is an American desert more bleak and desolate and famished than ever Western wind or ravening wolf howled over. Across its arid ridges capital puffs its flabby jowls in deadly peril, and gibbers like an idiot about the scenery and the sunset; and labor gasps and yelps and staggers and, with dry tongue protruding, snaps at friend and foe like a mad dog. It reeks with the blood of millions who would else have been stars

in the crown of Jesus Christ. It whitens with the bones of innocent women and little children dragged thither from our very altars by the greedy, red-mouthed pack of 250,000 saloons protected by the law. It is drunkenness, the *mauvaise terre*—the scourge, the pestilence, the perdition of living men, the wrath of God for violated harvests and mercenary public virtue. And we have been fleeing from it, or dancing about ridiculous incantation fires, or drinking wine and praising the gods of license gold. The hand of Jehovah writes upon the wall of the world in burning letters: "*Prepare ye the way of the Lord!*" *The liquor traffic ought to die; and any politics or any religion that postpones or ignores that ought to die, too, and be buried with it in the middle of the king's highway, and it will.*
—*John G. Woolley.*

17. THE JUG AN' ME AN' JIM.

"Thet ol' black jug up thar, eh! why keep it up on the shelf?"
"Broke—fire away?" Reckon not, sir; w'y, I'd ez soon lose myself
Ez thet ol' jug. Jes' you set down thar in the shade o' thet spreadin' limb
An' I ll tell you a leetle suthin' thet jug's done fer me an' Jim.

"Who's Jim?" W'y, Jim's my pardner, bes' feller'n all this place,
Stan's six feet'n his stockin's, an' got jes' the hones'est face.
Him an' me's jes' like two brothers—Jim hain't no rale brother, you see,
Sence the time when thet dretful thing happened to the jug an' him an' me.

'Twuz a turrible wild night, stranger, winter o' eighty-two,
The snow'd been a-peltin' down all day, an' now the wind it bloo
A regerler Nor'east blizzard, like nothin' so much in the world,
'Sif some o' them gret towerin' hills had up 'ith theirselves, an' hurled

'Ith the strength of a thousan' demons, the kiverin' o' ice and snow
They'd been heapin' up for years an' years, on us poor creturs below

In the gulch. Cold? Wall, yes, I reckon 'twuz cold, the wind an' sleet
Wus thet bitin' you'd a-froze, sir, 'fore you'd a-gone more'n two feet.

Tho', to tell the rale truth, stranger, nary one on us didn't much keer
Ef it did snow. Up to Jinkses' thar wuz plenty o' rum an' beer,
An' thar we'd all been a-settin' sence the airly part o' the day.
It felt so warm an' comferble like, we up'n 'lowed we'd stay.

So we jes' hitched up a bit nigher, an' Jim, he shuffled the ke-ards,
An' sez he to me, "Come, Bob, ol' chap, le's you an' me be pards.
We'll hev a regerler ol' fash—" but he never finished that speech,
For jes' then suthin' or 'nuther outside gin a mos' unairthly screech.

Jim drap'd the ke-ards mighty sudden, an' jumped up out'n his cheer.
"Wot wuz thet, Bob?" sez he, "wot wuz thet ar noise? did ye hear?"
"Hear?" sez I, "wall, I reckon I heerd, I ain't deef, not yit.
Thet ar wuz naught but the wind, Jim, don't you be skeered, one bit."

But whilst I wuz talkin', my teeth wuz hittin' together, click, clack,
An' my har stood up on end, like the quills on a porkypine's back.
Twict agin we heerd thet screech, 'bove the soun's o' thet awful night.
An' by thet time we's all on us eenymos' dead 'ith fright.

An' when, his eyes big an' starin', Irish Mike fell over 'gainst Jim,
Yellin' out, "Be the Holy Mither, 'twuz the Banshee callin' fer him."
W'y then, we jes' gin out ontirely, an' huddled all up'n a heap,
'Ith no more sperit amongst us'n you'd find in a passel o' sheep.

All the res' o' the night we sot thar, scurce darin' to breathe or to move,
The lamp flickered out 'fore daylight, an' the fire went down in the stove.
In the dark it seemed wuss'n ever, fer the wind kep' howlin' outside,
But thar wan't one on us fellers could ha' stirred a foot ef he died.

Byme-bye the sun riz an' sparkled, like dimon's all over the groun',
Jim an' me, we put on our gret-coats, an' 'lowed we'd tek a look roun',
But we didn't git fer — on the door-stun we foun' a gret snow-kivered heap,
'Ith suthin' so queer in its shape like, our flesh all to onct 'gan to creep.

We poked at the snow, sorter easy ; pretty soon we onkivered a head,
Then all 'twonct Jim keeled over agin me, 'ith a face like the face o' the dead.
"My God, Bob," he gasped, "it's my brother, my onliest brother, my Joe,
An' we sot inside thar, like heathen, whilst he died out here in the snow."

Then, 'ith one gret cry, like a heart-burst, Jim sorter went out o' his head,
An' begun a-jabberin' to "Josey," disrememberin' his brother wuz dead.
I called, an' the fellers come runnin', an' some on' em tended to Jim,
Whilst the rest on us fetched in his brother — our eyes mighty teary an' dim.

Thet night Jim come down 'ith the fever (Thank the Lord, I'd got him safe hum).
Ef he wa'n't jes' the craziest cretur drawed breath this side Kingdom Come.
Six long weeks it wuz 'fore he tottered to the winder, an' looked thro' the snow,
To whar, on' a ledge of the mount'n, we'd buried his poor brother Joe.

He begged so hard fer perticklers, I tol' him the hull harrowin'
tale,
How Joe, layin' out fer to s'prise him, had footed it over the
trail;
At a place, a few mile up the mount'n, he stopped to res' an'
git warm,
An' the folks they tried hard to 'suade him to 'bide a bit, 'count
o' the storm.

But he wouldn' hear to no reason, so anxious he wuz to see
Jim,
So they gin him a jugful o' whisky, "jes' to keep the cold out'n
him,"
An' not bein' customed to sperits, he drunk more'n he'd ough-
ter, you know,
An' los' his way, an' kep' wanderin' back an' forth, in the cold
an' the snow.

From some'eres 'way up on the mount'n he mus' ha' caught
sight o' the spark
O' light shinin' out'n our winder, an' follered it up in the dark;
An' when he'd nigh about reached it his foot likely slipped, an'
he fell
Off'n the rocks, right onter our door-stun, an' gin out thet tur-
rible yell.

We foun' thet black jug clost beside him; the han'le wuz
broke, ez you see;
When Jim seen it he cried like a babby, an' then he sez, turnin'
to me,
"Bob," he sez, "we'd bes' let it stan' thar on the eend o' the
shelf, don' you think?
Fer sorter a warnin' or pledge like, when we's hankerin' arter
a drink.

"Ef he hadn't a-drinked thet whisky Joe'd never ha' los' his
way,
An' ef we fellers'd been in our senses, he might ha' been livin'
to-day;
God helpin' me, Bob" he sez slowly, "I'll never tech licker
agin."
An' sez I, my han' laid in his'n, "I'm with you, ol' feller.
Amen."

Nigh ten years ha' passed sence thet mornin', but we hain't
    never broken our pledge ;
The posies is growin' and blowin' on thet grave up thar on the
    ledge.
We waters 'em out'n thet jug, sir,— w'y bless me, my eyes they
    is dim !
They allers gits so when I'm tellin' 'bout the jug an' me, sir,
    an' Jim.
— Eleanor Mayfield.

18. SENSE VERSUS LICENSE.*

Now, it is mad, it is driveling, to talk of regulating the traffic in intoxicating beverages. Raise the charge for license to $10,000 and enact that nobody but a doctor of divinity shall be allowed to sell, and you will have no material improvement on the state of things now presented, because so long as one man is licensed to sell thousands will sell without license. The law is robbed of all moral sanction and force by the fact that it grants dispensations to some to do with impunity, and for their own profit, that which is forbidden to others. If our laws allowed the five leading hotels in this city to disburse alcoholic madness only to moral, upright, discreet, thrifty men, upon payment of a license charge of $5,000 each per annum, there would be thousands of taverns, porter-houses, and groceries selling constantly and openly to all who would buy on the strength of that license, and public sentiment would say, " If one man is allowed to sell, why not other men ? Either stop all or give all a chance." But give us a strong law forbidding the sale of these maddening beverages entirely and we will drive the kegs and decanters out of public view the first year and pretty nearly out of existence within three years. This will involve a severe, arduous struggle — we understand that — but the men and the means are ready ; and, with such an act as Gov. Seymour has just vetoed, we will make rum selling as shy as gambling or harlotry now is within the three years aforesaid. That all liquor selling will be stopped in a city like this we do not anticipate ; but we will make it a stealthy, hidden, guilty business, so prosecuted that he who will drink must sneak down back stairs and through underground passages to find the liquor ; and whenever that shall be the case there will

* From The Tribune, April 4, 1854.

not be one glass drank where ten glasses are now, nor one new drunkard manufactured where there are now a hundred. And in spite of executive complicity with the vote-gathering groggeries this shall yet be! — *Horace Greeley.*

19. THE VICTOR.

It is not he that proudly stands
Upon the heights of mountain lands,
And waves his stainless banner where
The world can see the pennon fair.

It is not he who seeks to stay
At shrines of worship all the day,
And then goes to his peaceful rest,
With head upon the Master's breast.

But it is he who bravely goes
Out in the world to meet his foes,
And fight for right, till God shall win,
And faith shall triumph over sin.

It is the one, with stern-set face,
That enters in the earnest race
To win life's goal, as sets the sun,
Then shall the victor's crown be won.

It is the one that does the deed
Of love, to him in direst need,
Who soothes the wounded, aching soul,
But crushes sin by strong control.

This is the victor, great and grand,
Who ever works with heart and hand
Among the throngs of weary men,
Just as the Master worked with them.
— *M. A. Holt.*

20. THE CERTAINTY OF PROGRESS.

We live in an age of democratic equality; for a moment, a party may stand against the age, but in the end it goes by the board; the man who launches a sound argument, who sets on two feet a startling fact, and bids it travel from Maine to Georgia, is just as certain that in the end he will change the government, as if, to destroy the Capitol, he had placed gunpowder under the senate-chamber. Natural philosophers tell us that if you will only multiply the simplest force into enough time, it will equal the greatest. So it is with the slow intellectual movement of the masses. It can scarcely be seen, but it is a constant movement; it is the shadow on the dial, never still, tho never seen to move; it is the tide, it is the ocean, gaining on the proudest and strongest bulwarks that human art or strength can build. It may be defied for a moment, but in the end Nature always triumphs. So the race, if it can not drag a Webster along with it, leaves him behind and forgets him. The race is rich enough to afford to do without the greatest intellects God ever let the Devil buy. Stranded along the past, there are a great many dried mummies of dead intellects, which the race found too heavy to drag forward.

— *Wendell Phillips.*

21. THE QUEST MAGNIFICENT.

  In the earlier traditions,
   In the myths of olden time,
  Glows this oft-repeated legend,
   With its meaning all sublime —
  'Twas a youthful hero, noble,
   With a message to the king,
  Sought the far-off city royal
   With the monarch's signet ring.

Great the task to him entrusted!
 Fit for poet's rime to sing,
Else within his keeping never
 Glowed the signet of the King!
In disguise the hero journeyed —
 Secret was his mighty quest —
With a peasant's garments folded
 O'er the jewel in his breast!
And as near he drew and nearer
 To the monarch's proud abode
He was cautioned as he journeyed:
  "There are dragons in the road!"

Ever watchful of his dangers,
 Ever quietly prepared,
Ever confident, courageous,

Day by day he onward fared
Till one evening, as the sunset
  On his pathway redly glowed,
There he saw, with sudden tremor,
  A fierce dragon in the road!

But no turning back, nor fainting
  For his trust so brave and bold;
Never coward in that country
  Held the jeweled band of gold.
Swift his faithful sword was lifted,
  Strong the strokes that he bestowed
As a quick and ready greeting
  To the dragon in the road.

Fallen was the horrid monster,
  Useless scale-like armor bright,
Gleaming teeth and claw and venom;
  'Twas a long and weary fight.
But, at last, the youth, triumphant,
  On his way exulting strode;
He had met and he had vanquished
  One fierce dragon on the road!

It was morning, and the dewdrops
  Hung on flower and leaf and tree,
And the sun uprose in splendor,
  And the birdlings sang in glee,
When beside a sparkling fountain
  Stooped our traveler to drink;
Lo! he started back in horror
  At the dragon on the brink.

Flashed his sword, and long the combat,
  Till at last a weary load
Bore the youth a horrid trophy!
  "Second dragon in the road,
I will place your head up yonder
  On that cliff, that all may see
More than you it takes to keep me
  From the court of majesty."

It was evening, calm and silent,
  And the moonlight softly lay

On each tree and shrub and fountain,
   And the hill tops far away.
All was peaceful, naught suggested
   Scene of strife or source of wrath,
Till the youth could see before him
   Crouched a dragon in the path !
Long — oh, long that weary combat !
   But the rays of morning showed
That the youth again was victor
   O'er the monster in the road !

And at last he gained the palace,
   Showed the monarch's signet ring,
Told his mission, high and noble,
   In the presence of the king.
And with honors thick upon him,
   Forth in triumph then he rode,
Who had borne the signet safely
   Past the dragons in the road !

There's a moral in this fable —
   'Tis an easy one to reach
In the Present's hurried accents,
   Or the Past's more solemn speech.
Heed the lesson, youthful list'ner !
   For the Monarch gives to thee
Gifts so many and befitting
   Solemn pomp and majesty.
In thine eyes benignant shining,
   In their urgent questioning,
Lo ! I see the mystic jewels
   Of the Master's signet ring !

Oh ! a trust by far transcending
   His of fable and of song,
It is thine, to keep thy jewel
   From the enemy so strong !
To the mansions that are sacred,
   To the monarch's blest abode,
Journey with a soul untainted
   Past the dragons in the road !

Thou must have sublimest courage
   Weary combats to endure ;

Thou must hold a faith triumphant,
   Labor in that faith secure.
When God calls his chosen hero
   To a high and sacred quest,
Lo! that purpose is the jewel
   With the Monarch's seal impressed!

And, however poor and lowly
   The deliverer's disguise,
Be his mission high and holy,
   He shall win at last the prize —
He who labors for his fellows,
   Fearing never jest nor goad,
In the midst of persecution,
   Countless dragons in the road.

'Tis a task divine-appointed —
   On his mission he must go,
With his weapon sharp and ready
   He must batter down the foe!
Till, at last destroyed, beheaded,
   Is the Serpent in the way,

And the Present wreathes her laurels
   For the hero of to-day!
For the one whose onward journey
   To the Palace of the King
Is beset with fiercest dragons,
   Each with ready claw and sting!
With that two-edged sword, the ballot,
   Shall the fiercest foe be slain,
That no longer he shall fatten
   On his victim's heart and brain!

Heroes, meet without a murmur
   This vast monster and unclean!
Brazen front and fangs of poison
   Ye must face with brows serene!
Slay the monster of intemp'rance!
   Ah! He meets you here and there!
He waylays you at the roadside
   And he tempts you to his lair!
And, tho seeming sorely wounded,
   Seeming to be slain indeed,

    Yet, reviving, he attacks you
      In your hour of deepest need!

Monster dragon and insatiate!
  Like the Minotaur of old,
Claiming tribute of the fairest,
  From thy noisome dungeon hold!
But the Theseus, the Deliv'rer,
  From the people's ranks shall rise,
And at last the stroke is given
  And the wounded monster dies;
And the poet of the future
  Shall relate in song and ode
All the deeds of those who conquered
  Rum's red dragon in the road!
                — *Lelia Belle Hewes.*

22. THE ONLY CONCLUSION.*

We thought we meant business years ago in this warfare [against drink], but I hope God will forgive us for our weakness, for we went into the battlefield without sufficient resolution. We labored under the fatal mistake that we could argue out the question with the liquor-sellers. We imagined there was some power in moral suasion, that when we should show them the evil of their ways they would abandon the traffic. We have seen there is no hope of improving in any shape or form the liquor traffic. There is nothing now to be done but to wipe it out completely. I have lost too much of my time striving in the past to repair the fearful wrong of the liquor traffic. I have lost too much time in speaking of total abstinence in hall and pulpit to men who, while listening, were with me, but who, out in the streets, would be invited by the saloon-keeper to come, and take a drink, and forget their resolutions. Well, some of us are growing old, and do not intend to be throwing away our time in arguing with people who will not be converted, and I for one am going to go in with terrible earnestness in the future in this war against liquor in all shapes. I mean business this time.

                —*Archbishop John Ireland.*

---

* From an address before the Minnesota Total Abstinence Association.

23. BACK TO HIS CHRYSALIS.

The garden beds I wandered by
  One bright and cheerful morn,
When I found a new-fledged butterfly,
  A-sitting on a thorn;
A black and crimson butterfly,
  All doleful and forlorn.

I thought that life could have no sting
  To infant butterflies,
So I gazed on this unhappy thing
  With wonder and surprise,
While sadly with his waving wing
  He wiped his weeping eyes.

Said I, "What can the matter be?
  Why weepest thou so sore?
With garden fair, and sunlight free,
  And flowers in goodly store —"
But he only turned away from me
  And burst into a roar.

Cried he, "My legs are thin and few,
  Where once I had a swarm!
Soft, fuzzy fur — a joy to view —
  Once kept my body warm,
Before these flapping wing-things grew,
  To hamper and deform!"

At that outrageous bug I shot
  The fury of mine eye.
Said I, in scorn all burning hot,
  In rage and anger high,
"You ignominious idiot!
  Those wings are made to fly!"

"I do not want to fly," said he;
  "I only want to squirm!"
And he drooped his wings dejectedly
  But still his voice was firm;
"I do not want to be a fly!
  I want to be a worm!"

O yesterday of unknown lack!
  To-day of unknown bliss!

I left my fool in red and black ;
  The last I saw was this :
The creature madly climbing back
  Into his chrysalis.

And still we hear, in voices firm,
  The self-same, dismal cry,
" I only want to be a worm,
  I do not want to fly !
I'd rather wriggle, twist, and squirm
  Than raise Truth's banner high ! "

The temperance voter soon, no doubt,
  Will wiser grow than this,
But now, we watch him twist about,
  Toward what he dreams is bliss,
And madly cling to his worn-out
  Old-party chrysalis.
    —*Adapted from Charlotte Perkins Stetson.*

24. VOT DER VOOMANS HAF TON.

In Poston, you remember,
  Pout six dousand years ago ;
Berhaps it is not quide so long,
  Bud you know vot is so.

Der voomans vouldn't make der tea,
  Der mens, dey vouldn't drink it ;
Dey hit upon a happy blan,
  Und concluded dey vould sink it.

Der English didn't like it much
  To see dem take dot stand,
Bud dey said, " ve're in vor brinciple,"
  Und dey stood vor it shust grand.

Der English kept on getting mad,
  Und Shonny got his gun.
He dought he'd dake it back agin,
  Und started on de run.

Anodder dime in Poston,
  Boud vive dousand years ago,
Dey vere dalking apoud slafery,
  Und said dot it must go.

Und Mr. Phillips don'd gare much
  Poud dot question anyvay,
Cause he's peen du college always,
  Und god monish effery vay.

Bud he got no vife du lofe him;
  Und id don'd zeem right zomehow;
So he hunt him ub a gretchen,
  Und already she's his vrow.

She didn't keep some slafery,
  Cause she didn't dink dwas right;
Und she vouldn't sleep on gotten sheets
  Ven she laid her down at night.

Vor she knew it took some slafery
  Dot gotten goods to made,
Und she vouldn't do vone single ding
  Du help dot slafery trade.

Now, she told to Mr. Vendell
  All she dought apout dose dings;
Und Mr. Vendell du her side
  Ride offer himself prings.

Und Mr. Vendell und die rest,
  Dey made an awful row.
Und beoble said, "Id is no good."
  — But vere is slafery now?

Still annoder dime in Poston —
  Nod yet quite two years ago —
Der vimmens met togedder
  Und said dot rum must go.

Dey said, "Vee von't valk on sidevalks
  Und vee von't burn street lighds,
If visky money puys dose dings
  Und dakes prains du make it right.

"Und whoever zells his products
  Du our uncle's visky mill,
Ve pelieve is shust as guilty
  As der mon dot runs der still.

"Now dis question is pefore us
  Und vee haf to do our pest;

Und ven der still is ousted
  Vee vill gif der still a rest.

"If vee can make dis come out,
  Like dose oder questions do,
I dink it vil pe glorious ;
  Und I know dot you do too."

Perhaps, I gif der vimmens
  Some more credit dan deir share ;
But ven der voomans dells der tale
  Der voomans kills der bear.
                  —Jennie Fleming.

25. AN ANTI-SUFFRAGIST'S LAMENT.

    There was once a good old time,
    In a not far distant clime,
When man was man indeed, and held his own, sir.
    He believed the noblest toil
    Was to cultivate the soil ;
But now, alas ! those good old times have flown, sir.

    Yes, the man he knew his rights,
    There were no such scandalous sights
As " Woman's Suffragists in mass convention."
    Then a woman knew her "sphere,"
    And man held her there, that's clear,
And to keep her always there was his intention.

    Man was once allowed to plow
    With a woman and a cow,
And the woman pulled her share and ne'er did falter ;
    But those good old times have flown,
    And we'll surely have to own
That the woman has contrived to slip her halter !

    Have the men been half asleep,
    That they've let these changes creep —
Let this cry for " equal rights " gain such wide hearing?
    And it's " equal laws " they sing,
    " Equal, equal ",— everything !
And we'll never get those good times back I'm fearing.

    Close the college doors, I pray,
    Quite against them ; take away

All the high-up notions that we've been allowing;
    If we give an inch, you see,
    They will take two ells, or three,
So we'd better put the creatures back to plowing!

    Stop the pulpit — that will tell —
    Hush the mighty press as well,
Close the schools, else on results there's no relying,
    And give us back our plow,
    With the woman and the cow —
Those good old times for which we all are sighing!
                    — *Hattie Horner Louthan.*

26. THE BRAND OF CAIN.

It is true that no one voter in New York State has the power to outlaw the liquor traffic. Is he then responsible for its existence? Yes, if the power which he does possess, as a voter, is used to assist in the legalization and protection of the traffic. The man who assists in a crime is responsible for the whole crime. The 30,000 saloons are to-day prosecuting their business not only with the consent of the law, but under the broad egis of its protection. It is a lawful business. There is no inherent right, says the United States Supreme Court, to sell liquor. But every liquor seller has a commission issued to him by the public officers who received their authority from the voters of the State, and act under a law continued on the statutes by the representatives of the people. All the legal authority and force that are behind this legalized "traffic in human blood" are there by virtue of the action of the voters of this State. There alone is the power to remove them. There is the responsibility for all the iniquitous results.

The brand of Cain — where, then, is it to be found to-day? As God lives and reigns, it is on the forehead of every man who by his vote consents to and assists in the continuance of this atrocity of drunkard making. There goes a minister along the streets of New York City. Who is he? One of the foremost Methodist ministers and a prominent candidate for Bishop in the last General Conference. Look close and you will see the brand of Cain upon his forehead. There goes another. Who is he? The noted preacher in a Presbyterian church on Fifth avenue — the wealthiest in the country. Look close and the brand of Cain will be visible. Here is a third — rector of that rich and historic Episcopal church on lower Broadway. Look — the brand of Cain again! Walk the streets and you see it everywhere — a community of Cains, conspiring and assisting in the debauchery and death of their fellow creatures. Cains, do we say? Why, all that Cain did was to slay the body; but these men who believe that there is a soul in every man and a hell waiting for it are yet, despite all this, assisting to send thousands each year to that eternal doom.

Oh men, men, God forgive us if we are writing un-Christian and uncharitable words, but if the cries of utter misery and horror that well up from the depths day after day and year after year can't awaken you, what is left us to do but to say these things? Somebody is responsible for all this shame and sorrow, and it is not God. Somebody is doing this thing, commissioning men to prosecute the work of hell, and protecting them in it, and it is neither God nor the devil, for neither makes the laws on our statute books or votes for those who do.

The curse of Cain is resting on this Nation, and as sure as righteousness is right and sin is sin, there must come a day of reckoning. Look to yourself, voter; are you carrying the brand of Cain? — *The Voice, Oct. 1, 1891.*

27. THE COMING ERA.

Low in the dust and silence, low in earth's virgin breast,
    Rigid and cold and senseless there in their slumber deep,
The victims of drink are lying in a mute and soulless rest,
    And sealed are the lips that dying asked for a peaceful sleep.

Grasses wave above them and heavy with twilight's tears;
    The roses, wan and weary, lean over the vernal slopes,
To hear the spirit voices that come from the by-gone years —
    That speak of human ruins and the ghosts of murdered hopes.

They tell of the mystic shadows that crouch by hearths aglow,
    Where wives are sobbing wildly and mothers sigh in pain,
Where dregs of bitter memory fill up their cup of woe —
    Where all their prayers for lost ones are uttered but in vain.

Of manhood's deadly grapple and subsequent defeat,
    With one weird dancing demon in a blood-red habit decked;
Of merry hearts that drifted out on billows wild and fleet;

Of hearts dashed on sin's hidden reefs, of hearts forever
    wrecked.
And the life and love of many a home have gone to the distant
    skies,
    Like mist that coils from the river or the incense of battle's
        fray.
Oh, hard is the lesson we gather when the drunken father dies,
    Leaving the curse behind him, perhaps for many a day.
The wail of the orphan is drowned in the ceaseless din of the
    street,
    While rivers of wine flow down the throat of the rich and
        the proud;
And rampant the evils and crime which everywhere we meet,
    And the shuttle of death keeps weaving the poor inebriate's
        shroud.
Reeking the cells of the prisons with the poison breath of the
    wretch,
    Filled is the almshouse with paupers and tramps tattooed with
        shame;
Souls are pawned for a trifle, and honor for what it will fetch,
    And duty bleeds with ghastly wounds she gets in pleasure's
        name.

    *   *   *   *   *   *   *

Over the Union, Progress, calm as the stars above,
    Rides in her golden chariot, behind her chargers grand,
The banners of Heaven bearing the gilded message of love
    Inscribed thereon by the angels to the outcasts of our land.
And ne'er will she pause in her journey along the future's track,
    Till dramshops are changed to mansions, where joy and peace
        can dwell.
When souls are redeemed, homes restored, and the virtues of
    men come back —
    Ah! then will smilingly pause and say to all our land, "It is
        well!"

    —*Leon Mead.*

28. A CASE OF "PERSONAL LIBERTY."

Do you know what a five-year-old little girl is? Have you one of your own? Do you know her helplessness in this big world of complex and terrible forces? Do you know how dependent she is upon careful protection and nurture? If you do read this short item from *The Times*, Jan. 30 :

"A drinking couple named Michael and Mary Cluney, who live at 228 River avenue, Hoboken, were arrested yesterday for brutally beating their five-year-old daughter. The child was sent out daily to beg. When she did not bring home money enough to keep the couple in rum she was beaten with a heavy harness strap. Yesterday the neighbors, who had grown tired of rescuing the child, notified the police. The little girl and her three-year-old brother were taken in charge by the wife of the janitor at Police Headquarters, and the Cluneys were locked up. The girl's body is a mass of cuts and bruises. The case will be sent to the Grand Jury."

Nothing wonderful about that, you say. No, and that is why we call attention to it. It is a *common-place* occurrence. It is happening every day. It is such a usual thing that it is only worth 15 lines in the daily paper, and they are generally skipped by the average reader. There are impassioned orators of various kinds trying to make the people of America see certain evils and feel certain wrongs that they might not either feel or see but for the oratory. Here is an evil that needs no oratory to make it seen and felt. It is tangible. It is on all sides and at all times. We have no sermon to deliver over it, no gush to get rid of ; but we want to say this, that if you are a big, strong, healthy man, and are helping to protect and perpetuate a system that is doing such things as this to little five-year-old girls throughout this land, you ought to go and grovel on your face in an ash-heap till you make up your mind to fight such a damnable system against, if need be, all the powers of the world, the flesh and the devil.

— *E. J. Wheeler.*

29. COLUMBIA.

O grand, fair country, rich in bounteous blessing,
    Sweet Freedom's crown upon thy regal brow ;
From sea to sea the land of thy possessing,
    Looks to the sun and smiles in plenty now.

Of all the millions claiming thy protection,
    Not one will answer to the name of slave —
Buried the memory of thy defection
    Beneath the sod that marks the soldier's grave.

Sacred to Heaven, the Church gives message tender ;
   On every side thy halls of learning stand ;
Yonder white dome upreared in glistening splendor,
   Bespeaks the promise of a peaceful land.

Across the waters in a friendly greeting,
   Thy sister countries send the kindly word ;
In place of war the world's great good defeating,
   The grand Te Deum and the prayer are heard.

Ah, prayer and praise befit thy queenly seeming,
   And both are due the power that bid thee live ;
But pray as well to awaken from thy dreaming
   And clear-eyed reason to thy future give.

That future shrinks beset by many a danger,
   Lurking, half-fledged to rise strong-winged at last.
O trust it to the friend and not the stranger,
   To guide thee safe the dreadful breakers past !

Cling to the old, the tried and true that love thee,
   And bid new lovers prove their fealty —
Cling to thy birthright which the God above thee
   Sealed with the blood of martyred loyalty.

Ay, trust thine own, but bid them pledge thine honor
   In the pure glass that leaves the reason clear ;
Let all thy legions bear the snow-white banner,
   From out whose folds no foul-breathed demons leer.

Blot out the wrongs that cry for Heaven's bewailing,
   Crush wild-eyed License 'neath an iron heel ;
Bid Virtue rise, assured of help unfailing,
   And skulking Vice thy full displeasure feel.

Speak to thy sons in words whose lofty meaning
   Shall thrill them through with an undying fire ;
Shall fit their souls for boundless fields of gleaning
   And mighty effort that shall never tire.

High to God's throne upraise an ideal holy,
   And bid thy children look to that for light,
While pressing onward with a spirit lowly
   And patience boundless as the vault of night.

So in God's own good time thy gracious seeming,
  Shall every truth speak out to aid the world;
And larger hope upon thy fair brow beaming
  Smile 'neath the flag of purity unfurled.
— Fannie E. Ostrander.

30. THE TEMPERANCE REVOLUTION.*

Whether or not the world would be vastly benefited by a total and final banishment from it of all intoxicating drinks, seems to me not now an open question. Three-fourths of mankind confess the affirmative with their tongues; and, I believe, all the rest acknowledge it in their hearts. Ought any, then, to refuse their aid in doing what the good of the whole demands? . . . There seems ever to have been a proneness in the brilliant and warm-blooded to fall into this vice — the demon of intemperance ever seems to have delighted in sucking the blood of genius and generosity. What one of us but can call to mind some relative, more promising in youth than all his fellows, who has fallen a victim to his rapacity? He ever seems to have gone forth like the Egyptian angel of death, commissioned to slay, if not the first, the fairest born of every family. Shall he now be arrested in his desolating career? . . . If the relative grandeur of revolutions shall be estimated by the great amount of human misery they alleviate and the small amount they inflict, then, indeed, will this be the grandest the world shall ever have seen. Of our political revolution of '76 we are all justly proud. . . . But . . . it . . . had its evils too. . . . Turn now to the temperance revolution. In it we shall find a stronger bondage broken, a viler slavery manumitted, a greater tyrant deposed — in it more of want supplied, more disease healed, more sorrow assuaged; by it no orphan's starving, no widow's weeping. . . . And what a natural ally this to the cause of political freedom; with such an aid its march can not fail to be on and on, till every son of earth shall drink in rich fruition the sorrow-quenching draughts of perfect liberty. . . . And when the victory shall be complete, when there shall be neither a slave nor a drunkard on the earth, how proud the title of that land which may truly claim to be the birth-place and the cradle of both those revolu-

* From address before the Washingtonian Temperance Society of Springfield, Ill., on Feb. 22, 1842.

tions that shall have ended in that victory! How nobly distinguished that people who shall have planted and nurtured to maturity both the political and moral freedom of their species!
— *Abraham Lincoln.*

31. A TRAMP'S VIEWS.

I may be a drunkard, an idler, a tramp—
   I'm sure you would think so to look at me now;
But once I was dressed as you dress to-day,
   And had the Lord's seal of a man on my brow.
I had a fine home and a dear little wife,
   And a babe, just as bright as that dear babe of yours;
But now I'm an outcast, alone in the earth,
   My roof, Heaven's dome, and my home "all out-doors."

What brought me to this?—why, the devil of drink;
   Cold water don't murder our children and wives,
Nor drive sober men out of sunshiny homes,
   To beg and to steal and to tramp all their lives.
They had an election where I lived one day,
   To decide as to whether or not a saloon
Should be opened to help on the town,
   In business and life—a much needed boon.

Deacon Brown made a speech on the matter, and said:
   "A tavern well run was a help to the town,
Bringing trade from all the country around,
   And he hoped that the people would not vote it down."
The minister told us a fee would be paid,
   By the man who was ready to open the place;
And the money for license would pay half our debt;
   And he'd vote for the tavern; he would, "by God's grace."

The merchants all said it would fine business make,
   And increase every line of legitimate trade;
And so when the ballots were counted that night,
   The question was carried and the license was paid.
The tavern was opened, and all of us went
   To the "house-warming," so it was called in the papers.
No charges were made and we drank pretty free,
   And the stuff made us cut some ridiculous capers.

The trade built up fast, and the people were pleased,
   And business looked better than for many a year;

But I went home one night and the cheek of my wife
    Was as pale as the dead, and on it a tear.
Now that made me mad, so I gave her a talk,
    And demanded that she should not look like one dead.
But she told me she feared it could not be helped,
    As long as our cupboard was empty of bread.

It was true—the devilish drink at the bar
    Had made me its slave ; and every cent
That I earned, when sober enough to do work,
    Which was not very often, to the tavern it went.

But why tell it all? My trade was soon killed—
    A drunkard is fit for no business or toil ;
My wife and my baby grew paler, and soon,
    I found we were all wrapped in Alcohol's coil.
And one night, while I sat at the tavern and drank,
    With the very last penny I had to my name,
My baby, poor starveling, went home up to God,
    And only the next week my wife did the same.

STARVED TO DEATH, to make business for our little town,
    Business for men who must bury the dead ;
Business for those who grow fat and grow rich,
    As they gather the money that should go for bread ;
Business for judges and juries and jailers,
    Business for vampires who fatten on wrong,
Business for men who sell heartaches for money,
    Who make others weak that they may be strong.

The license was paid, two hundred good dollars,
    But to it I've added my dead babe and wife.
To it I've added the manhood I've lost,
    To it I've added this much of my life.
Christians may pray and preachers may preach ;
    But the Kingdom of Christ will never prevail
So long as for dollars we license foul murder
    And legislate citizens into the jail.

There are thousands like me who still want to be saved,
    Who long for the manhood they lost at the bar.
But I see no hope for us this side of the grave
    So long as the Christians our life-chances mar
By working for wrong, while they pray for the right ;

By talking for good, while they work for the evil;
By frowning on sin, while they license its grasp;
By praying to God, while they vote for the devil.

—*Lou J. Beauchamp.*

32. A RED NIAGARA.*

Two years ago we had a fit of national hysterics, because Coxey's weaponless petition in boots tramped from Ohio to Washington; to-day we coolly watch, marching through the land, an army mightier than general ever marshalled on the battle-field. An army that sways parties, rules city councils, controls legislatures, dominates Congress, dictates to the Supreme Court how to interpret the constitution, controls the church and gags its pulpit. This army's recruiting-station is the club-house, its drill ground the barroom, its barracks the jail, its soldier's home the poorhouse, its national cemetery the potter's field, its uniform rags, its step a stagger, its battle-cry Rum. This army enlists for life; the promotions are rapid — moderate drinker, hard drinker, drunkard, sot. Every saloon-keeper is a captain, every brewer a colonel, every distiller a general, the devil himself is its commander-in-chief. The continent is at its mercy; it gives no quarter. Attention, stagger forward, march! Rum, rum, rum. Two million five hundred thousand drunkards are on their funeral march; past home, past honor, past hope; over the blighted lives of wife and child; over the graves of broken-hearted mothers; down, down to a drunkard's death and a drunkard's hell.

The saloon says it is a profit to the nation; it pays $200,-000,000 a year for license; the nation pays $2,000,000,000 for liquor. It returns eight cents of every dollar it is licensed to steal. It also returns 25,000 lunatics, 50,000 paupers, and enough criminals to fill 50 penitentiaries and 2,000 jails. The nation has to pay $5,000,000 to support its lunatics; $10,000,000 for its paupers; $200,000,000 for its criminals. It loses the value of tens of thousands of men slain and hundreds of thousands rendered idle. Has it not a right then to say whether the saloon should be allowed to carry on this lunatic-pauper criminal manufacturing company? Is the liquor-dealer's right to get rich paramount to a drunkard's right to life, to his wife's

---

* Prize oration in the college contest at the National Prohibition Convention, Pittsburg, May 26, 1896.

right to bread and coal, to his child's right to be well born, to the state's right to an uncorrupted suffrage?

You say these evils must stop; but how? The old parties will never stop them; the saloon controls them both. The Democratic Party wept over a billion-dollar Congress, but it does not even shed a crocodile tear when the saloon robs paupers of $1,200,000,000. The Republican party will compass heaven and earth to protect the workingman's dinner pail, yet it permits the saloon to rob him of his dinner without protest. It sees 100,000 pieces of American bone and sinew buried annually by the saloon and it is silent. It will protect things, not men. The nation has a hundred lighthouses along her coast, but around the awful rocks of intemperance, on which unnumbered lives have been beaten out, she has nothing but licensed pirates. Neither the Republican nor Democratic captain of the Ship of State will pick up a drowning drunkard. Three million Republican and Democratic Christians might pray every night that the liquor traffic may be abolished, and it will go on unchecked; but if on election day 3,000,000 Christian men pray with their ballots, their prayer would be answered by nightfall. For a century a certain man on his way from Jerusalem to Jericho has regularly fallen among thieves. The Republican priest and the Democratic Levite have passed by on the other side. If you want to be a Good Samaritan, do not merely take this man to an inn and pay his board, but get your friends and go back along that road, determined to arrest the gang of thieves that have been robbing every one that passes down that way. Notify the liquor-dealers through the ballot-box that the workingman must go from his cottage to his work without passing a single saloon — that is Prohibition. The saloon-keeper may tell you that Prohibition does not prohibit. He is a reliable source of information, isn't he? If Prohibition does not prohibit, why is he so bitterly opposed to it? Why has it emptied the jails of Kansas; reduced liquor-drinking in Iowa? Why does liquor capital halt at the border of a Prohibition state? Why did Maine, after a trial of 30 years, make Prohibition a part of her constitution? Why does the party grow stronger at every election? Local Option — one dry town surrounded by ten wet ones; state Prohibition — a rock in a sea of rum — these may fail, but let us have prohibition in every state and territory in the Union, and a drunkard will be as rare a sight as a Democratic candidate for the Presidency. God has anointed this little David to sink the stone of Prohibition deep into the skull of this bragging Goliath, Alcohol. Throw your ballot away by voting for the Party? Not while God's throne stands. Your ballot is the way you can help him make America better. What does He care about the little partizan wrangles about the tariff, how many coppers to tax a foreign coat for an American dude, when men whom He gave His only begotten Son to save are sinking down into drunkard's graves on every hand? Votes were needed for independence in 1776, for Union in 1860; they are needed for sobriety, now! Now, when the continent trembles beneath the drunkard's tread — now, when children in their cradles are stung by this viper — now, when it dooms a million women to lonely and unpitied martyrdom.

A river of rum, a mountain of gold, a cloud of tears, a boulevard of broken hearts, a red Niagara, down which the best blood of the nation is pouring, a valley of dry bones, white with a million rum-made skeletons. This is the terrific indictment against this infernal traffic.

Oh, Christian men, reach out your iron arms and clutch with your steel fingers this foul and baleful harlot, and stamping deep upon her leprous forehead the burning titles of her shame, plunge the dagger of Prohibition to her heart and shrouding her in the curses of 70,000,000 people, bury her so deep she will never hear the trumpet of resurrection!

—*Charles S. Morris.*

33. SHOVEL OUT.

The blizzard had its lessons, which were borne upon the wind,
And dropped at many a door-step in the thought it left behind.
It reigned a very monarch, with an undisputed sway,
And chained the wheels of commerce for a nation in a day;
It made its crystal messengers a conquering brigade,
To force its proclamation for a general blockade,
And brought to every homestead with a morning song and
    shout,
The truth that they were captives, if they didn't shovel out.

It's just an illustration of another sort of "blow,"
Which hedges many lives about with something else than
    snow,

And turns a pleasant prospect, which is everything that's fair,
Into a sudden tempest with obstructions everywhere;
And makes of their to-morrow, what might seem like prison walls,
Heaped high with disappointments where the mass of driftage falls;
But rarely, like the blizzard, is there heard the warning shout,
That those within are captives, if they do not shovel out.

And yet the fact is patent, there's a power in the spell
Of sudden great reverses that may prove a captive's cell;
A sort of soul concussion seems to paralyze the brain,
To bind the will with fetters, and to kill out hope with pain,
And look out on the driftage in an aimless sort of way,
Heaped high about the doorsill from the hopes of yesterday;
While ears are dull and listless to the voice of any shout,
That there may be deliverance if they will shovel out.

But, brother, if a blizzard has swept over all your plains,
And piled the driftage higher than your upper window-panes,
A tiling lifted from the roof will bring the welcome sight,
That everywhere, outside of you, the world is full of light,
And you can, with your shovel, and a purpose brave and stout,
With sturdy and persistent work, soon tunnel your way out;
But if you wait the action of time's equalizing law,
You'll have a lonely waiting, and may die before a thaw.
  —*Almon Trask Allis, in his book, " Uncle Alvin at Home and Abroad."*

34. THREE VIEWS OF THE WHISKY BOTTLE.
FIRST VIEW.

(The speaker brings the bottle apparently containing liquor, and holds it in his hand during his recitation; then places it on the table, and steps to one side of the platform.)

I bring you some of the most wonderful whisky that ever drove the skeleton from the feast, or painted landscapes in the brain of man. It is the mingled souls of wheat and corn. In it you will find the sunshine and the shadow that chased each other over the billowy fields; the breath of June, the carol of the lark, the dews of night, the wealth of summer and autumn's rich content, all golden with imprisoned light. Drink it, and you will hear the voices of men and maidens singing "Harvest Home," mingled with the laughter of children.

Drink it, and you will feel within your blood the startled dawns, the dreamy, tawny dusks of many perfect days. For forty years this liquid joy has been within the happy staves of oak longing to kiss the lips of man. —*Robert G. Ingersoll.*

SECOND VIEW.

(This speaker takes the bottle from the table and holds it in his hand during his recitation ; then replaces it upon the table, and joins first speaker.)

I bring you some of the most wonderful whisky that ever brought a skeleton into the closet or painted scenes of lust and bloodshed in the brain of man. It is the ghost of wheat and corn, crazed by the loss of their natural bodies. In it you will find a transient sunshine chased by a shadow as cold as an Arctic midnight, in which the breath of June grows icy, and the carol of the lark gives place to the foreboding cry of the raven.

Drink it, and you shall have "woe," "sorrow," "babbling," and "wounds without cause"; "your eyes shall behold strange women," and "your heart shall utter perverse things." Drink it deep, and you shall hear the voices of demons shrieking, of women wailing, and worse than orphaned children mourning the loss of a father who yet lives. Drink it deep and long, and serpents will hiss in your ears, coil themselves about your neck, and seize you with their fangs ; for "at the last it biteth like a serpent and stingeth like an adder." For forty years this liquid death has been within staves of oak, harmless there as purest water. I bring it to you that you may "put an enemy in your mouth to steal away your brains," and yet I call myself your friend. —*J. M. Buckley, D.D.*

THIRD VIEW.

(This speaker advances to the table, wraps the bottle in a paper representing a ballot and holds the package in his hand at the beginning of his recitation, but soon unwraps it and replaces the bottle upon the table, while holding the ballot up repeatedly before the audience.)

I show you a bottle of licensed whisky in the foul embraces of its creator, a license party ballot — just such a ballot as the foregoing speakers sweetly unite in voting.

It is the most wonderful ballot that ever consented when sinners enticed. It is the sheet-music of coiled vipers hissing,

"Vote for splendid sin, and thou shalt *not* surely die!" It is the mingled souls of Judas and Ananias, of Pilate and the strange woman. It is the inscription from the portals of the temple of mercenary politics: "Abandon conscience, all ye who enter here!"

In this ballot you will find the gloom of midnight, full of all nameless horrors, and the glare of the pit, revealing the tempted and fallen. Vote it straight, and you multiply this bottle by millions all over our land. Whatever ills that bottle holds, this wicked ballot unseals and pours in wrath over happy homes and prosperous hamlets, withering them as by a blast from the pit.

Vote it steadily against conscience and prayers, and you breed rings here, and mobs there, and Tammanys elsewhere; and when the cover is lifted anywhere, you find scrolls bearing the names of deacons, and vestrymen, and stewards, and teachers, all calling for the open bottle in new neighborhoods.

For 30 years this license-party ballot has been electing "its perennial but nameless candidate, the saloon." For thirty years it has transformed our election day from a holy day of patriotism into a saturnalia of crime, a wild orgy of debauchery For 30 years the rustle of these ballots into our Government has kept time with the rustle of departing angel-wings of purity, honor, patriotism, piety, and home-life from our land.

Take this ballot with all its foul record. Vote it, in spite of everything. Cling to it on your death-bed; carry it in your bony clutch to your God. Justify it there, if you dare! Plead your puny party policies; whimper that you did not intend the known inevitable result of your wicked deeds, if you can — but do not insult a sham-hating God by saying, "I thought that ballot right." — *A. R. Heath.*

35. EXACTLY OF A SIZE.

Have you seen a sort of puzzle,
   They are giving at the store?
Two little cardboard pieces
   Three inches long, or more;
So shaped with curves and angles,
   Almost any one would swear
That this ticket here is larger
   Than its fellow over there;
But 'tis simply an illusion

That deceives the best of eyes,
  You put 'em both together
    They're exactly of a size.

You have seen the two old parties,
  There is not a doubt of that ;
The woolly-eyed Republican
  And moss-grown Democrat ;
With histories so different,
  They stand out, side by side,
One looking pusillanimous,
  The other grand and wide ;
But, appearance is deceiving,
  And, to your great surprise,
You put 'em both together,
  They're exactly of a size.

These parties build their platforms
  Of old worm-eaten planks,
Expressing, quite ambiguously,
  Anathemas and thanks
On ill-assorted entities
  From silver down to sin,
All worded most adroitly
  To draw the voters in ;
There seems to be some difference,
  But if you're sharp and wise,
You put 'em both together,
  They're exactly of a size.

And then, how soon there follow
  The candidates of each,
To fill the streets with torchlights,
  The atmosphere with speech,
To tickle all the rabble
  With their antiquated straws,
And crack old mildewed chestnuts
  'Mid the wildest of applause ;
You think they differentiate
  Between their party ties,
But put 'em both together,
  They're exactly of a size.

Is not this the greatest puzzle,
    Yes, the most satanic game,
That things can look so different,
    And yet be just the same?
That Christians are so blinded
    As never to compare
The license that they sanction
    With the whisky that they share!
Let us leave the league unholy,
    And combat it till it dies!
For, you put 'em both together,
    They're exactly of a size.

—*Rev. P. J. Bull.*

36. A VESSEL IN DANGER.

That vessel in danger is our National Prohibition Temperance ship. Caught between the teeth of the legalized rum traffic of the State, and the consistent and intelligent temperance (moderate drinking) of the church. Just in the harbor of victory, the fierce winds of opposition seek to drive this gallant bark, heavily freighted with the lives of millions, on to the dreadful breakers. Many anchors have been cast out from bow and stern, to hold the good ship. Sons of Temperance, Rechabites, Good Templars, Daughters of Temperance, Drunkard's Pledge, Holly Inns, Reading Rooms, etc., etc.; all of which were good anchors in ordinary weather, but in the present dread storm their cables are too short, and their "flukes" don't bed in the soil deep enough.

No! with all these, the good ship has drifted. Something better is needed! What is it? The single anchor of *Prayer*, and the long cable of *faith* and *works* in alternate links. "Praying with all supplication in the spirit"; "the effectual fervent prayer"; "praying without ceasing." "*That* anchor holds!" says Tennyson. Yes, it does: prayer takes hold on God's power as with the grip of a giant. And the cable of faith and works is strong and long. "Have faith in God"; "all things are possible to him that believeth"; "ask what ye will in my name"; "be not weary in well-doing, for in due season ye shall reap if ye faint not"; "knowing that your labor is not in vain in the Lord." The Woman's Christian Temperance Union in our land is the call of God to all who are working for the deliverance of our country from the curse of the slavery of rum, to acknowledge Him as the leader in this crusade; to put no confidence in the flesh, but by prayer, look for wisdom and victory from Him; to exercise strong faith, continuous confidence, that by His right arm shall the dreadful foe be overthrown; and to work mightily in the strength of this faith for the closing up of the halls of death, the saloons of the murderers of their brothers, and for the perpetual prohibition of the infamous traffic. With that anchor, and this cable, the ship will stand the storm; upon her strong sides the elements will exhaust their rage in vain. "We will not fear, tho the earth be removed, and the mountains be carried into the midst of the sea; tho the waters thereof roar and be troubled, tho the mountains shake with the swelling thereof. The Lord of hosts is with us; the God of Jacob is our refuge." The sun shall burst forth in beauty and glory over the dark abyss; the good ship, "Perpetual Prohibition," spreading all sail, shall stand up the harbor of victory and cast her "head lines" over the pier-head of *National Emancipation from the slavery of the rum-power.* —*Rev. Wm. H. Boole, D.D.*

37. FAITH AND LIBERTY WITH LOCKED HANDS.*

The Statue of Liberty at the New York gates of the ocean and the Statue of Faith on the Plymouth shore are sisters. I never pass through New York Harbor or visit Plymouth Rock without seeming to hear the two statues converse with each other. The Statue of Liberty I always overhear repeating Webster's aspiration: "Liberty and union, now and forever, one and inseparable!" And the Statue of Faith replies: "Liberty and union, now and forever, one and inseparable; but these are possible only to a people whose God is the Lord." And to-day I hear both Liberty and Faith uttering in unison the words of Neal Dow, with which we all agree and which, God grant, the future may endorse: "We forbid the banns between rum, religion, and politics. But, in the name of God and humanity, we proclaim a union, holy and indissoluble, of affection as well as of interest, between temperance, religion, and politics, of every party and every sect."

---

* Rev. Joseph Cook's oration on Neal Dow closed with this passage and original poem written by Mr. Cook at Prohibition Park as the bells of University Temple were ringing for morning service.

Rapt vigil keeping, day and night,
In panoply of grace and might,
Two stately sisters solemn stand
And guard a great and goodly land :
Fair Faith on Plymouth's sacred shore,
Where Pilgrim ghosts float evermore ;
Tall Liberty, where Commerce waits
The tides of vast Atlantic gates.

With velvet feet, the years go by,
And Liberty, with torch on high,
Saith : "Give me freedom, or I die !"
But Faith points upward with a sigh,
And answers : "Hallowed be His Name,
Who gives to every star its flame."
"My torch illumines land and sea ;
I lead the sphere," saith Liberty.

"Who lights your torch?" fair Faith replies.
"Your hand with mine lift to the skies.
All torches lit from nether fire
In God's deep breathing must expire,
No torch not lighted at the stars
Can rule on land or ocean bars.
Join hands with me, tall Liberty,
And so shall we be one and free."

The sisters join their fateful hands
Above the seas and severed lands,
And woo the world to unity ;
And God fills all the canopy :
The blue flames lit from nether fire
In Liberty's wild torch expire.
No winds can quench, no darkness mars,
Her torch when lighted at the stars.
—*Rev. Joseph Cook.*

38. A SERMON IN A SAW-MILL.

Waal, 'Squire, I see yer runnin' of yer saw-mill right along,
Rippin' off yer slabs an' scantlin' to the same old pleasin' song ;
An' the crick still keeps a rushin' on the noisy water-wheel,
An' goes dancin' down the tail-race to a new Virginny reel.
Yer a pilin' up yer lumber, an' yer sawdust, too, I see ;

But the buzzin' of the saw-mill is the ruin of the tree.
An' I'm goin' to preach a sermon while yer greasin' up the cogs,
For ter keep the saw a runnin' thro' yer old saw logs.

I have heerd yer say, frien' Will'am, that this cruel liquor trade
Is a necessary business, an' it never can be stayed;
But I'm here ter tell yer, Will'am, that no matter what yer think,
The vile business can not flourish 'ceptin' some one buys the drink.
An' as sartin' as you've got ter have some logs ter run yer mill,
Jes' so sartin' must these liquor men have boys ter fill the till.
An' we bring the human timber, an' they saw it up, yer see,
Until by an' by we're minus both the timber and the tree!

O, ther' is a sort o' hummin' which I know yer loves to hear,
When the slabs are fallin' that way an' the laths a pilin' here,
When the lumber's movin' out'ard an' the cash's a comin' in,
An' when everything's a prosperin' an' times is good ag'in.
Ah! but when the dives be hummin' an' the wheels of sin go round,
Ther's a splendid lot of fellows that I know are being ground.
You're a slashin' down the forest, but they're slashin' down our joys,
An' the rushin' of the business is the ruin of the boys.

O that buzzin' saw o' ruin keeps a thrummin' right along.
It's a tearin' thro' the helpless an' it's tearin' thro' the strong.
An' the sawdust that is fallin' is the tears an' blood an' woe,
Droppin', drippin' in the waters that's a surgin' down below.
But the mill-wheels still keep thrummin', an' the slabs are flyin' free,
An' the dust of blood has fallen till it's sprinkled you an' me,
An' our boys are droppin' deathward like yer forests on the hills,
But we still keep up the timber for the runnin' o' the mills.

You can saw yer logs, frien' Will'am, so that when the work is done
They are worth far more in money than afore the work begun.
But for every gash these liquor fellows make upon our boys,
There's a blood-red gash o' ruin thro' our own domestic joys.
An' we're all a stan'in' back of 'em, an' helpin' 'em along,

An' a votin' liquor ballots to perpetuate the wrong.
For I tell yer it's the voter that manipulates the saw,
When he regulates the business with his tax or license law.

Yes, the party wins by voters, an' the winners make the law,
An' the law is the machinery that agitates the saw.
An' this peerless Christian nation, with a heart as hard as steel,
Takes the dealers' cash an' turns the rushin' water on the wheel.
Then all the mills go buzzin', and the tears begin to flow,
An' the homes begin ter crumble, an' the land is full of woe.
But I tell you all the sufferin' an' sorrow that we feel,
Is because the Christian voter stands himself beside the wheel.

— Rev. D. R. Miller.

39. AN INDICTMENT THAT STILL HOLDS GOOD.*

The record of the liquor business, the creed of the brewers, the admissions of their advocates, show conclusively that the dramshop is a bulldozer, a rebel, a defiant outlaw, which assassinates business, character, or life, as it may deem best, to intimidate opposition and prevent investigation of its record and effects. These cowards are universal bulldozers. I never knew the liquor business to do a manly thing in the world. I never knew it to make a manly fight. I never knew it to stand squarely on an issue. Its whole defense is a show of defiance, a show of bravado, a show of bulldozing, a show of braggadocio; and when these fail the defense is private, cowardly assassination. What is the first argument brought against the amendment in this State? "You cannot prohibit the sale of liquor." What does that mean? Rebellion.

— John B. Finch.

40. THE FIRST DUTY OF CITIZENS.

The first duty of citizens in reference to the liquor traffic is to free the country from the political control of the saloon. So long as the saloon is in power intemperance will run riot, and wax daily more defiant and more destructive. Let your vote be never given to put a liquor dealer in office; it is not to be expected that he will forget, in the service of his country, the interests of his own traffic; these will naturally be uppermost in his own mind. Discard the saloon candidate; he who

---

* From an address at Moore's Opera House, Des Moines, Iowa, April 23, 1882.

will owe his election to the saloon-keeper will retain kind remembrance of his benefactor, and serve him as occasion may offer. Keep out of office the timid man who will fear to do what he believes to be right lest he offend the saloon-keeper. To brave men only, to men of principle and conscience, can we safely entrust the reins of government. The first and most necessary step towards reform is to reduce beer and whisky men and their friends to private life, to wrest completely from their hands the helm of government.

— *Archbishop John Ireland.*

41. OUR BENEFICENT LICENSE LAWS.

I took my seat in church one day to hear God's law expounded,
 The pastor chose the eighth command, which says, "Thou shalt not steal."
He closed the Book, drew in his breath, and on the pulpit pounded,
 And said, "My hearers, I propose that statute to repeal.

"For it is plain the eighth command for us was not intended,
 The people now will not endure prohibitory laws;
So it must be repealed outright, or very much amended;
 At least there ought to be attached a heavy license clause.

"Now I have been your pastor for ten long years or more,
 I have watched you very closely (unflagging is my zeal);
And four I found there were that lied, and six that often swore,
 But, worst of all, it now appears that ten of you will steal!

"What shall we do to stop this drain upon the congregation?
 My pay is back a year or two, the church debt's never paid;
Suppose we license one of these (who has the reputation
 Of being quite respectable while working at his trade).

"And let him steal from all who fall within his lawful clutches,
 Provided ten per cent. of what he steals from you is given
To help the church of God along and save poor sinful wretches,
 By showing them the narrow way that leads direct to Heaven.

"This will reduce the thieves to one. The idea it is pleasing!

The other nine will be reclaimed, your property protected;
The church finances much improved by this cute plan of leas-
    ing,
While all the morals of the church will quickly be perfected."

You stop your ears and cry aloud in righteous indignation,
    To think that man should interfere and trample on God's
        law;
And substitute, in place thereof, one of his own creation,
    As though the Lord had made mistake and placed therein a
        flaw!

But if it is a righteous thing to license whisky selling,
    In order to restrict the same and lessen our taxation,
Then show me, if you can, the wrong this pastor did in telling
    His church to license one to steal, to help the congregation!

And if the truth shall ever dawn, upon this rum-cursed nation,
    That license laws do not restrict the sale of liquors strong;
But only serve to block the way to full annihilation,
    Then tell me if you think it pays to compromise with wrong!
            —*Rufus C. Landon.*

42. THE FORCES OF BATTLE.

Against any great evil in a community the forces are drawn up in this order. Immediately confronting the evil, on the very battle's edge, is a comparatively small company of men whose consciences are perfectly clear. With them all doubt and debate are at an end. They have but one cry, so intense and relentless that it falls on duller consciences like a storm of hail. Sin! sin! sin! War to the knife and no quarter. These are the radicals, the fanatics, the cranks, the fools, God's fools, who "turn the world upside down."

Back of these is the great host of the eminently respectables, good souls, well meaning men with half-informed consciences, timid, conservative, inclined to calmness and particularly given to hard sense. Among them originate all the compromises, the make-shifts, the substitutes, the half measures. They love to pass resolutions, and if they get as far as "ringing resolutions" they seem to think that the walls of Jericho have forgotten their ancient manners if they do not instantly fall flat. Back of this half-converted host stretches the great mass of the indifferent, shading off into the blackness of darkness and the shadow of death. This is the order of battle. Now comes the process. The conscience, that little band of radicals and cranks down at the front, keeps up an incessant racket. They rest not, day nor night. They run to and fro discussing, declaring, hurling fire-brands of incendiary literature right and left. They hold forlorn little meetings in most unheard-of places, but manage to so stir things up that their little place becomes suddenly interesting, as a house afire. They define, explain, teach, exhort. They drag us poor, limp ministers out of our "splendidly null" pulpits, and when we get down into their inflammable atmosphere, before we know it we have used "injudicious language." And when a minister reaches that point his course is rapidly downward. He is soon shouting and waving a torch with the worst of them. He is at last among the prophets. So by degrees the conservatives are won over and catch the divine madness until conscience has an irresistible host under command. It moves steadily on to the occupation of the conquered territory, and then follow the more peaceful tasks of clarifying conviction, establishing customs and framing righteous, efficient laws. What the Abolitionist was to slavery, that the Prohibitionist is to strong drink — a sleepless, remorseless conscience with a naked sword in hand, smiting in the name of God.

— *Rev. Dr. J. H. Ecob.*

43. THE REFORMER.*

All grim and soiled and brown with tan,
   I saw a Strong One, in his wrath,
Smiting the godless shrines of man
      Along his path.

The Church, beneath her trembling dome,
   Essayed in vain her ghostly charm:
Wealth shook within his gilded home
      With strange alarm.

Fraud from his secret chambers fled
   Before the sunlight bursting in:
Sloth drew her pillow o'er her head
      To drown the din.

"Spare," Art implored, "yon holy pile;
   That grand, old, time-worn turret spare";

---

* By permission of Houghton, Mifflin & Co.

Meek Reverence, kneeling in the aisle,
    Cried out, "Forbear!"

Gray-bearded Use, who, deaf and blind,
    Groped for his old accustomed stone,
Leaned on his staff, and wept to find
    His seat o'erthrown.

Young Romance raised his dreamy eyes,
    O'erhung with paly locks of gold,—
"Why smite," he asked in sad surprise,
    "The fair, the old?"

Yet louder rang the Strong One's stroke,
    Yet nearer flashed his axe's gleam;
Shuddering and sick of heart I woke,
    As from a dream.

I looked: aside the dust-cloud rolled,—
    The Waster seemed the Builder too;
Up springing from the ruined Old
    I saw the New.

'Twas but the ruin of the bad,—
    The wasting of the wrong and ill;
Whate'er of good the old time had
    Was living still.

Calm grew the brows of him I feared;
    The frown which awed me passed away,
And left behind a smile which cheered
    Like breaking day.

The grain grew green on battle-plains,
    O'er swarded war-mounds grazed the cow;
The slave stood forging from his chains
    The spade and plow.

Through vine-wreathed cups with wine once red,
    The lights on brimming crystal fell,
Drawn, sparkling, from the rivulet head
    And mossy well.

Where the doomed victim in his cell
    Had counted o'er the weary hours,
Glad school-girls, answering to the bell,
    Came crowned with flowers.

Grown wiser for the lesson given,
  I fear no longer, for I know
That, where the share is deepest driven,
    The best fruits grow.

The outworn rite, the old abuse,
  The pious fraud transparent grown,
The good held captive in the use
    Of wrong alone,—

These wait their doom, from that great law
  Which makes the past time serve to-day;
And fresher life the world shall draw
    From their decay.

O, backward-looking son of time!
  The new is old, the old is new,
The cycle of a change sublime
    Still sweeping through.

Take heart! the Waster builds again,—
  A charmed life old Goodness hath;
The tares may perish,— but the grain
    Is not for death.

God works in all things; all obey
  His first propulsion from the night:
Wake thou and watch!— the world is gray
    With morning light!
                 — *J. G. Whittier.*

44. AN UNFORTUNATE TRELLIS.

Beyond any question the present effrontery and power of the saloon are due to the license laws.

At my old home a vine of bitter-sweet came up at the root of a fine young elm tree. It was a pretty, delicate, twining thing, and I turned it so it might climb the tree. It did climb in graceful spiral rings to the very top, and the tree was beautiful. The long tendrils of the vine hung down on every side. I pinched off the tender shoots as they multiplied so as to obstruct the path, and the more I did so the stronger grew the trunk coils. I planted vines by all my young trees; it made them look so brave and lively. I thought, "How strange nature has not planted vines and trees in pairs!" I have seen "why" recently. My beautiful elm is a dead stalk, with the vine embedded in its body, itself spiral now, conformed to the constricting cord of the beautiful thug. So the Christian Republic — guileless, devoted trellis of the liquor traffic for so many years — stands all deformed and corkscrew-shaped to-day, in the deadly spiral of commercial and political whisky rings; but alive, thank God! and still powerful, for her good right hand, tho atrophied by long disuse, is free. The Church is its palm; the Women's Christian Temperance Union, the Young People's Societies of Christian Endeavor, the Salvation Army, and the Society for the Prevention of Crime are the fingers, and the Prohibition Party the thumb. I see it reaching out for "the sword of the Lord and of Gideon." I see it closing on the hilt. I see the blade poised aloft, all gleaming. I read upon it, "Gideon," "Washington," "Grant." O strike, Excalibur! Cleave to the marrow the murderous parasite, and set this nation free!

It is not the union of Church and State I advocate, but *union of the Church to save the State.*
— *John G. Woolley.*

45. RESPONSIBILITY OF INDIVIDUAL VOTERS.

In every reform from intemperance, from vice, from crime, each individual citizen is responsible to the degree of influence which he has, and if he does not exert it he is responsible for a neglect of duty, a binding duty. He is bound to create a public sentiment that shall work for virtue. He is bound to drain the community of all those evils that run together and form a channel for vice and crime. It is not a matter of election; it is a matter of obligation, and because there are the most respectable classes in the community that don't do it, it doesn't set you free. Because the man of riches and the man of power and the man of standing in society don't do it, the poorest laboring man in the community if he does not, under the direction of his reason and conscience, labor for the purification of the commonwealth, he is responsible to God. He is bound to do it. If his individuality on the one side has shielded him against aggression, it brings with it also certain obligations, and he is bound to meet them. All parties hold their members only subject to the corrected judgment and moral sense of the individual. If they go with their party on the general ground that it is going right and is doing right, as far as the limitation of human ignorance and human power are concerned traveling in the right direction, although with many imperfect steps and many imperfect elements, he may justly go on with it; but if he is committed, as were the parties of slavery, to so atrocious a wrong as that which violated the fundamental rights of the whole human family, a man is bound to fight the party, in it and out of it; in it by correction, out of it by protest and opposition. And merely because he can say "The party did it, I did not," he is not relieved of responsibility. Inasmuch as you knew what was right and did not do it, so much you are involved in the guilt; and there was a great deal of guilt. The church itself was involved in the same — dumb pulpits, uncirculated Bibles, a corrupt and vicious public sentiment.

— Henry Ward Beecher.

46. TWISTING AND TURNING.

It was only a sign on a countryman's shop,
   Standing out in bold letters, uneven and queer,
But I read and reread, as I came to a stop,
   "All kinds of twisting and turning done here."

Now this man of the shop was a turner by trade,
   And his ladles and butter-bowls sold far and near,
But his sign's in demand farther yet, I'm afraid,
   "All kinds of twisting and turning done here."

There is that big convention that planes off its planks
   To please both church members and brewers of beer,
In order to hold every sort in its ranks,
   "All kinds of twisting and turning done here."

There's the State Legislature, and Congress no less,
   With higher officials in places so dear,
They are just covered up with this flag of distress,
   "All kinds of twisting and turning done here."

There are even Church papers, and ministers, too,
   Who try on two horses to ride and to steer;
'Twixt gospel and license they've all they can do,
   "All kinds of twisting and turning done here."

I see some are twisting and turning to-night,
   Because of God's message, so loud and so clear;

Well, twist from old parties, and turn to the right!
"All kinds of twisting and turning done here."
—*Rev. P. J. Bull.*

47. VOTING VS. RESOLVING.

King Alcohol's vanquished;
  The Church has decreed it;
Then let us rejoice
  And be glad when we read it.
They've resolved and whereas'd
  That the traffic must go,
In language so plain
  That a fool ought to know.

"It can not be licensed,"
  They say, "without sin";
Why, friendly old chestnut,
  Come, where have you been;
And "where were you at"
  In the conflict last fall?
I really don't think
  That you voted at all.

If you did, did you vote
  As you've just resoluted?
Now figures won't lie
  If rightly computed.
Say, what was the number
  Of votes you recorded
Against this great monster,
  So remorseless and sordid?

I've seen an old scarecrow
  Standing out in the field;
It became so familiar
  That no power it could wield
To frighten the birds
  That came every morn,
And from under its nose
  Took the farmer's good corn.

But the farmer came out,
  You could see he was "hot,"
And with an old gun

Filled the birds full of shot.
The birds then decided
  To have nothing to do
With the business-like end
  Of that living scarecrow.

Your resolves are the scarecrow,
  The old parties the birds;
'Tis but little they care
  For your empty, wise words.
They feel very certain
  You will do nothing rash,
But will vote at the crack
  Of the old party lash.

And you are the farmer,
  The hand is the gun;
The ballot's the shot
  That will "make things hum."
A vote will weigh more
  When cast for the right,
Than all the resolves
  You could make in a night.

—*J W Rowe.*

48. SIX BOYS.

We all went to school together in the old brick academy in a country town, years ago.

We grew up, separated, went our different life roads.

But I have been meeting my old schoolmates lately, and it is strange how the whisky curse has divided the six.

I stood not long ago on the platform of the chapel in a penitentiary to talk to the prisoners. On the front bench, in spite of his stripes, his close-cut hair, his prison pallor, I recognized one of the six. We used to occupy the same desk at school.

He was a prisoner for life, and was drunk when the murder was committed.

Picking up the paper one morning I noticed that a tramp had been pushed from a train on one of our railroads, had fallen under the wheels, his right arm crushed, and that the surgeon at the hospital had amputated it at the shoulder. Recognizing the name I went down to the hospital and found in one of the wards a miserable one-armed tramp — my old schoolmate.

I tried to talk to him, to pray with him; he would not listen. I telegraphed his brother, a well-to-do farmer. He came on to the city, took the poor fellow home with him, gave him a good suit of clothes and said to him: "Brother, as long as you live you can have a good home here with me. You shall not want for anything, but you must not go to the city."

He stayed there three days, and then wandered off. He is to-day a miserable, one-armed bloated wretch, a whisky tramp, drifting toward a drunkard's grave.

There was another, a bright boy full of life, the wit of the school, sunshiny, bubbling over with laughter. He grew up to be a wild, drinking young man, but later on I learned that he had reformed and was in the temperance work.

I heard him one night, and went on the platform to speak to him.

I said: "Are you a Christian?"

"No," he said, "but I am not afraid of whisky."

A few months afterward I heard of his conversion.

Again I met him, an earnest, active, intelligent Christian worker.

I said in my heart: "My friend is safe."

Alas! No man is safe in a land where whisky is sold.

My friend had been working as an evangelist in the West. He had some money, and he started home to visit his old father and mother. He was within twenty miles of home, on the train. He was taken sick. A gentleman in the seat with him said: "Are you sick?" "Yes." "I am taken that way myself sometimes, and I always carry a little good whisky with me. Suppose you take a little; it will do you good." "No," said my friend; "I used to drink, and will never touch the stuff again."

The man got up, went to the water cooler, poured a little whisky in the glass and brought it to my friend. He held it under his nose and said: "Don't be a fool; drink it."

The old devil in my friend jumped at the bait. Very eagerly he swallowed the poison.

It was like putting a spark in an open keg of powder.

At the next station my friend got off, eight miles from

home. He stayed there in a saloon until, crazed by delirium tremens, the saloon-keeper sent him to a hotel.

He was put in a second-story corner room and served with all the whisky he wanted, for he still had some money. One day the delirium devils chased him to the window, out of the window headlong down on the sharp palings.

They found him there, bruised, bleeding — dead.

Within eight miles of home!

At the next station his old father had waited every day for his boy.

He said: "He will come to-morrow."

And to-morrow came at last, and a rough wooden box was pushed out on the platform.

The father saw his son's name on it. He had the box opened, and he found all that remained of his only son.

So three of my old schoolmates went the downward way of death.

One in the penitentiary for life; cause, whisky.

One a wanderer on the face of the earth; cause, whisky.

One gone to a drunkard's eternity; cause, whisky.

Now for the brighter side.

Not long ago I looked down from the gallery of the House of Representatives upon a session of Congress.

At his desk I noticed a man whose name is known all over the Union.

The breath of suspicion has never touched him.

He is without fear, without reproach — an active Christian worker.

Another one of my schoolmates.

One Sabbath morning I entered a church in a little Virginia town, and had the pleasure of hearing another one of my old schoolmates preach.

The sixth one of the boys is myself, a sinner saved by grace, living in the sunshine, trying to make the world brighter, happier, better.

Here are the other three:

One an honored Congressman; cause, cold water.

One a minister of the Gospel; cause, cold water.

One A WORKER FOR THE RIGHT.

—*A. W. Hawks.*

49. "FEED MY SHEEP."

Peter the fisherman toils all night,
  He and his fellows toil in vain;
But lo! a word in the morning light,
  And at loaded nets they tug and strain.

Peter the fisherman cries aloud,
  "It is the Lord!" and springs to the shore;
What are his nets and the finny crowd?
  Naught recks he of the plentiful store.

Calmly the Lord prepares the feast;
  Down on the shore they break the bread;
Served by hands from the cross released,
  Never such viands as these outspread.

Eager Peter, his heart on fire
  With a mingled tumult of love and shame,
Longs to utter his strong desire,
  Longs to honor the blessed Name.

Could he but do some wonderful deed,
  Give his life as an offering free,
Stand once more in an hour of need!
  Questions the Master, "Lovest thou me?"

What shall he do? The Master's word,
  That could awe to quiet the stormy deep
When all its passionate waves were stirred,
  Answers him quietly, "Feed my sheep."

Nothing great for Peter to do;
  Only to follow, by night and day,
Where pitfalls are many and shepherds few,
  Seeking the sheep that go astray.

Not with the ninety and nine to rest,
  But to walk alone in desert ways,
Bearing the wounded, the weak, on his breast,
  With none to aid him, with none to praise.

So, O Lord, from Galilee's shore,
  Comes thy word as it came of old;
Show us how we may serve thee more,
  Loving and seeking the lost from thy fold.

      —*B. E. S., in "Golden Rule."*

50. WHAT J. M. B. THINKS.

Methodis' women air not very bad,
   Their virtues he'd not for one moment despise,
The blessin's the church in the past's frum them hed
   Reely brings the tears to his eyes ;
        But J. M. B.,
        Conservative, he
Sez we can't go to Gineral C.

I s'pose that settles it ; orter, indeed,
   Purvided assertion is better'n proof ;
If only each voter to him would give heed
   This troublesome question would soon keep aloof ;
        For J. M. B.,
        Conservative, he
Sez we musn't go to Gineral C.

Why ? Thet's a sticker ; as near's I can tell
   Because we've dun so well in the past ;
It's true thet logic don't seem to fit well,
   But thet's our fault, not his'n at the last ;
        For J. M. B.,
        Conservative, he
Sez it's as plain as A, B, C.

The church hes heaped blessin's all over our ways ;
   We've bin let speak in meetin', and raise money, too ;
We've c'lected the salary on warm and cold days,
   Washed dishes at socials and cushioned the pews ;
        And J. M. B.,
        Conservative, he
Sez, if we ain't satisfied *now*, wen will we be ?

It's true we've done all them things well,
   An' they'd sort uv miss us ef we should step out ;
But then, you never kin reely tell
   In any new movement, what may come about ;
        And J. M. B.,
        Conservative, he
Sez, it's a dangerous experiment for we !

My ! how thet frightens us ! S'posin' it's true,
   Jist s'posin' we git on the conference floor
An' all our sweet graces jist melt like the dew,

Till we git cuttin' up, like our brethren before!
    For J. M. B ,
      Conservative, he
Thinks thet's the use of Gineral C.

Better not resk it ; fur better stay hum
  An' work fur the church in the orthodox way ;
No matter ef 't does seem a trifle humdrum
  An' wen things go wrong, we would like our say ;
    Mind, J. M. B.,
      Conservative, he
Sez thet there is an awful idee !

It's true thet we sorter remember, you know,
  A hearin' thet kind uv logic before,
An' the church, sumhow, seems to hev weathered the blow
  Uv hevin' lay delegates onto its floor.
    But J. M. B.,
      Conservative, he
Sez thet there argyment don't hit we.

It's true, wen you give your mind to the thing,
  It does seem a trifle onreasonable, too,
Thet we'll git to be bishops, all in one spring,
  And remand man ministers back to the pew ;
    But J. M. B.,
      Conservative, he
Sez thet ther's the very idee.

We've sorter suspicioned all through the years,
  Thet the question wus much like the " Heathen Chinee";
" Brethren, gird on your armor, give wings to your fears ;
  There only air places enough for we !"
    And J. M. B.,
      Conservative, he
Sez God meant men to boss the Gineral C.

It's true there has been a lot other talk,
  'Bout Mary an' Martha, an' 'bout Phœbe, too;
Till you really would think, ef you dared to take stock,
  Thet we might be trusted outside uv the pew ;
    But J. M. B.,
      Conservative, he
Sez, "they didn't know everything down in Judee."

Wall! we must settle it, trustin' the Lord ;
   Somehow, we've not lost faith in His might
Who ruleth men's hearts, and by whose spoken word,
   All darkness shall yet give place to the light.
        Yes, J. M. B.,
          Conservative, he
May find God rules,— even Gineral C.
              — *Katharine Lente Stevenson.*

51. DREAMING AND WAKING.

Beside the road I dreamed of Heaven ;
   I heard its far-off fountains play ;
I heard the song of souls forgiven,
   Like birds that chant the birth of day.
I dreamed I saw an angel come
Down from those heights to lead me home.

His eyes were kind; his robes dropped dew
   And fragrance of that unknown land.
He spoke, but in no tongue I knew —
   No language I could understand :
And with a glance of pitying pain
He turned him back to Heaven again.

A pilgrim passed. "And didst thou hear,"
   I asked him, "what the angel said ? "
Whispered the traveler in my ear,
   Ere onward into light he sped,
"I heard the angel sigh, 'Not yet ;
This soul knows not love's alphabet.'

"Oh, comrade mine, thou dreamest in vain
   Of Heaven, if here thou hast not found,
In soothing human grief and pain,
   That earth itself is holy ground.
Unpractised in love's idioms now,
A foreigner to Heaven art thou.

"Cold wouldst thou walk, and blind, and dumb,
   Among those flaming hosts above,
A homesick alien ; for the sum
   Of all their thoughts and deeds is love.
And they who leave not self behind,
No Heaven in Heaven itself can find.

"Rejoice that with the sons of men
  A little while thou lingerest yet.
Go, read thy Book of Life again;
  Go back and learn Love's alphabet
Of Christ the Master. He will teach
Thy lips to shape the heavenly speech."

I looked within; a dreary scroll
  Of loveless, dull, self-binded days,
I saw my humbled Past unroll.
  Not even my fellow-pilgrim's gaze
Could I uplift my eyes to meet,
Such glory played around his feet!

He went his way. I turned again,
  Ashamed and weeping, to the road
Thronged by the suffering sons of men,
  A beckoning Face among them glowed,
Sweeter than all the harps of Heaven
I heard a voice: "Thou art forgiven!"

"Come follow Me, and learn of Me,
  And I will teach thee how to love."
My Master! now I turn to Thee;
  I sigh not for a Heaven above.
These human souls are angels bright;
Thy presence here is Heaven's own light!
— *Lucy Larcom.*

52. NOT A MUSHROOM PARTY.

The Prohibition party is not a party of mushroom growth or evanescent existence. For twenty-one years it has withstood the storms of abuse, vilification, and malicious misrepresentation, and in spite of these has had a steady and substantial growth. It has beheld other parties rise, flash past it like a rocket to fame and disappear like a stick. But it has held its ground, kept true to its principles, and moved faithfully onward. The power of its cohesion and the vitality which it exhibits is due to the fact that it applies to the government of a political party the same law of conscience which governs the individual. Is it wrong to steal? Then it is wrong to belong to a political party or any other combination of individuals that will steal. It is wrong for the individual to oppress the poor by establishing monopolies and trusts? Then it is wrong for him to belong to a political party that by its legislation establishes and protects oppressive monopolies and trusts. Is it wrong for the individual to run a saloon? Then it is just as wrong for him to cast his ballot with a party that makes laws which legalize, protect, and perpetuate the saloon. Because of the application of conscience to politics, the Prohibition party becomes an indestructible force, until the wrongs in government, which made its organization necessary, have been overthrown. —*J. J. Ashenhurst.*

53. A BATTLE RALLY.

Abolition had its martyrs,
  Men who dared to do or die,
Freely giving voice and life-blood
  To the slaves' despairing cry.

Lovejoy, in his gory garments,
  Roused the Northern sense of right;
John Brown, swinging on the scaffold,
  Nerved her legions in the fight.

Prohibition has its martyrs,
  Men of equal strength and truth,
Who have kept its banner flying
  In its weakness and its youth.

Gambrell, Haddock, Moffett, fallen!
  But their blood for vengeance cries
'Gainst the gory-taloned dragon
  That all righteousness defies.

Shall we ever wait or falter
  While the cause for action lives;
While the martyr meekly dying,
  Life to Prohibition gives?

No! the cause of God is with us
  And his truth shall win the day;
Hear we mutterings in the present
  Of the future's fearful fray.

—*George A. Fish.*

54. THE SAME OLD SWING.

A very wise man once fell among thieves,
  On a lone, dark way as he rode to town ;
They beat him and robbed him and sent him adrift,
  With nothing left save his steed and gown.
Then a stranger rode near,— " Sweet friend, dear friend !
  It must give you a pain to be treated so :
But I vow you a straight, smooth ride to town,
  If by my way you'll consent to go."

Then sadly the very wise man turned round —
  Sadly because he'd been treated thus —
With thankfulness for this kindness done,
  Went the other road with the smooth-tongued cuss.
He started, that is, but he hadn't gone far
  Till led by his guide to a second roost
Of robbers, who took his horse away,
  With a kick for the wise man by way of boost.

As the wise man weakly tottered off
  He called to his guide in tearful whang :
"You've broken the promises made to me,
  And I'm going to town with the other gang !"

" Yes, poor, dear friend, come back to us ! "
  Cried a voice from the dense, tree-shaded track.
" You shouldn't have trusted that smooth-tongued cuss ! "
  He went — and they took the coat from his back !
" Oh, my, that's rough ! " sobbed Number Two ;
  " It breaks our hearts to see this sin !
Come here, and we'll clothe and give you wealth ! "
  He went — and the rascals grabbed his skin.

And all this time the straight highway
  Shone smooth and right and broad and safe.
And the watchmen called, " This road is plain !
  Why tread dark, devious paths, weak waif ? "
Then the very wise man smiled a raw, sad smile,
  And shook his gory, dismantled head :
" I've been going these ways to town so long,
  If I'd think of a change I'd fall down dead !

" These two great parties assure me now
  That by one of these roads I shall reach the town ;

  And each has promised to give me back
   My wealth and my horse and my hide and gown.
  'Tis true that their ways are twisted and dark,
   And they've lied to me every time — strange men!
  But they say they love me so tenderly,
   And I think I'll just try the old way again."

So the wise man once more turned away
 From the honest lights and the highway straight;
And again we'll hear his shrieks of pain
 As he meets his usual, well-known fate.
They will boil him down for his tallow and bones,
 And chuckle again to view his pains.
But where, in his whole anatomy,
 Will they find the things he calls his brains!
         — *Edna C. Jackson.*

55. QUEER, ISN'T IT! *

Lo, a Northern forest burns,
And the startled nation turns,
Views with wonder and with fear
Desolation far and near;
Sees the homeless people flee,
Counts the loss of property,
Shudders at the ruin rife,
Sad bewails the loss of life.
Then toward the stricken land
Stretches prompt and helpful hand.

There's a wilder, hotter fire,
Sweeping farther, leaping higher,
Round the nation, through the land,
Each saloon a burning brand.
Loss of life there is, and home;
Women, children, hopeless roam;
Lo! there follow in the glare,
Ruin, madness, grim despair.
She may count, if loss she seek,
Twenty millions every week!

---

* The saloon burns up $23,000,000 of our national resources every week — and yet we are excited over a few forest fires. — *Editorial note in The Voice.*

But the nation only sighs,
Folds her hands and shuts her eyes!
— *Hattie Horner Louthan.*

---

56. THE DEACON'S MATCH.

There was a man out West who owned a calf. That is nothing new, because I knew a man out there that owned two. And the man had a ten-year-old boy, and the boy carelessly let the bars down and let the calf out of the lot. And the calf strayed over the railroad track, and an engine came along and struck him and doubled him all up, and it was not worth anything as a calf after that; but the owner of that calf was somewhat vexed. He was not very particular whether the "sun went down on his wrath" or not, and he sued the railroad company, and after lawing away the price of a hundred calves, the company beat him — as the company usually does in such cases — and the man got madder; and coming home from the trial he said to the church deacon:

"I am going to get even with that railroad company."

"How?" asked the deacon.

"I am going to burn that bridge crossing the chasm just out of town."

"Why!" said the deacon, "you would never do that, would you?"

"Yes," he said, "I don't propose to let any rich corporation run rough-shod over me."

And the deacon, in telling his wife about it, said the man intended to burn the bridge that night at nine o'clock, and the time came around, and the wife, who was a member of the Woman's Christian Temperance Union, said that they had better go down and see about it; but the deacon said he would not burn it — he was just in a passion when he said he would. "Well," she said, "let us go down and see about it, anyway." So they started down toward the bridge, and sure enough, the man was there, and he had just finished saturating a portion of the bridge with kerosene oil, and just as they reached him he felt in his pocket and found he had forgotten to bring matches. He turned to the deacon and asked him for a match.

"What are you going to do with it?" inquired the deacon.

"Going to burn the bridge," said the man, "as I told you I would."

"Well," said the deacon, "now I propose to show you the difference between a man who has made his peace with the Lord and a man of the world. If I loan you a match to burn the bridge," said the deacon, "I would be as guilty as you are."

"Well," said the man, "there are plenty of matches, I will have them if I want them, you know; there is no doubt about that. Why, deacon, I know where I can buy matches at different places, right here in the village. You can't suppress the sale of matches, deacon, and I must have the match. I tell you what I will do: I will give you a dollar for a match."

"Well," said the deacon, "are you going to burn the bridge anyway?"

"Why, yes," said the man, "I told you I would burn it, and you might just as well have a little revenue as anybody out of this transaction, don't you see? Exactly so, I am going to burn it anyway."

"Well," said the deacon, "if you are going to burn it anyway, that puts an entirely different light upon the whole question."

And he reached into his pocket for a match, and his wife caught him by the coat and said: "Here, husband, you would not sell the man a match to be used in burning the bridge?"

And that broke the deacon all up, and he said: "Nancy, that is just the way with you Christian Temperance Union women. You are a lot of fanatics, always going to extremes in everything. It is your business to attend to household affairs and it is my business to provide for the family, and when I have an opportunity of making an honest dollar, I don't want you coming round and putting your oar in." And he hands over the match to the man, and the man passes him back a big wagon-wheel silver dollar, and the deacon shoves it away down in his pocket, ond then turns to the man and says:

"Are you going to burn the bridge?"

"Why, of course I am," said the man, "that is what I bought the match for."

"Well," said the deacon, "May God have mercy on your soul; I wash my hands of the whole business."

And the match is lighted and the bridge is ablaze, and the

cars come along at the rate of forty miles an hour and dash into the chasm and one hundred lives are lost.

Who is guilty when it comes to the judgment bar of God? The man who sold the match is just as guilty as the man who lighted it and fired the bridge! And he who gives way to the plea that "we are going to settle this question on a high license basis"— that we can not effectually prohibit the liquor traffic, and goes to the polls and uses his ballot to represent the deacon's match, and votes for a license party, and the saloon system continues, homes and immortal souls are destroyed, when it comes before the judgment bar of God, will be just as guilty as the man who keeps the saloon. My friends, there is no compromise ground in this matter.

— *John P. St. John.*

57. THE BOUNDARY POST.*

A vision of ice-bound barrens,
   'Neath the midnight sun's weird glow,
A band of tyrant's hirelings,
   Hearts cold as the Polar snow —
Crouching in dread of their mandates,
   A sorrowful helpless host,
On their knees, and with prostrate figures,
   Before the boundary post!

Oh! dreadful is man's oppression
   In the tropic's genial glow.
'Mid the temperate zone's rich fruitage,
   As well as 'mid northern snow!
He plunders the home of his brother,
   Enslaves him; and tyrants boast
They have stolen his soul, his manhood,
   Who dies at the boundary post!

It riseth, solemn and stately —
   A symbol that draws the tear —
A tall white column majestic,

---

* It is related by sympathetic Americans, who deplore what they call the tyranny of the Czar, that when the convicts sentenced to Siberia reach the boundary post on the Russian frontier the stoicism of the very sternest character gives way, and the old and young, sage and simple, noble and peasant, reduced to one rank of misery, mingle their tears and sighs, realizing that their journey's end is reached.

That marks the Russian frontier!
Through the first dim shadows of morning,
  Its outlines of pain appear
To the exile who marcheth eastward
  On the road that is long and drear!
Trembling, through cloud-bank or mist-veil,
  It comes, like an awful ghost,
And blasts the sight of the gazer —
  The dreadful boundary post!

With blood are their sandals sullied
  As they painfully drag along;
Not an exile heart may be merry,
  Not a voice awaken a song!
'Neath the whip of the brutal driver
  The staggering convict goes
Who follows the path of oppression
  To Siberia's wastes and snows!
But the keenest throb of his anguish
  That his torn heart feels the most
Is to fall 'neath the strokes and the woundings
  At the tall white boundary post!

He dreams, as he travels in silence,
  That yet there may be a reprieve!
He cannot be sent to the toiling
  In the mines and the valleys to grieve!
But the sight of the landmark uplifted,
  'Mid the Northland snow and frost,
Only bids him: "Your hope you must bury
  At the foot of the boundary post!"

*   *   *   *   *   *   *

A vision of palsied fingers
  That touch not the poet's pen;
A story of genius fallen
  Of one who was great among men,
The poisoned cup hath enslaved him!
  His journey of woe is begun,
The Garden of Eden he planted
  Is waste 'neath the midnight sun;
The glare of his evil passions
  Illumes a road more drear

Than the weary convict follows
  Afar to the east frontier!
O tempted soul, though the wine-waves
  Flash keener than Northland frost,
Pause ere thy soul lieth panting
  And wrecked at the boundary post!

A tyrant, relentless and cruel,
  'Neath tropic or polar star —
King Alcohol — gathers his minions
  And mocks at the might of a czar!
A boundary line there obtaineth
  'Twixt virtue and vice, as we know!
Here lie the harvest-fields, vineyards —
  There, are the wastes and the snow!
Tempted thou art, yet refraining?
  Oh, cast thou the tempter away!
And naught have to do with the spoiler
  Who watcheth by night and by day!
O sin-ridden soul, yet an effort,
  A prayer! From the dram-drinkers' host,
Thou hast paused on the road to perdition
  This side of the boundary post!

—Lelia B. Hewes.

58. MORAL SUASION NOT SUFFICIENT.

But we are told we should use moral suasion. Yes! but the question is, when moral suasion should be applied. The tiger springs from the jungle, strikes down a man, begins crunching his arm and drinking the life-blood from his very heart. Shall he then begin to stroke that tiger's head, to fondle him, and to reason with him? "Now, tiger, it's very unkind, very ungentlemanly, very unreasonable for you to chew my arm in that way." Suppose his friend comes out and sees what is going on; shall he lecture the man who is down, and say: "Now you ought to have known better than to get into such a position. You ought to have watched and taken more care." No, let him snatch out his dagger and strike it in to the hilt in the heart of the destroyer. Then there will be time for talk and warning. I arraign the saloon as the wild beast of our civilization, with blood-stained teeth and claws, still raging unchecked through our land, and entire Prohibition is the only effective remedy. Let Prohibition be echoed everywhere. — *Rev. Thomas Dixon.*

59. WORRIED ABOUT KATHERINE.
GRANDAM.

I'm glad that it suited you, Schoolma'am, to spend a few days here with Kate :

You're both of you fine-wove and crisp-like, an' take to each other first-rate.

When woman-hearts tangle together, they twist round again and again,

An' make up a queer sort o' love-match, I never have noticed in men.

And, Schoolma'am, I'm thriftily anxious about this smart gran'-child o' mine,

An' want to talk candid about her, with present an' future design.

She's hungry for other folks' knowledge, an' never too full to be fed ;

She's packed every book that I know of, all open-leaved, like, in her head ;

The 'rithmetic makes its home with her ; the grammar is proud of her tongue ;

She spells words as if she had made 'em, 'way back when the language was young.

She knows all the g'ography found yet ; she'd feel in a manner at home,

If dropped in the streets of Jerus'lem, or woke up some mornin' in Rome.

She's studied the habits of planets — knows how to call names at a star —

She's traced their invisible railroads, an' tells what their timetables are,

She's learnin' the words of old heathens that good-minded people abhorred —

A-thwartin' the old Tower of Babel — undoin' the work of the Lord.

Yes, Teacher, our dear, pretty Kath'rine is very sleek-minded an' smart ;

But still I can't help but to worry concernin' the breadth o' her heart!

TEACHER.

Why! sympathies need not to narrow, because the brain clambers above;
The more that a genuine heart knows, the better it knows how to love.
A gem was all crowded with splendor, unseen in the gloom of mines:
'Tis not now the less of a diamond, because it is polished, and shines!
The flower that was hunted by wild weeds, thinks never to bloom the less fair,
Because it is borne to a garden, and tended with wisdom and care.
A lamp in the sky had been tarnished by cloud-birds that flew from afar;
The wind swept the mist from its brightness — it gleamed, all the more of a star!
Whate'er is at fault in your grandchild, her learning makes easier withstood;
Whatever is good in your grandchild, her learning makes only more good.

GRANDAM.

That's nice, soothin' sentiments, Schoolma'am, an' helps all that works in your line;
It's one o' your golden opinions — I wish that it also was mine!
But, Teacher, suppose that she marries — the knives of her brain bright an' keen —
An' knows all creation, excep' how to keep her house cosy and clean!
Suppose when her husband comes home tired, the cheer o' her table to seek
She feeds him with steak that is soggy, an' tells him its meanin' in Greek?
Suppose that her coffee is muddy as if it was dipped from a trench:
Will that make his stomach less homesick, because she can tell it in French?
Suppose that her help is her master, along o' the things she don't know:

Can algebra make up the diff'rence, or grammar books give her
    a show?
Oh, Schoolma'am, those women keep house best (with nothin'
    to say ag'in *you*),
Who've learned to keep house o' their mothers, an' worked all
    its alphabet through!

TEACHER.

Your grandchild must take for her husband, a man with an
    intellect wide,
Who makes of the well-guarded body a place for the soul to
    reside;
Whose home is a God-made cathedral, with heart-blessings
    clear-voiced and sweet;
Who comes back at night for soul-comfort — not simply what
    he can eat.
Who thinks with her, feels with her, helps her; has patience,
    for both of their sakes;
Who celebrates all her successes, and takes stock in all her
    mistakes.
Who treasures her well-taught advantage o'er one who unstud-
    ied begins;
Who welcomes with sweet-whispered pleasure each step of the
    race that she wins.
Who leads her to minds that are kindled with brands from the
    watch-fires of fame;
Who's glad that her lamp has been trimmed well, to catch the
    clear sanctified flame.

GRANDAM.

An' if she shouldn't find this cur'os'ty?

TEACHER.

Then let her as single be known;
And thank God her training has taught her to work out life's
    problem alone.

GRANDAM.

But, Schoolma'am, admittin' your arg'ment (if one can "ad-
    mit" what one don't)
We'll say that she'll marry an angel (tho likelier 'twill happen
    she won't);
But s'posin' she does, an' her children are sent, same as others,
    to school:

I'm worryin' 'bout whether she'll let 'em be taught by the brain-stuffin' rule.
It hurts me to see 'em build over a child into somebody's pride,
Through givin' him heart-aches each week-day, by poundin' his head from inside!
They make 'em bite books with their teethin'; grown studies run all through their play;
They're killin' the children by inches, with five or six studies a day.
They load 'em with large definitions — as big as the children are small;
Ah me! it's a wonder the poor things twist up into grown folks at all!
There's many a poor little cre'tur' with other folks' words over-filled,
Not only "made mad" by "much learning" but weakened an' sickened an' killed!
There's many a green little grass-mound, whose tenant would say, could it talk,
"I died by their tryin' to run me, before I was able to walk!"

TEACHER.

A blessing's no less of a blessing, because by some 'tis abused;
The air, fire, and water *can* murder — and yet they all have to be used.
The steed that we drive to the river is tempted, not tortured, to drink;
The child should be given thought-burdens — but only to teach him to think.
Take comfort from now for the future; for Katherine, with all that she knows,
Is bright as a dollar just minted, and fresh as a new-blossomed rose.

GRANDAM.

But, Teacher, I'll tell my main trouble (though less than the ones I have said);
I'm gettin' behind the times daily, while Kate keeps a gettin' ahead.
She'll grow a fine lady, and nothin' between us in common there'll be;
Now don't you think, some time or other, that Kate'll be 'shamed, like, o' me?

6

KATE (entering, and kissing GRANDAM).

Ashamed of you? Never!—I'd give more for one silver hair of your head,
Than all of the studies I know of, and all of the authors I've read!
Do you know, you absurd dear old Grandma, your heart and your brain are more aid,
Than all of the sciences heard of, and all of the books ever made!
No process that man has discovered will act out affection's pure part;
The brain of the head is a failure, compared to the brain of the heart!
Ashamed of you? Let your grand life-work an answer unqualified be!
Pray God that my life may be lived so you'll never be " 'shamed like " o' me!

— *Will Carleton, in " Ladies' Home Journal."*

60. A CHRISTIAN ENDEAVORER'S POSITION.

WHAT SHALL CHRISTIAN YOUNG PEOPLE DO AGAINST THE SALOON?

The question is its own perfect answer, and I can only give it back expanded, as one may blow a rosebud into bloom.

First of all, *I will be a Christian.* I will keep *myself* pure. I will, as to this thing, abolish the word "temperance." It is the Pharisee of grammar, the arch-hypocrite of the vocabulary of this reform, the blood-guiltiest common noun in the language, a quagmire of definition not to be trusted by the foot of reason, or crossed by any but an empty vehicle of thought. I will be a *Christian.* Henceforth I'll stand upon the mountain top of Paul's great verse, of which the familiar version is: "If meat make my brother to offend, I will not eat meat enough to hurt *myself* tho the world perish; but which *is written,* "I will eat *no meat* while the world stands." And drinking wine *does* cause my brother to offend. From the first, the strong, clean, moderate drinker has been, and is to-day, the weak man's schoolmaster, to lead him to the gutter. Am I saying that one who drinks is not a Christian? No; but he is not *such* a Christian as can help in this endeavor.

I will be a man — an active, definite, persistent, self-respecting and respect-compelling *man;* no flunky to a party or a sect ; no toady to a majority ; no trimmer to the popular breeze ; no lisping baby-talker to committees ; no whimpering petitioner of my own servants ; no whispering, apologetic preacher, with a gag ; no wire-puller's Punch and Judy penny puppet annex to a party show ; no straddling, small and easy reformer ; no driveling camp-follower of the world's forward march ; no dreary spouter of the Concordance ; no Christian whose convictions require editing ; no sniveling moral coward trembling at a politician's sneer ; no pastor whose politics are queer ; no crayfish pietist backing under a creed at the approach of a new thought. *I will be intelligent;* I will take a Prohibition newspaper and read it. I will have an opinion and express it. *I will be consistent;* I will let no man despise me. I will not despise myself ; if I keep political company where saloon keepers feel at home, I will be man enough not to pray "Thy kingdom come on earth." I will be too much a man to talk of taking the world for Christ while I am consenting to farm out the highways of my own country to saloons and live on the rentals. I will hold no politician's coat while he stones a prophet or denies full citizenship to a woman. By the grace of God, I will be a Christian and a manly man.

I WILL BE AGAINST THE SALOON

and anything that favors, fears, or ignores it. The liquor traffic is the foot-rot of civilization. Saloons are the progeny of cities betrayed by party politics. I will renounce utterly and forever all allegiance to any political party in municipal government. I will not be bound by a caucus. But when a citizens' meeting conflicts with my prayer-meeting, I will miss the prayer-meeting. I will trust no man in city politics who winks at the saloon in national politics.

In national affairs I will belong to a party and be true to it, so true that when it goes wrong I will leave it and go straight ahead until it catches up. I will scratch the wickedness out of its ticket and then throw the ticket away, unless I can stand with it upon a clean, brave, open platform. A man who is false to himself can not be true to *anything*, and a party that asks a man to belie himself and *speak easy* his convictions, will in time betray both him and the country. A coward is potentially a traitor. I will square my politics to my church, or leave the church. The man, the ticket, or the party that expects or desires votes from the saloon shall have no vote from me. Let who will win this election, sell the licenses, and administer the all-pervasive paltry-treason of the spoils; when the clean church comes, whose right it is, she will take, without a rival or a question, the scepter of the world and reign. I will be for *that*. These hands are hers, only two of millions; but I will wash *them*, by the grace of God, and keep them clean for her. *No sales, no spoils, no saloon votes in Christian Endeavor !*

— John G. Woolley.

61. A FANATIC.

"Fanatic!" they said; yes, he stood for the truth,
  Defended it always by day and by night;
He wrought for the good of the children and youth,
  Well knowing the worth of their souls in God's sight.

Fanatic was he? Yes, he spent time and strength
  In labors of love for the tempted and tossed,
No toil was too great, no trifle too small
  To offer to Him for the souls that were lost.

Fanatic was he? Yet he cheerfully gave
  Of his income so small, to those who had less,
And the poor and the lowly, the sad ones of earth,
  Had cause this "fanatic" to love and to bless.

Fanatic was he? Yes, the world flitted by,
  With its laughter and song, its jest and its jeer;
They pitied him so, so they said as they went,
  For they fancied his life bitter, cheerless, and drear.

For they had their pleasure, their wine and their glee,
  And life was to them gay, and merry, and bright,
They lived for themselves, while he toiled for those
  Whom, born in the darkness, he brought to the light.

Ah! little they knew how the peace God doth give
  Dwelt deep in his heart, sweet, abiding, and strong,
And how, when in sorrow o'er those whom he loved,
  God gave in the night-time His presence and song.

And one day he died, and they laid him to rest
  On the sunny hillside, 'neath the grass and the flowers,

In the sorrowful hush of a heart-broken throng,
  Where lovingly God keepeth watch through the hours.

Ah! happy forever, no longer to toil
  Alone, and in sorrow, and misunderstood,
No longer "fanatic," but heir to a throne,
  With all the redeemed, the rejoicing and good.

O Soul! thou hast won — and thy hard race is o'er,
  Time's years are but few, and Eternity's long;
Thy service of love for the sin-stricken earth
  Shall blossom forever in gladness and song.
— *Maria L. Underhill.*

62. A GLORIOUS MONUMENT.

An artist, seeing a little boy, with rosy cheeks and laughing face, playing with his toys, was so charmed with the beauty and happiness of the child that he requested the privilege of taking its portrait. Permission being granted, he transferred the features of the beautiful boy to his canvas, and placed it in his studio, as one of the first specimens of his cherished art, and of the beauty, innocence, and happiness of childhood.

Many years afterward the same artist desired to find a subject that should be the very reverse of this. After a long search, on going into a prison, he there saw a man who, in a drunken frenzy, had murdered his own wife, and was soon to be executed as the penalty for his crime. His countenance was the picture of agony, remorse, and despair. The artist transferred the features of that wretched culprit to his canvas, and placed it in his studio, side by side with that of the beautiful and happy boy he had taken many years before. On retracing the history of that wretched man back to his childhood, he proved to be the same innocent boy whose happy and smiling countenance now exhibited a striking contrast by the side of that of the condemned criminal.

This is but a picture of what our youth may become, unless parents educate them to shun the vices and temptations of the liquor traffic. Such, fond parents, may be the fate of that little cherub boy you are now dandling on your knee, unless you, like an ancient heroine, make him "swear eternal hatred" to the liquor traffic. Cherish not the fond hope that he may not be allured and fall by the same insidious foe. All along life's perilous pathway may be seen the wrecks of thousands, whose early training and prospects were as bright and hopeful as are his. Oh, what is that bitter wail which is heard from fond parents' hearts all the earth over? Is it not like that which escaped from the lips of the king of Israel: "Oh, my son, my son! Would God I had died for thee, my son, my son!" Is it not the wail of blighted hopes and ruined prospects arising over the victims of a legalized curse?

Father's, brothers, will you stand with folded arms and silent tongues, and see this boa-constrictor, the liquor traffic, crush out the lives and hopes of your fondest affections? "*No?* No!" Methinks I hear a thousand reply: "No! *It must not be!* IT SHALL NOT BE!" If all who acknowledge the evils resulting from this nefarious business, and the necessity of its utter annihilation, would engage in its extirpation with heart, hand, and ballot, it would be exterminated — certainly, speedily, and effectually. Its accomplishment would be the grandest event the world has ever witnessed. It would be perpetuated in eloquence, poetry, and song, and transmitted to posterity by some master historian, written with an eloquent pen, on a spotless page, in a golden era.

Its achievement would constitute a monument far more glorious than any which the genius of antiquity has ever bequeathed to the generations that were to follow. Moldering and dilapidated are the pyramids of Egypt, the Mausoleum, and the temples of Athens and of Rome. Lost are the cities of Ninevah and Babylon. Forgotten are the countless millions that have figured upon the earth, and taken their exit. But the prohibition of the liquor traffic will be a monument which the devastating jaws of Time can never demolish. With foundations resting on the eternal principles of truth and justice. this memorial will remain when all the temples of the earth are demolished and Nature's great temples retain not a stone; until the promised era, foretold in prophecy and invoked in poetry, when the Angel of Time, standing on sea and land with uplifted hand, shall swear by Him that liveth forever and ever. Time shall be no longer! For tho its pedestal be on earth, its glorious apex towers unto heaven.

— *Prof. Chas. W. Sanders.*

63. DRINK!

Drink! spend your hard-earned wages for Death!
Drink! for a foul, obnoxious breath!

Drink! for health and morals shattered!
Drink! for raiment thread-bare, tattered!
Drink! that the Publican and his wife,
May wear rich jewels, bought with your life!

Drink! that the mob may jeer you!
Drink! that the good may fear you!
Drink! that you may be known as a fool,
By the smallest tot that goes to school!
Drink! that men may say of you —
Not your own mother could love you!
Drink! that your days may end speedily,
And earth, for your absence, better be!
  —*Translation from the Persian of Omar, by H. G.*

64. STAND FIRM.

Stand firm when the enemy charges
　　Your ranks in all his might,
When sore indeed is the danger
　　That lies in the hot, fierce fight.
Cower not in that hour of conflict
　　When the test comes unto you;
But in that hour of hours
　　To God and yourself be true.

Stand firm, and not for an instant
　　Let the coward's thought be yours,
Or the heart that is weak and trembling
　　The heart that not endures;
But steel your breast to the conflict,
　　And with courage your soul endue;
And in that hour of hours
　　To God and yourself be true.

Stand firm, and so shall falter
　　The enemy at last,
Grow weak, and yield the conquest;
　　And the trial will be past.
And so shall glorious victory
　　O'er sin come unto you,
Since you, in that hour of hours,
　　To God and yourself were true.
　　— *George Newell Lovejoy, in " Golden Rule ".*

65 "I'VE GOT IT!" OR, THE RUMSELLER JUBILANT.

"I've got it! I've got it!" he shouted with joy,
And chuckled and danced like a half-witted boy!
And what has he gotten — this boaster? pray tell!
Why, license to send his weak neighbors to — well,
  Rum-drinking, idleness, shiftlessness, shame,
  Ultimate ruin of fortune and fame!

"I've got it! I've got it!—they signed it last night!"
And what does this document grant? Why, the right
Intoxicant liquors of all kinds to sell,
To rake in the dollars and send men to — well,
  Drunkenness, penury, gross self-neglect,
  Loss of their own and of others' respect!

"I've got it! I've got it! I've got it!" And now,
How came he to get it? *You* ought to know how!
Your ballot instructed the city to sell
The right to recruit for the armies of —well,
  Mendicants, criminals, suicides — all
  Who under the curse of the rum-traffic fall!

"I've got it! I've got it!" Ah! yes, so he has!
And thousands of others have "got it," alas!
And millions of people are rushing pell-mell
Into these licensed recruit shops of — well,
  Why don't you stop it? Why vote for the men
  Who vote for saloons? Don't do it again!
                           —*Lorin Ludlow.*

66. THE LAND OF PROHIBITION.

No broken windows or hanging doors,
No greasy walls or dirty floors,
But pretty homes and gardens gay,
Scent of sweet flowers miles away
    In the Land of Prohibition.

No "raggit weans," no weary wives,
No women in fear for their wretched lives,
But merry maids and bonny boys,
And streets alive with gladsome noise
    In the Land of Prohibition.

No aching hearts and dragging feet,
No unemployed in any street,
But bounding step and cheery song,
Work for the willing, brave, and strong
    In the Land of Prohibition.

No frowning jails or prisons drear,
No criminals in training here,
But far and wide our banner waves
O'er men who never shall be slaves —
    In the Land of Prohibition.

No public debt to make men frown,
No breaking banks to crush them down,
No empty coffers in the state,
For debts are small and incomes great
    In the Land of Prohibition.

Dear, far-off country of my birth,
The grandest spot upon the earth,
Oh, may I live to see the day
When all thy woe shall pass away,
And glorious, beautiful, and free
Thou shalt arise victoriously —
    The Land of Prohibition.
      — *Mrs. Harrison Lee, Victoria, Australia.*

67. THE NECTAR OF THE HILLS.

We poetize about it when we see the water dancing in the shower, or flashing in the lake, or impearled in the hoar frost, or enthroned in the rainbow; but how little ordinarily we think of the necessity which it supplies. No one but the infinite God could mix this elixir commonly called water. In right proportion are its elements combined, or instead of life it would be death. So simple it seems, that, poured out in a cup or standing in a pitcher, it excites no remark. But what Divine mingling of chloride of sodium, chloride of magnesia, sulphate of lime, carbonate of soda, sulphate of soda, phosphate of alumina, and many constituent parts that I have no time to name. The human hand and the human brain can manufacture liquids deleterious or liquids that may be pleasant and refreshing for a while, but it took a God to mingle this wine of the hills, which never intoxicates and has no baleful reactions, and is so superior to all other beverages that whatever else we taste, with water we close the feast, banishing all other tastes from our mouths with a sip of this divinely-mingled liquid. Its importance God indicated when, in the formation of the earth, He put into it two and three-fourths times more water than dry land. You thank God for bread, why not thank Him for water? The one is as great a necessity as the other.

And here let me say there is no excuse for any American city being short of supply when there are great lakes of fresh water and great rivers of fresh water North, South, East, and West. Why does New York dip its cup into a puddle a few miles up, when it might pour Lake George and Niagara Falls into its chalices? If a small part of the money misappropriated in half the cities were devoted to the bringing down of more abundant waters, there would be in no city of America any threat of water famine. But for the present necessity, let us ask God for rain. Elijah's prayer brought down the showers, and your prayers and the prayers of all the people can do as much. In answer to supplications already ascended, I think the skies are now preparing for a great rain, and the windows of heaven will be opened, and the reservoirs will be filled.

Water — study it. One glass of it is enough to confound the chemist and overwhelm the Christian. Meanwhile, never partake of this superb and delicious liquid without emotion of gratitude to God. Stand around this nectar of the hills, and drink, all of you, to the praise of Him who brewed it among the mountains. I rejoice that the Bible is all asparkle with fountains and wells and rivers and oceans. They toss up their brightness from almost every chapter. Solomon exclaims, "As cold water to a thirsty soul, so is good news from a far country." Isaiah, speaking of the blessedness of Christians, says, "They shall spring up as willows by the water courses." In the canticles, the church is often spoken of as a "well of living water," and "streams from Lebanon." The prophet, glowing with anticipation of the millennium, says, "Streams shall break forth in the desert"; and to make heaven the more alluring to those who have lived on the banks of rivers, and are fond of landscapes ribboned and glorified with bright streams, St. John says, "He showed me a pure river of water of life, clear as crystal, proceeding out of the throne of God and the Lamb." — *Rev. T. De Witt Talmage.*

68. WHY?

He couldn't write, he couldn't read,
   He little knew nor cared
About the people's wrongs and need;
How others lived he took no heed,
   Nor how they fared.

The big saloon he couldn't pass,
   Nor pools of any type,
He couldn't live without his glass,
And he was miserable, alas!
   Without his pipe.

On public streams, whiche'er the way,
   He could do naught but float;
And on the questions of the day,
He couldn't think, he couldn't pray —
   But *he could vote.*

She couldn't drink, she couldn't swear,
   She couldn't even smoke;
Nor could she open wrongs declare,
Nor with a ballot did she dare
   The right invoke.

She loved the people and she knew
   The questions passing by
Were weighty; her conclusions drew —
And out of these convictions grew,
   The *how* and *why.*

She kept herself outside the rut;
   From leading minds could quote;
She had opinions clearly cut;
Could write and read and reason — but
   She could not vote.
                 — Hattie Horner Louthan.

---

69. THE SUPREME CURSE.

   The supreme or capital curse of the nineteenth century is summed up in the one word "saloon," because its influence extends in all directions; and wherever it is felt, human misery, degradation, and moral eclipse follow. It is the devil-fish of our civilization, whose every tentacle crushes to death. It pollutes politics; it degrades manhood; it makes a possible murderer of every victim; it fills the slums with want and wretchedness; it crowds our jails to overflowing, and is a leading factor in populating insane asylums, almshouses, and the Potter's fields; it destroys the physical strength of manhood; it beclouds the intellect; it obliterates moral integrity. But, towering above all this, its crowning evil, and that which makes its existence the national crime of the age, is its effect upon the guiltless. The innocent wife, the prattling children, and the unborn baby all feel its cruel curse. This is the phase of the problem which makes its toleration a crime of measureless proportions. The supremacy of the saloon affords a most impressive illustration of the possibility of a whole nation becoming morally anæsthetized by a curse constantly before its vision, and whose wealth is lavishly used to quell all opposition which would deal it mortal blows. We build insane asylums and incarcerate madmen, for the protection of the lives of their families and others; but here we find a so-called Christian nation giving the stamp of legality to a traffic which takes from thousands of innocent people every gleam of hope and happiness, clothing bodies in rags and minds in perpetual fear. If the saloon cursed only its victims the case would be different; but it is the gloved hand behind the automatic victim which is responsible for a large proportion of the crimes committed yearly against the innocent. — *B. O. Flower.*

70. THE SPEECHLESS.

Ye call them dumb, and deem it well,
How e'er their bursting hearts may swell,
They have no voice their woes to tell,
    As fabulists have dreamed.
They can not cry "O Lord how long
Wilt Thou, the patient Judge and strong,
Behold thy creatures suffer wrong
    Of these thy blood redeemed?"

Yet are they silent? need they speech
His Holy sympathies to reach.
Who by their lips could prophets teach,
    And for their sakes would spare;
When, wrestling with His own decree,
To save repentant Nineveh,

He foun..
　　　So "ma..,

Have they no language? Angels ..
Who take account of *every blow*:
And there are angel hearts below,
　　　On whom the Eternal Dove
His penticostal gift hath poured,
And that forgotten speech restored
That filled the garden of the Lord
　　　When Nature's voice was love.

Oh, *blest are they the creatures bless!*
And yet that *wealth of tenderness,*
In *look,* in *gesture,* in *caress,*
　　　By which our hearts they teach.
Might well the thoughtful spirit grieve,
Believing — as we must believe —
How *little* they from man receive,
　　　To whom they give *so much.*

They may be silent, as ye say,
But woe to them who, day by day,
Unthinking for what boon they pray,
　　　Repeat "Thy kingdom come."
Who, when before the Great White Throne,
Shall plead that *mercy* may be shown,
Find *awful voices drown their own,*
　　　The voices of *the dumb.*
　　　　　　　　— *Anna Drury.*

---

71. WHAT DO YOU CARE?

Strong men are falling on every hand,
Havoc appalling is wrought in the land;
Pestilence, famine, and war are outdone —
Never more damning ill under the sun —
Highest and lowest are caught in the snare;
Statesmen and patriots, *what do you care?*

Women are weeping worn hearts away,
Fasting and watch keeping day after day;
Tremblingly waiting steps that were dear,
Love soured to hating, hope chilled to fear;

...est can bear —
., what do you care?

. are crying for love and for bread,
Needlessly dying, happy when dead;
Carrying friendless hearts made for fun
Through shadows endless, life just began:
Aimlessly wandering, hungry, and bare;
Fathers and mothers, *what do you care?*

Babes are polluted, cursed from their birth,
Parents embruted fixing their worth,
Infancy prized by the Spirit of Wine —
The modern Moloch — is burnt at his shrine;
Daily his priests for their altars prepare;
Champions of Christendom, *what do you care?*

Daily the weak to slavery sink,
Vainly they seek escape from the drink;
Household and neighbor, involved in their thrall,
Fruitlessly labor to break the fall;
Piteously rises the victim's prayer;
Lovers of freedom, *what do you care?*

Jesus by dying liberty gave;
Love self-denying only can save;
Light to its strength is the temperance cross,
Glorious at length the gain of its loss;
Passion and triumph Love asks us to share;
Friends of the Saviour, *what do you care?*
— *I. F. B. Tinling.*

72. DEACON BEERY'S PROTEST.

Deacon Beery went into the commissioner's office where licenses for selling liquor are sold. He was off in one corner reading Bishop Molehill's tract on "High License." Being a little near-sighted in his ears, he failed to hear correctly what the next applicant for license said, but he thought he heard the following:

"Mr. Commissioner, I want a license to get drunk. I want to get drunk for a year, and make myself dangerous to all. I want to pay for all the crime I shall commit, and I want to pay for it in advance. What's the bill?"

"One hundred dollars," was the reply.

The man took the license and departed. The deacon was paralyzed with horror. Coming to the desk he said:

"Is it really possible that you let a man commit a crime by paying his fine in advance? What a state of morals we have reached! It seems to me the avenging hand of justice must be near. Shame! Everlasting shame and contempt on such laws!"

"You don't understand," said the clerk. "The man does not want a license to do wrong; he simply wants a license to make other people commit crime. He himself is a very moral man. This money I just received is needed to pay damages arising from—"

"From what?" shrieked the deacon.

"From the liquor traffic," said the clerk. "In fact," continued the clerk, "out of every $17 damages from liquor, we make the dealers pay one by the way of a tax — some call it license."

"And the people?" said the deacon.

"Pay the $16," was the calm reply.

The deacon put the tract in the stove and started downstairs, saying, "'Lead us not into temptation'; and if the welfare of Thy Kingdom demands that I should refuse to lead others in, even tho my party should lose a vote, yet I say, True and righteous are thy ways altogether, O Lord.'"

The deacon was converted. — *Home Gazette.*

---

73. EVE'S RECOMPENSE.

A woman once, in Paradise, 'tis said,
Sinned, and brought countless curses on her head;
And not alone she suffered, but on all
Her race bestowed the harvest of her fall.
Her husband, too, shared the disastrous sin,
And brought the whole family of mankind in.
He, timid soul, was fearful of his life,
And whispered faintly, "Lord, it was my wife —
She tempted me!" O father of the race!
That speech but added more to thy disgrace!

To think a member of the "weaker sex"
Should have such power his mighty soul to vex!

Because her opportunity was first
Ere his, why is she more accurst?
Perhaps her lord was jealous that not he
Was offered first the fruit of wisdom's tree.
But woman, for the wit she paid in pain,
Resolves the sacrifice shall not be vain;
And, tho her trials high as heaven mount,
Decides they shall be turned to good account.

First in transgression, first repentant, she
In works benev'lent ever first will be.
Experience-taught, all Satan's wiles to shun,
She longs to shield her husband, brother, son.
Satan, too wise to try his former plan,
Tempts, in another way, the race of man.
Foreseeing in the apple no excuse,
Decides, this time, to try the apple's juice.
Through this, to wine and beer, the danger grows,
Till all man's shame is written on his nose.

Now woman comes to thwart the demon's plan,
Abolish alcohol, and save the man;
First moral suasion tries, but little gains,
But scorn and ridicule for all her pains.
The man, so willing to be *led*, of yore,
By Eden's queen, now wills *to go before*.
Now, to be led by woman is a shame,
The world will laugh, 'twill hurt his manly name.
Next, woman thinks by law to thwart the Devil,
And by her ballot to undo the evil.

But Satan, in a politician's coat,
Cries out in terror, "Don't, don't let her vote!"
For tho he has a throne in every land,
The Devil dreads a blow from woman's hand.
But she, who suffers most beneath his reign,
Predestined is to forge his final chain.
She who first sinned is set apart by fate
To banish wrong and her sin expiate.
For righteous laws and equal rights we stand,
For God and home, our own and every land.

—*Mabel R. Winter.*

74. "DORLESKY'S ERRENTS."

(Dialogue, arranged from the interview between Samantha and the Senator, in Josiah Allen's Wife's "Sweet Cicely.")

Senator (*bowing profoundly*): "Shall I have the inexpressible honor and the delightful joy of aiding you in any way? If so, command me."

Samantha (*impressively*): "Dorlesky Burpy sent these errents to you. She wanted intemperance done away with — the whisky ring broke right up. She wanted you to drink nothin' stronger than root-beer when you had company to dinner, she offerin' to send you a receipt for it from Jonesville; and she wanted her rights, and she wanted 'em all this week without fail."

SLIGHT PAUSE.

Samantha: "Now, can you do Dorlesky's errents? and will you?"

Senator (*examining corner of Samantha's* "*mantilly*"): "Am I mistaken, or is this the trimming called piping? or can it be Kensington tatting?"

A PAUSE.

Senator (*continuing*): "Have I not heard a rumor that bangs were going out of style? I see you do not wear your lovely hair bang-like, or a pompidorus! Ah! women are lovely creatures, lovely beings, every one of them." (*Sighing.*) "*You are very beautiful.*"

Samantha: "I shall do Dorlesky's errents, and do 'em to the best of my ability; and you can't draw off my attention from her sufferin's and her suffragin's by talkin' about bangs."

Senator: "I would love to oblige Dorlesky, because she belongs to such a lovely sex. Wimmen are the loveliest, most angelic creatures that ever walked the earth: they are perfect, flawless, like snow and roses."

Samantha: "That hain't no such thing. They are disagreeable creeters a good deal of the time. They hain't no better than men. But they ought to have their rights all the same. Now, Dorlesky is disagreeable, and kinder fierce actin', and jest as humbly as they make women; but that hain't no sign she ort to be imposed upon. Josiah says, 'She hadn't ort to have a right, not a single right, because she is so humbly.' But I don't feel so."

Senator: "Who is Josiah?"

Samantha: "My husband."

Senator: "Ah! your husband! yes, women should have husbands instead of rights. They do not need rights, they need freedom from all cares and sufferings. Sweet, lovely beings, let them have husbands to lift them above all earthly cares and trials! Oh! angels of our homes — fly around, ye angels, in your native haunts! mingle not with rings, and vile laws; flee away, flee above them."

Samantha: "Dorlesky would have been glad to flew above 'em. But the ring and the vile laws laid holt of her, unbeknown to her, and dragged her down. She didn't meddle with the political ring, but the ring meddled with her. How can she fly when the weight of this infamous traffic is a holdin' her down?"

Senator: "Ahem! Ahem, as it were — as I was saying, my dear madam, these angelic angels of our homes are too ethereal, too dainty, to mingle with the rude crowds. We political men would fain keep them as they are now: we are willing to stand the rude buffetings of — of — voting, in order to guard these sweet, delicate creatures from any hardships. Sweet, tender beings, we would fain guard you — ah, yes! ah, yes!"

Samantha: "Cease instantly, or my sickness will increase; for such talk is like thoroughwort or lobelia to my moral stomach. You know, and I know, that these angelic, tender bein's, half clothed, fill our streets on icy midnights, huntin' up drunken husbands and fathers and sons. They are starved, they are frozen, they are beaten, they are made childless and hopeless, by drunken husbands killing their own flesh and blood. They go down into the cold waves, and are drowned by drunken captains; they are cast from railways into death by drunken engineers; they go up on the scaffold, and die of crimes committed by the direct aid of this agent of hell.

"Women had ruther be a flyin' round than to do all this, but they can't. If you want to be consistent — if you are bound to make angels of women, you ort to furnish a free, safe place for 'em to soar in. You ort to keep the angels from bein' meddled with, and bruised, and killed, etc."

Senator: "Ahem — as it were, ahem."

Samantha: "I am sorry for Dorlesky, sorry for the hull

women race of the nation. Can you, and will you, do Dorlesky's errents?"

Senator: "Well, so far as giving Dorlesky her rights is concerned, natural human instinct is against the change. Certainly modern history don't seem to encourage the scheme."

Samantha: "We won't argue long on that point, for I could overwhelm you if I approved of overwhelmin'. But I merely ask you to cast your right eye over into England, and then beyond it into France. Men have ruled exclusively in France for the last forty or fifty years, and a woman in England: which realm has been the most peaceful and prosperous?"

Senator: "Well, but you people seem to place a great deal of dependence on the Bible. The Bible is against the idea. The Bible teaches man's supremacy, man's absolute power and might and authority."

Samatha: "Why, how you talk! Why, in the very first chapter, the Bible tells how man was jest turned right round by a woman. It teaches how she not only turned man right round to do as she wanted him to, but turned the hull world over.

"A few years later, after men and women grew wiser, when we hear of women ruling Israel openly and honestly, like Miriam, Deborah, and other likely old 4 mothers, why, things went on better.

"And, as I said before, if God called woman into this work, He will enable her to carry it through. He will protect her from her own weaknesses, and from the misapprehensions and hard judgments and injustices of a gain-saying world.

"Will you do Dorlesky's errents? Will you give her her rights? And will you break the Whisky Ring?"

Senator: "My dear madam, I would love to do Dorlesky's errands. You have convinced me that it would be just and right to do them, but the Constitution of the United States is against them. As the laws are, I can not make any move towards doing either of the errands."

Samantha: "Can't the laws be changed?"

Senator: "Be changed? Change the laws of the United States? Tamper with the glorious Constitution that our forefathers left us — an immortal, sacred legacy? Can it be that I heard my ear aright? or did you speak of changing the unalterable laws of the United States — tampering with the Constitution?"

Samantha: "Yes, that is what I said. Hain't they never been changed?"

Senator: "Oh, well, yes; they have been changed in cases of necessity."

Samantha: "The laws have been changed to benefit whisky dealers. And you jest said I had convinced you that Dorlesky's errents wus errents of truth and justice, and you would love to do 'em."

Senator: "Well, yes, yes — I would love to — as it were — but, really, my dear madam, much as I would like to oblige you, I have not the time to devote to it. We Senators and Congressmen are so driven, and hard-worked, that really we have no time to devote to the cause of Right and Justice. I don't think you realize the constant pressure of hard work, that is ageing us, and wearing us out, before our day.

"As I said, we have to watch the liquor-interest constantly, to see that the liquor-dealers suffer no loss — we *have* to do that. Taking it with other kindred laws, and the constant strain on our minds in trying to pass laws to increase our own salaries, you can see just how cramped we are for time. And though we would love to pass some laws of Truth and Righteousness — we fairly ache to — yet, not having the requisite time, we are obliged to lay 'em on the table, or under it."

Samantha: "But just think what you are a doin'. You are a keepin' Dorlesky out of her rights all this time that you are working for your own rights, and other folkses. It don't seem reasonable. I don't believe in it, nor Dorlesky don't. It hain't honest."

Senator: "My dear madam, in public affairs it would never do to be *too* honest. Dishonesty in matters like that you mention has come to be considered nothing serious; especially when it pays so well. It should be remembered that there are *different degrees* of dishonesty. We senators find it so."

Samantha: "I don't know how many degrees of dishonesty there may be, but you won't convince me that any one of 'em is right. Howsumever, it is perfectly clear that there are different degrees of insane craziness, and that you are a sufferin' from a voyalent attack. I am dretful sorry for you, and for your folks, but I must be a goin'. I must hunt up somebody who can and will do Dorlesky's errents."

75. "IF."

If you want a red nose and dim, bleary eyes;
If you wish to be one whom all men despise;
If you wish to be ragged and weary and sad;
If you wish, in a word, to go to the bad;
                Then drink!

If you wish that your life a failure may be;
If you wish to be penniless — out at the knee;
If you wish to be houseless, broken, forlorn;
If you wish to see pointed the finger of scorn;
                Then drink!

If you wish that your manhood be shorn of its strength;
That your days may be shortened to one-half their length;
If you like the gay music of curse or of wail;
If you long for the shelter of poorhouse or jail;
                Then drink!

If your tastes don't agree with the "ifs" as above;
If you'd rather have life full of brightness and love;
If you care not to venture nor find out too soon
That the gateway to hell lies through the saloon!
                Then *don't drink!*
                    — *William Howard.*

76. A SONG OF MARTYRDOM.*

The King of a boundless empire,
    To his council chamber came;
He summoned His loyal princes,
    He named them each by name;
For His heart is the heart of a father,
    And He knoweth His own by sight;
And He gave them the cross of the legion,
    The badge of the blameless knight.

As ever, the brave are the tender,
    As ever, the loving are strong,

---

* "I believe that in so doing I take my life in my hand."—*Geo. C. Haddock.*

And to him of the heart of the lion,
   Do the graces of pity belong ;
And the King, to the Prince of the Fearless,
   Gave order and sign of command ;
For He knew what manner of hero
   Had taken his life in his hand.

Then spake He, the King, to His chosen —
   "Go wage ye a warfare of peace ;
Proclaim to the children of sorrow,
   The beautiful year of release ;
They have gathered the grapes of my gladness,
   And drunken the wine of distress ;
They have garnered the grain of my plenty
   For famine and bitterness.

" And the strength and the beauty of nations
   Have plighted their faith to the foe
That bringeth the honor of manhood,
   The virtue of womanhood, low ;
And out of the cradle of promise,
   A childhood, dishonored and weak,
Goes forth with a brand on its forehead,
   And shame on its innocent cheek."

Then answered the Prince of the Fearless —
   "I am ready, O King ! for the fight ;
My life not so dear have I counted
   To myself, as the triumph of right."
But alas ! for the Prince and his army,
   And alas ! for the hands that have slain,
Tho he sought not the blood of the basest,
   His own was poured out like the rain.

But out of the dust of the martyr
   Ariseth, immortal and strong,
The angel of vengeance and mercy,
   With only a sword for the wrong.
The sinner, He lifteth and saveth,
   For He loveth the children of men ;
'Tis the soul of the Prince of the Fearless
   Who leadeth His army again.   — *O. F. B.*

77. CUT DOWN THE TREE.

Yes, cut down the tree, tear up the roots — destroy the rum traffic. Why longer waste strength and precious time lopping off the branches and dragging them away, by trying to restrict by license that which *will not* be restricted? Why longer pursue each individual drunkard to his hiding place and with pleadings — too often ineffectual — seek to reclaim him? *Cut off the damning supply from him, and he will thank you, and you will save his soul alive.*

It is too little known how many victims of intoxicants fairly long for the total success of the present forward movement to dry up the streams of the rum trade.

They are bound hand and foot, soul and body, in the iron fetters of appetite now beyond the control of their will, which in its turn has become the slave of its tyrannical master; and they are ready to welcome any means, any remedy by which this dreadful "inward craving" shall be no longer satisfied.

A friend of mine related to me the following incident which took place only a few weeks since in the city of New York.

He stepped into a coffee saloon early one cold morning and called for a cup of coffee. The saloon had a liquor bar attached, and the proprietor in handing the coffee to my friend said, "Will you have something else?" "Nothing else," was the reply, "I drink nothing stronger than coffee." While he was drinking of the cup a well-dressed man whom he had observed walking the floor, stepped up to him and said, with an earnest manner, "Sir, I would give all I am worth to be able to do what you are doing." "How so, what am I doing that you can't do?" "Why, sir," spoke the earnest man, "you can drink your coffee with a zest, and refuse the rum at that bar; that's what I can't do; no, sir, *I can't do that.*"

Build "Inebriate's Asylums" of stately proportions, a thing of beauty in architecture, of Philadelphia brick with marble facings, as the graceful building you see on Randall's Island in the East River, New York — build such at immense cost for the drunkards, if you will — send out your missionaries in the cities to gather in and convert others, drunkards too poor to be sent to the marble palaces; do all this heroically, and while you are doing your best, for every man and woman cured, and every one saved, *the legal-*

ized rum traffic, *supported by the government of this nation, is turning out one hundred ready-made confirmed drunkards!* O, tell it not in Gath, lest the Philistines rejoice over the people of the living God.

In India twenty thousand human lives are annually destroyed by the bites of venomous reptiles. The government, careful of the interests of its subjects, pays a certain sum for the head of every venomous reptile killed by any person.

In this Christian nation *seventy thousand* human lives are destroyed annually by the venomous reptile found in every glass or cup of alcohol drank in the land, yet this government, instead of offering a premium for the head of this destroyer, keeps it in a national cage and feeds it on the finest of the wheat, and corn, and barley, and offers a premium for the preservation of its life, while the huge rattlesnake is swallowing the precious lives of our households. This is no time for argument ; the case doesn't admit of it ; it is life or death to the tens of thousands. A premium for the death of the monster ; a price on his head! Cut down the tree! Forward, pioneers, with your axes! — *Rev. Dr. W. H. Boole.*

78. PROHIBITION'S BUGLE CALL.

Men of purpose, sound the tocsin
    For the fray — for the fray.
Men of courage, raise the war-cry,
    Lead the way.
Through the darksome forest streaming,
Lo! the dawn of thought is gleaming,
And the sun of action beaming
    Into day — into day ;
Men of purpose, truth, and courage,
    Lead the way.

Lo! the waiting ground is ready
    For your toil — for your toil ;
Men of purpose firm and steady,
    Break the soil ;
Thickly sow the good seed over,
Straight and true the furrows cover,
Rout the hungry birds that hover
    For the spoil — for the spoil.

Woman's friend and children's lover,
    Break the soil.

Foemen strong, with roar and rattle,
    Flock around — flock around;
Soldiers in the coming battle,
    Stand your ground!
No time now to halt or blunder,
Cleave their gleaming ranks asunder,
While the nations watch and wonder,
    Smile or frown — smile or frown.
Through the cannon's smoke and thunder,
    Ride them down!

Men of purpose, sound the tocsin
    For the fray — for the fray;
Men of courage, shout the war-cry,
    Lead the way!
Hand in hand in strength outgoing,
Heart to heart, with love o'erflowing,
Breast to breast, with fervor glowing,
    Lead the way — lead the way;
Men of purpose, strength, and courage,
    Win the day!

                      — *Lide Meriwether.*

79. A PLACE IN HEAVEN.

Behrynge, the pilgrim, lifting up his head,
Saw the Death Angel standing near his bed,
And heard him say in accents calm and cold,
"The names I write within the Book of Gold
Are names of those whose place in heaven is won.
To gain this place what hast *thou* ever done?"
Behrynge, the pilgrim, struck upon his breast,
"Alas! full many a law have I transgressed,
Yet at God's feet, for creatures He hath made
Both mute and helpless, all my life I laid,
And prayed Him daily that my strength might be.
Their faithful safeguard, as He guarded me.
The dumb beast's cause I plead through all the land,
And stayed the torture of the oppressor's hand.
My life, my all, to the great work I gave,
Yet know I not if deeds like these can save."

The angel vanished. When at heaven's gate,
Behrynge, the pilgrim, sadly came to wait,
Lo! the pearl portals flew asunder far.
A light shone round him like a glorious star,
And a voice said, "Thy sins are all forgiven,
Love for the helpless won thy place in Heaven."
— *Nat'l W. C. T. U. Dep't of Mercy.*

80. THE "PERSONAL LIBERTY" CRY.

Guizot tells us in his admirable work, the "History of Civilization": "Civilization is characterized by no one thing more clearly than by the voluntary concession of the liberties of the individual citizen that he may enjoy something richer and better than civil liberty or organized liberty."

I have very little patience and but small respect for the argument against Prohibition based upon the cry of personal liberty. You and I may suffer curtailment of our private rights and have our personal liberties invaded constantly.

Some farmer five miles out comes into your city on Monday morning and consults an attorney. He says: "I have an animal that died on Sunday morning. Now, is there anything that stands in the way of dressing that diseased animal and using it for food in my own family?" and the man, wise in the law, tells him, "No, sir; but as a friend I would not advise you to do it, but as a matter of law you have a perfect right to do so." "But," said he, "there is more than I can consume; may I not dress it and put it on the market?" "No," says the lawyer, "We have a prohibitory statute in the state against the selling of diseased meat."

"But," says the proposed seller, "I will advertise it as such; the purchaser shall buy it with full knowledge of the facts." "No," the lawyer tells him, "the knowledge and consent of the purchaser in no way relieves you of the obligation you have assumed, and you can not put diseased meat upon the market and sell it even with the knowledge and consent of the purchaser."

Here our personal liberties are hedged again. I see that beautiful horse passing along the green yonder, and I have no doubt were the gentleman in the carriage behind him to put him to the very top of his speed there would be none to say him nay; but let him take him down to the city and speed the animal at the very top of his speed, and he would not go two blocks before some policeman, if he were doing his duty, would have the horse by the bit, and another policeman would have the driver by the coat-collar, and he would lug him up to the police office — his personal liberty invaded. Why? At the behest of the public good.

Smallpox breaks out in your family and your personal liberty is at once restrained. You can not go out of your door and up and down the street as formerly. Why? Because your personal liberty must give way before the demand of a higher good, the preservation of the public health.

I will go some of these days over to New York City after Prohibition prevails, and it gets fit for a gentleman to live in, and I will be on such excellent terms with the citizens that I can get their endorsement at the bank for $100,000; I will spend half of it in buying an elegant building lot right in the heart of the city, and then I will accumulate a great quantity of building material, and some beautiful morning a gentleman with a blue coat and brass buttons will wait upon me, and he will say:

"Sir, are these your premises?" I tell him they are. "Is this your building material?" I assure him it is. "Now," he says, "will you show me your plans and specifications?" I refuse. He persists and I yield. He looks them over. "Now, sir," he says, "I see you intend to build a four-story frame house."

I assure him he is correct. "Now, sir," he adds, "it is my official duty to serve upon you a notice that you can not build a frame house on this lot." I say, "This is a strange proceeding," and I talk about the Fourth of July and *E Pluribus Unum*, and the blood of our forefathers, and the stars and stripes, and the personal liberty of the individual citizen, and I say: "Things have come to a pretty pass, if on my own real estate I can not build any sort of a house I please."

But I rave as long as I will, talk as loudly as I care to, I will run right up hard against a prohibition that within the fire-limits no frame building shall be erected.

Now, when my friends talk, as they very likely will, about Prohibition interfering with the private rights of the individual citizen, they will not be discussing the question we are here to examine. Prohibition does not contemplate the individual drinking man. Prohibition does not propose to interfere with the private rights of any citizen. It takes a broad, comprehensive, statesmanlike view of the situation. Prohibition must and will prohibit for the good of the people.

— *Prof. Samuel Dickie.*

81. THE PRESENT CRISIS.*

We see dimly in the present what is small and what is great,
Slow of faith how weak an arm may turn the iron helm of fate,
But the soul is still oracular; amid the market's din,
List the ominous stern whisper from the Delphic cave within —
"They enslave their children's children who make compromise with sin."

Count me o'er earth's chosen heroes — they were souls that stood alone,
While the men they agonized for hurled the contumelious stone,
Stood serene and down the future saw the golden beam incline
To the side of perfect justice, mastered by their faith divine,
By one man's plain truth to manhood and to God's supreme design.

By the light of burning heretics Christ's bleeding feet I track,
Toiling up new Calvaries ever with the cross that turns not back,
And these mounts of anguish number how each generation learned
One new word of that grand *Credo* which in prophet-hearts hath burned
Since the first man stood God-conquered with his face to heaven upturned.

For humanity sweeps onward; where to-day the martyr stands,
On the morrow crouches Judas with the silver in his hands;
Far in front the cross stands ready and the crackling fagots burn,
While the hooting mob of yesterday in silent awe return
To glean up the scattered ashes into history's golden urn.

---

* By permission of Houghton, Mifflin & Co.

'Tis as easy to be heroes as to sit the idle slaves
Of a legendary virtue carved upon our fathers' graves;
Worshippers of light ancestral make the present light a crime;
Was the Mayflower launched by cowards, steered by men be-
    hind their time?
Turn those tracks toward past or future, that make Plymouth
    Rock sublime?

New occasions teach new duties; Time makes ancient good
    uncouth;
They must upward still, and onward, who would keep abreast
    of Truth;
Lo, before us gleam our campfires! we ourselves must Pilgrims
    be,
Launch our Mayflower, and steer boldly through the desperate
    winter sea,
Nor attempt the Future's portal with the Past's blood-rusted
    key.   —*James Russell Lowell.*

82. A CURTAIN LECTURE.

My wife and I had jest gone to bed,
When a curtain lectur' to me she read:—
"Ef I was a man," sez my wife to me,
"I think I should be a man," sez she.
"Why, wot is the matter, Jane?" sez I.
"Matter enough," was her reply.
"I wouldn't go preachin' temperance
An' votin' for license, both ter wunce!
I wouldn't stan' up in church an' pray
Fer the curse of drink to be took away;
Fer the Lord in marcy to look an' bless
The needy widder an' fatherless,
An' then march up to the polls nex' day
An' vote jest eggsackly the other way!
I think I should have at my command
At least jest a leetle grain of sand;
An' whenever a pollytishun showed
His rum-blossom nose 'round my abode,
An' commenced his blarney to get my vote,
A-singin' the song he'd learnt by rote,
I'd spunk up to him an' tell him wot
I thought of him; an' ez like ez not

I'd jest perlitely show him the door,
An' invite him to never call no more!
I think I'd know enough," sez Jane,
"When a rumseller works with might an' main
To gain a p'int in the town elexshun,
To see that it wasn't jest my complexshun!
An' what he wanted so awful bad
Was the very thing he ortn't to have;
An' I'd work ag'in it, tooth an' nail,
My motto, 'No such word as fail!'
An' wouldn't care one cent in cash
Ef the publicrat party went ter smash!
I'd hev my conshens clear an' sound —
An' know I was treadin' on solid ground."
"Ef I was a man," sez Jane, once more,
But I had already begun to snore.
I wasn't asleep, but then I meant
She'd think I was; for her argyment,
I own, I couldn't quite answer it,
Tho it struck right home to me, every bit,
But Jane, she groaned when I didn't cheep,
And then turned over and went to sleep.

— Union Signal.

83. THE FIRST REFORM.

Before any reform can be secured, its friends must unite against the enemy of all reforms — the saloon.

Would you secure ballot reform? Prohibit first the liquor traffic, which degrades the citizen, corrupts the voter, and makes him the tool of politicians for base political ends. What profit would inure from a State printed and furnished ballot and secret voting, if the candidates are to be named by the saloon, platforms framed in a pothouse, and votes cast by a hand guided by a sodden brain?

Would you have civil service reform? Prohibit first the liquor traffic, which names the candidates for public office and corrupts the integrity of officers. Prohibit the saloon, through whose influence offices have become positions to which "no wage worker need apply," because he can not afford to "set 'em up for the boys" and control the slum vote.

Would you abolish usury and monopolies? Prohibit first the saloon, through whose door monopoly and its purchased minions ascend to the throne of political power.

Would you nationalize industry ? Prohibit first the liquor traffic, and let us have men who know what they want, how to get it, and how to keep it — men who can make a government in which every man's good will be each man's care, and an injury to one the concern of all.

Prohibition is not a cure-all ; but so wide and beneficial is its operation that, with Prohibition once secured, the wage worker can rise to heights not otherwise accessible.

Himself a king, in his family a Providence, in the factory a freeman, in politics a law maker, in society an equal and a brother. — *John Lloyd Thomas.*

84. THE WHISKY DEACON.
(After "The Bird With a Broken Pinion," and More Particularly After the Deacon.)

I saw, in an opulent city,
   A church with a tapering spire,
With a most magnificent organ,
   And a highly salaried choir ;
The singing was operatic,
   And the preaching was out of sight,
And the deacon he climbed Mt. Pisgah,
   At the prayer-meetings, Wednesday night !
But when it came round to election,
   He voted for license then,
And the church with the whisky deacon
   Never soared so high again.

This church with the whisky deacon,
   As the wide awake citizens know,
Can boast of its powerful revivals
   Away in the dim long ago ;
Its shouts, they are all reminiscent,
   And its songs have a faraway tone,
A good deal as if San Francisco
   Should sing to New York through the phone.
I am glad that this church, in past ages,
   Had its hearty "Thank God !" and "Amen !"
But the church with the whisky deacon
   Never soared so high again.

The church with the whisky deacon
   Sat and dreamed of the beautiful stars,
All its membership riding to Heaven
   In Pullman and vestibule cars ;
Their warm hearts were broken and bleeding
   For Armenia, torn by the Turk,
And they got up a series of socials
   To rebuke such a horrible work.
There are "birthdays," and "neckties," and "aprons,"
   And "cobwebs," beyond mortal ken,
But the church with the whisky deacon
   Never soared so high again.

This church with the whisky deacon
   Was puzzled and mystified, sore,
To understand why the great masses
   Should never swing open its door ;
It baited the net of the gospel
   With barrels of good Sunday beer,
Then, having such poor luck afishing
   Seemed most unaccountably queer ;
Thus the groans of a languishing Zion
   Met the howls of the dive and the den,
And the church with the whisky deacon
   Never soared so high again.

But I afterward came to that city,
   And I found what was left of the flock,
Not even excepting the deacon,
   Had received a most wonderful shock ;
They were praying, and shouting, and singing,
   And the people around there for miles,
As if packed by Chicago's Phil Armour,
   Were jammed in the pews and the aisles ;
The church rolls were rapidly filling
   With true hearted women and men ;
Still the church with the old whisky deacon
   Never soared so high again.

Under God, a reformer had done it,
   He swept, like a whirlwind, the town,
And the Jericho walls took a tumble,
   And old Amalek had to come down ;

The deacon, he faithfully promised
  To vote Prohibition next fall,
And the rest of the male members, ditto,
  Was the long and the short of it all ;
But the drunkards to die in the parish
  Counted up to a hundred and ten ;
So that church with the ex-whisky deacon
  Never soars so high again.   — *Rev. P. J. Bull.*

85. SELF-GOVERNMENT.*

This is said to be an American government of the people, by the people, and for the people. . . . No such form of government can be a successful government which does not involve self-government. A man who governs himself governs others. If he cannot govern himself, he is not fit to govern a dog. Then if this is a government of the people, by the people, and for the people, the first element of its success rests on the intelligence, the morality, the character of the masses, and it is the duty of the government to develop, foster, and support institutions which try to build up character, strengthen morality, and develop intelligence. It is the duty of the government by the hand of law to suppress every institution which destroys character, ruins intelligence, and wrecks morality. Our free school system was developed by law, because of the necessity that the people of the United States should be intelligent. If we pay taxes to support our free schools and colleges, is it not the height of political folly and a blunder in political statesmanship to license antagonistic schools of vice and crime, from which the nation derives a revenue ?

We can never have a pure ballot till we have a pure citizenship, and we can never have a pure citizenship until there are no more schools of vice making drunken devils of our men of intelligence.   —*John B. Finch.*

86. THE CORE OF THE RUM QUESTION.

We hear much talk of the Maine law as interfering with men's natural rights, subjecting them to inquisitorial searches, reducing the profits of landlords, breaking up the business of distillers, etc., but no man has ever yet asserted, as far as we have seen or heard, that crime, misery, pauperism, vagrancy,

---

* From an address at Cooper Institute, Jan. 7, 1887.

and the other fearfully increasing social evils of our time would be increased by the passage of the act demanded of our legislature by the prayer of over 200,000 petitioners. On the contrary, if the rumsellers themselves were examined successively and compelled to make answer on oath, "Do you not believe that our jails, prisons, and poorhouses would be largely depopulated by the passage of the Maine law?" we believe a majority of them would be constrained to answer, "We do!"

Of what avail, then, are vague abstractions in the presence of such fearful facts as the rum traffic involves? Men in thousands are burning out their souls with the liquid madness, which fills their homes with unspeakable wretchedness and dooms their children to shame, destitution, and vice. Yet we stand pattering over foggy generalities as if it were a question concerning the rings of Saturn or the mountains in the moon.

We protest against this cold-blooded way of viewing the matter. The question on which our legislators are called to pass in considering the Maine law concerns the happiness of families, the prevalence of vice or virtue, the safety of human life. Of the last hundred murders in our state, it is perfectly within bounds to say that 90 would never have been perpetrated but for intoxicating liquors. Of the 1,600 criminals in our state prisons, fully seven-eighths are either the children of drunkards or themselves maddened by liquor when they were first impelled to crime. Of the 18,000 persons in one year arrested on charges of crime and misdemeanor, less than 50 were total abstinents, while a large majority were excessive drinkers. Of the denizens of our almshouse, nine-tenths have either been tipplers or were reduced to want by the tippling of others. Our gaming houses and haunts of infamy float their victims to perdition on a river of strong drink, without which they could scarcely and but meagerly exist. Yet in full view of these appalling facts, journalists coolly chop logic about the perils of excessive legislation, the proneness of lawmakers to intermeddle with what is none of their business, etc. They might as well call on our firemen to listen to a graceful and silvery-toned speech in the midst of a vast and spreading conflagration.

Patriot, you profess to love your country, and are ready to pour out your blood in her defense. But "he that ruleth his spirit is greater than he that taketh a city," and a people who have thoroughly conquered their own vicious appetites need fear no foreign enemy. The general adoption of the Maine law (Prohibition) by our states would add more to the strength, wealth, vigor, industry, and prosperity of our Union than a new Bunker Hill or half a dozen Buena Vistas. Help us, for your country's sake, to carry the Maine law!

Christians, when you pray "thy kingdom come," do you really mean anything? How is the kingdom of God to come except through the banishment and overthrow of social and moral evils? Can it ever really come into a world filled with grogshops and their concomitants unless these shall be cleared out to make way for it? How can you be indifferent or sluggish in view of the contest now in progress?

Moralists of all creeds, reformers of all shades, philanthropists of every name or nature, we claim your assistance, we ask your earnest and active cooperation. The triumph of this cause requires effort and sacrifice, but it is richly worth them. Help us to carry the Maine law.

— *Horace Greeley in " New York Tribune," Feb. 18, 1852.*

---

87. GENERAL NEAL DOW.
1804–1894.

Maine bids her sons and daughters join
   With those who dwell in distant lands,
In weaving fadeless garlands fair
   With loving hearts and willing hands,
     To crown her favorite son.
To-day we honor him whose life
   Has proved a blessing to all men;
And scanning his past history,
   We find, at four-score years and ten
     No duty left undone.

Faithful and loyal, true to right,
   He holds no compromise with wrong;
But with unbounded faith in God,
   And with a purpose firm and strong,
     He champions our cause.
Behold him in our "Capitol halls";
   And while the world with wonder looks,
He pleads — he fails — *at last he wins,*

And places on our statute books
    Maine's grandest law of laws!

Gaze on a picture dark and drear;
  It is the Maine of years ago:
Her wretched homes — her ruined farms,
    Her bar-rooms dealing death and wo,
        Distilleries on her soil.
From hillside, mountain, vale, and plain,
    Want spreads its gaunt and sallow wings;
While hard-earned dollars are exchanged
    For that which poisons, mocks, and stings
        Her hardy sons of toil.

But, oh, how different is the scene
  Since Alcohol has ceased its reign!
Prosperity and happiness
    Are known on every hill and plain,
        Contentment now holds sway.
Where once the old distillery stood
  And spread its ruin and disgrace,
A church, a school, or home now stands,
    And love beams in each honest face,
        And hearts are light and gay.

*   *   *   *   *   *   *

Heroic soul, from myriad hearts
  Who dwell upon Maine's sacred sod,
Full many an earnest prayer goes forth
  In humble gratitude to God,
        That thou hast lived so long.
The truly great can never die;
  Their work is of the world a part;
And needs no record carved in stone.
  For 'tis enshrined in every heart,
        Immortalized in song!
              — *William Grant Brooks.*

---

88. GIVE THEM JUSTICE.

Justice! Yes, give them justice. Surely every man must be anxious to give the liquor trade justice. The men in the business are men of intelligence and good judgment. They knew the results of the trade before entering it. No one compelled them to enter. Of their own free will they took up the fearful work, simply to make money out of the wretchedness and misery of others. They are responsible as social units for their social acts. They would not be in the business if it were not for the fact that it is the most profitable of trades. When one knows the actuating motives of the drunkard makers, and then looks at the destitute homes and ruined families of their victims, the only conclusion that can be reached is that to do justice would be to repeat the Shylock verdict, "Confiscation of property and death." But the wronged ones in this case are more merciful even than in that case, for they only ask that the guilty shall be stopped from continuing their crimes and are willing to leave with them all their ill-gotten gains. The liquor men ought to be happy to be let off so easily. The people only ask a verdict on the record that this accursed trade has made for itself. The ruined homes, the degraded men, the broken-hearted wives and beggared children made by the liquor dealers in their attempt to amass wealth are witnesses in the case. The results of the traffic, as shown by the police court, the almshouse, the penitentiary, and the scaffold, must all be considered in making up a verdict.

—*John B. Finch.*

89. A WARNING.

There is a time when man will not suffer bad things, because their ancestors suffered worse. There is a time, when the hoary head of inveterate abuse will neither draw reverence, nor obtain protection. I do most seriously put it to the administration, to consider a timely reform. Early reformations are amicable arrangements with a friend in power; late reformations are terms imposed upon a conquered enemy. Early reformations are made in cool blood; late reformations are made under a state of inflammation. In that state of things, the people behold in government nothing that is respectable. They see the abuse, and they will see nothing else. They fall into the temper of a furious populace, provoked at the disorder of a house of ill-fame; they never attempt to correct or regulate; they go to work by the shortest way. They abate the nuisance, they pull down the house. —*Edmund Burke.*

90. EFFECT OF MORAL COWARDICE.

There never has existed, and never can exist, either an administration or a political party, that would dare trifle with the *uttered* sentiments of the men of principle in the United States. . . . If you ask me why it is, then, that public wrongs are so frequently done, and the doers of them held scathless, I answer, it is because those sentiments *are not uttered.* There exists among us a fear of avowing our *moral* sentiments upon political questions, which seems to me as servile as it is unaccountable. It envelopes society like a poisoned atmosphere. It is invisible and intangible, but every virtuous sentiment that breathes it grows torpid, loses consciousness, gasps feebly, and dies. Our sentiments are worthless, not to say savoring of hypocrisy, unless they lead us to corresponding action. To this result every man contributes who withholds the expression of his honest indignation on every occasion of public wrongdoing. — *Francis Wayland.*

91. PRACTISE VERSUS PROFESSION.

To license the liquor traffic is to legalize it. Therefore, if it be a sin to license the liquor traffic, and if we, by our votes, uphold the license policy, then are we partakers of this sin. We, the ministers and members of the Methodist Episcopal Church, can not support a party "committed to the license policy, or that refuses to stand in open hostility to the saloon." A Christian man can not vote with a whisky party, can not support its candidates, can not be a party to the iniquity of the liquor-license business. We deeply regret that the practise of the majority of the church is so far in the rear of its profession. Its profession of hostility to the saloon stands in the front line of progress, while its practise, when the battle of ballots is joined, is eminently conservative.

We say we can not support a party "committed to the license policy," yet the votes of the vast majority of our membership are cast for political parties distinctly committed to the license policy. "Brethren, these things ought not so to be." We as a church insist upon the Bible law of divorce; let us continue to prosecute with renewed zeal, in the old Gospel court of equity, the writ of political divorcement of the church as libelant and the saloon as respondent. What God hath not joined together, let the church of God put asunder.

Our efforts as Christian ministers in prosecuting the work of temperance reform should be mainly in the church. For the time is come that judgment must begin at the house of God.

—*From report adopted by the Erie Conference of the Methodist Episcopal Church.*

92. WHICH ARE YOU?

There are two kinds of people on earth to-day,
Just two kinds of people, no more, I say.

Not the sinner and saint, for 'tis well understood
The good are half-bad, and the bad are half-good.

Not the rich and the poor, for to count a man's wealth
You must first know the state of his conscience and health.

Not the humble and proud, for in life's little span
Who puts on vain airs is not counted a man.

Not the happy and sad, for the swift flying years
Bring each man his laughter and each man his tears.

No; the two kinds of people on earth I mean
Are the people who *lift*, and the people who *lean*.

Wherever you go, you will find the world's masses
Are always divided in just these two classes.

And oddly enough you will find too, I ween,
There is only one lifter to twenty who lean.

In which class are you? Are you easing the load
Of overtaxed lifters who toil down the road?

Or are you a leaner, who lets others bear
Your portion of labor and worry and care?

—*Ella Wheeler Wilcox, in her book, "Easter, and Other Poems."*

93. ALL THE RIGHTS SHE WANTS.

She's got the right to handle a broom,
  And why does she want any more?
She may wash the dishes till day of doom,
  And why does she want any more?
She's got the right to cook and to scrub,
To play the piano, or rub-a-dub-dub

In a lowlier sphere, at the laundry tub —
   And why does she want any more?

She's got the right to teach and to sew,
   And why does she want any more?
(She's only two-thirds of a teacher, tho,
   And she mustn't ask any more.)
She may rock the cradle and mend the hose,
And solace her mind with dreams of clothes;
Or else to the Woman's Page she goes —
   And how can she want any more?

She's got the right to a clerk's employ —
   And how can she ask any more?
To take the place of a younger boy —
   She mustn't ask any more.
The right to labor as hard as she can,
Wherever they cannot afford a man,
And to get her pay on the half-rate plan.
   She mustn't ask any more.

She's got the right to a student's hat;
   Now, how can she want any more?
But somebody had to fight for that,
   And she mustn't want any more.
She's got the right to a choice of schools,
And to quite a respectable lot of tools,
Such as have never been used by fools —
   She can not want any more.

She's got the right to a soul — Oh, yes!
   And why does she want any more?
The right to be pious for two, I guess.
   Could any one ask for more?
She may hear the brethren preach and pray,
She may serve the Lord in a quiet way,
With schemes for raising the parson's pay —
   And why does she want any more?

She's got the right to be taxed — or hung —
   And nobody *can* have more!
She isn't forbidden to use her tongue;
   And she never can want any more.
And she has her representative now,

A piece of a man — somewhere, somehow —
Mixed up in all the political row —
  And how can she want any more?

But ah! how manners and times do change!
  Somebody's asking for more!
Something has happened that's utterly strange,
  Somebody's asking for more!
O Oliver Twist! Can it verily be
Your name is Olive? And what do I see?
A dreadful, unfeminine, malapert She,
  Actually asking for more!   — *Carl Spencer.*

94. DOES IT PAY?

Standing on a corner in this city not long ago I counted 14 doors leading to as many places of business in the block on the opposite side of the street. Three doors led to clothing stores, one to a millinery establishment, one to a barber shop, one to a telegraph office, and another to a bank. The other seven led to where strong drink is sold. Four places where the outer man and woman may be clothed, one place where the man may be shaved so as to look respectable and neat in his new clothes, one place through which he may send urgent messages and from which the daily papers receive their intellectual freight to place before the community, and one place where the savings of labor may be deposited when the wants of the home are supplied. It takes seven doors, seven places of business, to do all of this for the outer man. I came near forgetting to say that the bank occupies the floor above the barber shop and telegraph office. The other seven doors lead to where the inner man is supplied with that which deprives him of clothing, his wife of her bonnet, his children of their clothing and shoes. In any one of the seven will he find that which will reduce him to such depths of degradation that he will not care whether he shaves or not; indeed, he will not have the dime to give to the barber and no money to deposit in the bank above. Seven doors to open on those who clothe themselves and families, and seven other doors in the same block where memory, self-respect, honor, gratitude, and everything a man can esteem are washed into the sewer fed by crime and ending in oblivion.

As I stood contemplating the spectacle a young man crossed the street from one of the places where wet goods are sold and on recognizing me extended his hand in greeting. He wore an old well-worn suit of clothing. His coat was the counterpart of many the reader has seen in his time; it was sun-burned, short in sleeve and tail and well frayed out where the edges were not worn off altogether. No overcoat, no overshoes, no collar and no cuffs save those which misfortune, bad habits, and a worse appetite had administered to him. He asked for a nickel to pay for a ride home on a street car. I knew that a man who felt as tho he could fly did not want to ride on a street car, even tho it were propelled by electricity, and told him so. Inquiry elicited the following facts: He is a mechanic, but has not worked steadily for three years owing to intemperate habits. The suit of clothing he wore that night was three years old, his wages when at work were $2.75 a day, and he had an aged mother and helpless sister depending on him for support. He had lost during that month eight days for the reason that he "was on a breeze." His wages for the eight days would amount to $22. He informed me that it was no uncommon thing for him to lose a whole month through intemperance.

Had he been a total abstainer he would have purchased at least three suits of clothing instead of one in the three years, and a very good suit can be had for $20. In eight days he had lost $2 more than would provide him with a suit of clothes, but for three years his shadow did not rest on the floor of a clothing establishment. He buys no papers, contributes nothing to assist his neighbor, is himself an applicant for relief at the hands of the humane residents of the city who have organized a relief committee, for his name appears in the list of those who were served. Had he been sober and steady he would have purchased clothing and given employment to the tailor and cloth manufacturer. Had he remained sober he would have laid carpet on his mother's floor and kept the loom in motion a little while longer; had he remained outside of the saloon he would have read the papers and would know what his labor was worth, and as a consequence he would not drift into the ranks of the vicious and improvident from which Pinkertons are recruited in times of trouble. In eight days $22 were lost to labor, and in the loss industry received a shock which, tho slight in itself. became an earthquake when added to the hundreds of thousands of others like it as they occur in our centers of industry every year.

When workmen who desire to provide for their families in decency and comfort ask for an advance in their wages, they are told very often that money thus advanced is squandered, and such men as the one I described are pointed to as illustrations of what workmen degenerate into on an advance in wages. The fault, the example, of one drunkard has an evil effect on the prospects of hundreds of industrious workmen who do not drink. Is not industry the loser through the saloon? When the industrious of the community must contribute to support the family of the drunkard — and they do it in every community — is not industry the loser and sufferer through the saloon? When intemperate men are driven to want by their bad habits and thrown out of employment, is not industry the loser when the workers have to support the idlers through taxation on one hand, and face them, in the shape of Pinkertons, on the other, when they demand higher wages with which to meet the extra drains upon their resources? If one man in a small village is a drunkard, he is also an idler, for sooner or later he loses self-respect and employment. If he does not support himself some one else is forced to do so, and I know of no community in which a helpless wife and children will be permitted to want, no matter how worthless the husband and father may be. If the family is dependent on the charity of the neighbors, is not that a tax on them, and is it not a reduction in the wages of every workman who has to contribute to the support of the drunkard's family? Is not industry the loser when the saloon is permitted to make of every home an asylum and of every sober, careful man an almsgiver?

— *Terence V. Powderly.*

95. TO-MORROW.*

High hopes that burned like stars sublime,
   Go down the heavens of freedom,
And true hearts perish in the time
   We bitterliest need them.
But never sit we down and say,
   There's nothing left but sorrow;
We walk the wilderness to-day,
   The promised land to-morrow.

---

* This poem was a favorite with Gen. Fisk, and he frequently quoted from it. On his death bed he recited the first stanza to show his faith in the ultimate triumph of the Prohibition cause.

Our birds of song are silent now,
    There are no flowers blooming —
But life beats in the frozen bough,
    And freedom's spring is coming ;
And freedom's tide comes up alway,
    Tho we may strand in sorrow ;
And our good barque, aground to-day,
    Shall float again to-morrow.

Our hearts brood o'er the past, our eyes
    With smiling futures glisten ;
Lo ! now its dawn bursts up the sky —
    Lean out your souls and listen.
The earth rolls freedom's radiant way,
    And ripens with our sorrow ;
And 'tis the martyrdom to-day
    Brings victory to-morrow.

'Tis weary watching wave by wave,
    And yet the tide heaves onward,
We climb, like corals, grave by grave,
    Yet beat a pathway sunward.
We're beaten back in many a fray,
    Yet newer strength we borrow,
And where our vanguard rests to-day
    Our rear shall rest to-morrow.

Through all the long, dark night of years,
    The people's cry ascended ;
The earth was wet with blood and tears,
    Ere their meek sufferings ended.
The few shall not forever sway,
    The many toil in sorrow ;
The bars of hell are strong to-day,
    But Christ shall reign to-morrow.

Then youth flame earnest, still aspire
    With energies immortal ;
To many a haven of desire
    Your yearning opes a portal ;
And though age wearies by the way
    And hearts break in the furrow,
We sow the golden grain to-day —
    The harvest comes to-morrow. — *Gerald Massey.*

96. LIQUOR AND WAGES.

It is frequently stated in labor circles that drinking helps to keep up wages. On the plea that the average wages of labor tend to the sum just sufficient to supply the workman and his family with the necessities of life, it is claimed that cutting off the drink bill, which many workingmen regard as a sort of necessity, would tend to reduce average wages by just the amount which the workingman now spends for drink. There might be some truth in this claim were alcoholic drinks in the nature of actual necessities, and were the effects of drink productive of strength. health, and comfort, such as are the effects of food, clothing, shelter, etc. As it is, however, drinking tends to decrease instead of increase average wages.

And it does it in just this way : Habitual drinking, as most will admit, whether the drinker gets drunk or not, tends to stupefy, and brutalize, and benumb the finer faculties and desires. To just the extent which drink so stupefies, brutalizes, and benumbs, the drinker loses the desire to gratify the manifold and many-sided finer part of his nature. To illustrate, how much less does the habitual drinker care for pictures, music, books, lectures, and a hundred similar features of the best modern life than the man who abstains from alcoholic poison? With the loss or partial loss of such higher desires comes a lessened demand for better food, better clothing, better shelter, and better surroundings — all of which cost more money than poor food, poor clothes, poor shelter, and poor surroundings. But the better food, clothing, shelter, and surroundings come to be regarded by the abstainer, who has cultivated his finer nature, *as actual necessities of life*. When, therefore, we have as wageworkers an army of abstainers demanding these more expensive necessities, if it be true that wages tend to the level which will supply necessities, then wages must increase correspondingly to that of the increased cost of the necessities.

The drunken workman also tends powerfully to lower wages when he forces his wife and children out to service in order to help support the family. Everywhere the cry is going up that women and children are forcing down the wages of able-bodied men.

Let the wageworker then hesitate not to boycott strong drink. All the cumulative power of many-sided manhood is on the side of abstinence. Not the least of this power will be the ability to hold with firm grasp the principles underlying the social evolution, and to apply those principles in disciplined cooperation for the advancement of the masses.

— *C. De F. Hoxie*

97. MERRY CHRISTMAS!

Merry, because the brotherhood of man, taught by Him whose birth we celebrate, is more than ever before recognized as the ideal of those who pray, "Thy kingdom come on earth as it is in heaven." Merry, because a day is dawning when the meek who work for the good of their fellows, instead of the warlike who trample upon them, shall inherit the earth. Merry, because the peacemakers are looking to a time — not so far distant, let us hope — when even industrial strife shall cease, and all who contribute toward the world's wealth and happiness shall receive their just share of the world's cheer, even as "the children of God." Merry, for then, indeed, shall the mourners find comfort and the hungry be filled.

Merry Christmas, because the common people of our land are fast coming to the conclusion that a government of the people and for the people must embody first and foremost the principles of the Golden Rule, and that a State which licenses men to poison its subjects comes far short of the ideal of a Christian commonwealth.

So every Christmas day finds this old world in spirit, if not in action, nearer the Christmas ideal. It is the Christmas spirit which must finally triumph in spite of old habit, iron-bound custom, and unwise law.

Once again, "Merry Christmas!" — *The Voice.*

98. THE FUNDAMENTAL REFORM.

THERE'S A BETTER TIME COMING — AN ALLEGORY FOR REFORMERS.

Many long years ago a great ship set sail for the Port of Happiness, and on her voyage she ran aground in the darkness. But the passengers took no notice of it, and the officers, seeing that they would be blamed, denied that there was anything wrong. The weeds and barnacles grew about her so that it seemed that she had always stood still. As for the crew, they said, "What do we care if only we get our daily pay?" But the ship was straining and in danger of going to pieces. She pounded heavily upon the sand. "Those noises," said the captain, "are strikes. We have always had such troubles."

One day a fisherman came down to the coast, and when he saw the ship he began to push at it, while the passengers laughed at him. Others passed by, and to them he called, "Come and help us." And now and then one did join him. The officers said: "These people are disturbers of the peace. They must be arrested." And others said: "If you push the ship off, no one knows where she will go nor what will become of her."

Then a passenger stood up and shouted to those who worked: "You fools, your intentions are good, but you are ahead of the times. The wind is against you." The fisherman answered, "Yes, but the tide is rising." And still he cried aloud. Some of the passengers came and helped him push, and the timbers cracked. "That," said the ship's doctor, "is the necessary strife of nature." And some of those who were on board grew sick in the hot rays of the sun, so that their groans annoyed the officers, and they put them in the hold.

He who pushed cried out, "The Kingdom of God is at hand." They did not understand at all, so they put him to death.

Yet the commotion attracted many, and now and then one left his work and shoved or hauled or pried with a lever, or fastened a float under the ship. And some, tho meaning to strengthen the ship, fastened weights on its sides. These they called other reforms and charities. They said: "It is Utopian to try to get the ship off. Let us make the people as comfortable as possible, so that they will be quiet."

And as they worked wearily and almost discouraged, a wind from God came out of the West, and when all pushed the great ship moved off, and behold, it was almost in sight of the kingdom.

* * * * * * *

And many of those who were pushing died in the chill water, and some were drowned and many forgotten. But their names are written in the book of remembrance of Him who cried, "The Kingdom of God is at hand."

—*Bolton Hall.*

99. A CASE FOR CHARITY.

He was out at the elbows and out at the knees.
   But he had an old pipe in his mouth.
He was worse than a ragman by several degrees,
   But he had an old pipe in his mouth.
He was out of a job, and his plans had all failed,
He was "down in the mouth," and his luck he bewailed,
At the rich man he swore, at monopoly railed —
   But he kept that old pipe in his mouth.

He was woful and shabby and hungry and lame,
   But he had his old pipe in his mouth.
He had saved little money — he was not to blame,
   For he must have a pipe in his mouth.
He would "go out to market" — an everyday joke,
And you knew what he'd say ere a sentence he spoke,
"A penny for bread and five cents for a smoke,"
   Oh, he *must* have that pipe in his mouth!

His wife sewed by lamplight, to drive the wolf hence
   (And to keep that old pipe in his mouth),
And he said between puffs: "We must cut our expense,"
   But he kept that old pipe in his mouth.
Kind Charity, come, without further delay,
This woman may die — what will happen, then, pray?
Here's a case you must help. Shall I tell you the way?
   Just take that old pipe from his mouth!

— Hattie Horner Louthan.

100. THE DAWN OF MERCY.*

   The history of the world from the time when the first murderer swung his brutal club, until now, is largely a record of suffering inflicted by man. So-called heroic deeds of conquerors, hideous punishments inflicted by tyrants, and ever-recurring instances of love of revenge and thirst for blood, occupy much space in the chronicles of ancient times; in the history of the Middle Ages, and in that of succeeding centuries.
   One reads with a throb of pity and of horror of those unhappy days, when even the wise and virtuous, distracted with

---

* From address delivered before the Second Triennial Session of the National Council of Women of the United States, in Metzerott's Music Hall, Washington, D. C., Feb. 27, 1895.

anxiety and terror, found life so unendurable that in many cases they gladly welcomed an opportunity to end it. Men were afraid of knowing each other; even silence was a crime, and even natural affection. Tacitus states that the Roman Senate actually put to death a woman of advanced age because she wept for her son who had been executed. The age was a carnival of death and torture, and the general murmur was, "Will there ever be a day unpolluted with blood?"

But in a small corner of Rome's great empire was soon to be enacted a drama which began an era in human history, and which has exercised an ineradicable influence on the morals of a large proportion of the human race. That drama was the perfect life and the malefactor's death of one who founded a strange new sect which preached the gospel of *love*; of peace and of good will; and whose central principle of action was the Golden Rule. The simple, yet matchless record of the words and acts of Christ and of His followers, has for 1800 years been the guide of that portion of the human race to which the world owes all that is highest in literature and art, all that is best in invention, wisest in statesmanship, in benevolence and in social reform. Even limited and imperfect adherence to the Christian standard has brought the world's civilization to what it is. When dissension arose among the early Christians, it was because the precepts of the Author of Christianity were disregarded; in the centuries when the theological differences resulted in persecution rivalling that of paganism, it was because those who sought to *drive* their fellow-men forgot the exquisite gentleness of Him who said, "Come unto me," and men were cruel then and are cruel now because His command, "Be ye therefore merciful as your Father also is merciful," has been uncomprehended and disregarded. The earth is still a dark place of cruelty where His spirit is not. The bent of the human is toward selfishness and cruelty except as it is opened to the touch of the Divine. Christ's professed followers and those whose admiration of His example lead them to fight sin and evil, should lay the ax to the root, and work to promote universally the law of kindness and of mercy, recognizing that cruelty is the worst thing in the world. Show me a sin that you think worse than cruelty, and I will show you that it is bad in proportion to its cruelty, present or prospective. Wrongs which most infringe right are wrongs which most infringe *rights.* Is it conceivable that any human being who had been systematically and thoroughly trained to be kind would so infringe the rights of his neighbor's family as to sell him that which may turn him into a drunkard? Is it conceivable that if he were kind he would sell his neighbor that which may turn him into a fiend of cruelty to human beings and dumb brutes? None ought to work harder than temperance reformers to promote the law of kindness, and none ought to work harder than the humane to promote temperance reform.

— *Mrs. Mary F. Lovell.*

101. THE LEVEL OF CIVILIZATION.

The *London Times* proclaimed, twenty years ago, that intemperance produced more idleness, crime, want, and misery, than all other causes put together; and the *Westminster Review* calls it a "curse that far eclipses every other calamity under which we suffer." Gladstone, speaking as Prime Minister, admitted that "greater calamities are inflicted on mankind by intemperance than by the three great historical scourges — war, pestilence, and famine." DeQuincy says, "The most remarkable instance of a combined movement in society which history, perhaps, will be summoned to notice, is that which, in our day, has applied itself to the abatement of intemperance. Two vast movements are hurrying into action by velocities continually accelerated — the great revolutionary movement from *political* causes concurring with the great *physical* movement in locomotion and social intercourse from the gigantic power of steam. At the opening of such a crisis had no *third movement arisen of resistance to intemperate habits*, there would have been ground of despondency as to the melioration of the human race." These are English testimonies, where the State rests more than half on bayonets. Here we are trying to rest the ballot-box on a drunken people. "We can rule a great city," said Sir Robert Peel, "America can not"; and he cited the mobs of New York as sufficient proof of his assertion.

Thoughtful men see that up to this hour the government of great cities has been with us a failure; that worse than the dry-rot of legislative corruption, than the rancor of party spirit, than Southern barbarism, than even the tyranny of incorporated wealth, is the giant burden of intemperance, making universal suffrage a failure and a curse in every great city. Scholars who play statesmen, and editors who masquerade as scholars, can waste much excellent anxiety that clerks shall get no office until they know the exact date of Cæsar's assassination, as well as the latitude of Pekin, and the Rule of Three. But while this crusade — the temperance movement — has been, for sixty years, gathering its facts and marshalling its arguments, rallying parties, besieging legislatures and putting great States on the witness-stand as evidence of the soundness of its methods, scholars have given it nothing but a sneer. But if universal suffrage ever fails here for a time — permanently it can not fail — it will not be incapable civil service, nor an ambitious soldier, nor Southern vandals, nor venal legislatures, nor the greed of wealth, nor boy statesmen rotten before they are ripe, that will put universal suffrage into eclipse ; it will be rum entrenched in great cities and commanding every vantage ground.

Social science affirms that woman's place in society marks the level of civilization. From its twilight in Greece, through the Italian worship of the Virgin, the dreams of chivalry, the justice of the civil law, and the equality of French society, we trace her gradual recognition; while our common law, as Lord Brougham confessed, was, with relation to women, the opprobrium of the age and of Christianity. For forty years, plain men and women, working noiselessly, have washed away that opprobrium ; the statute books of thirty States have been remodelled, and woman stands to-day almost face to face with her last claim — the ballot. It has been a weary and thankless, tho successful, struggle. But if there be any refuge from that ghastly curse, the vice of great cities — before which social science stands palsied and dumb — it is in this more equal recognition of woman. If, in this critical battle for universal suffrage — our fathers' noblest legacy to us, and the greatest trust God leaves in our hands — there be any weapon, which, once taken from the armory, will make victory certain, it will be, as it has been in art, literature, and society, summoning woman into the political arena. — *Wendell Phillips.*

102. THE GREATEST MISSIONARY NEED.

We hear from missionaries that there are open fields calling for Gospel light. "China and Corea asking for more missionary teachers." India, Africa, and the islands of the sea are in need of more missionaries *and less rum* from Christian America. The cry comes to us from Turkey, where in Armenia ten thousand Christians have been brutally butchered during the last year by Mohammedan swords; from the Freedmen of the South and the Indians of the West, both in need of churches and schools, while we have young men and women educated for this work, and many generous hearts daily responding to the call for means to support them.

Yes! let us send forth these missionaries. Let us send them, with the American flag, and these American institutions, the church and the school, that they may plant them abroad, and in our own South and West. But there is *one* American institution that was not included in the recent appeals for more help. That institution is protected by the American flag, and stands as a barrier to every Christian enterprise. It stands in the very gateway of our land. At Ellis Island, for ten thousand dollars paid annually to our government by a single man, strong drink is forced upon emigrants at high prices, when many of them would gladly choose good water if they could get it. Is it any wonder that emigrants are ready to go into the liquor business to recover the money thus wrung from them under the very torch of liberty?

Take the American flag, and those American institutions, the church and the schoolhouse, and plant them in the South and West, *and another* can take the *same flag* and that American institution, the legalized saloon, plant it beside the church and school, and send more souls to perdition than the others can save.

Legalized iniquity in this land of ours destroys tenfold more victims than Mussulman swords in Armenia, and with quite as fiendish cruelty. All the horrors of heathen lands pale into insignificance when compared with this institution of Christian America maintained by the hand of Christian citizens in their idolatrous worship of corrupt political parties, whose victims number about one hundred and twenty-five thousand annually.

How can we Christianize heathen lands until we receive sufficient Gospel light to keep us from being a part of such a worse than barbarous system?

In China's determined struggle to keep out English opium, it was a well-known principle of the Chinese government *not to license* what they condemned as immoral; and the mandarin who advised that a tax and a heavy duty be laid on opium as a measure of expediency was promptly banished to Tartary as a suitable reward for his infamous proposition. It would be well for Christian America if those who advocate the same policy of legalized iniquity were compelled to share the same fate. The Chinese glory in the superiority of their own government as to principle, and scorn the Christian governments that tolerate these vices for the sake of public revenue. It was declared by the high commissioner of China that tho the oar should break in his hand, or the boat should sink from beneath him, yet would he not stay his efforts until his work, the expulsion of opium, was accomplished.

The Chinese are a practical people, and glory in their ethical teachings. Christianity, as it comes to them, must likewise be intensely practical, proving its innate worth by presenting, above all else, a morality superior in theory and practise to that which they already have. With what an awful force must these facts appeal to the logical, intelligent Celestial! The moral debt which Christian lands owe to China can never be computed. — *A. Morehouse.*

103. THE DIFFERENCE.

What a difference Prohibition will make to thousands of women who have now only the wretched rooms with bare floor, whose gaps and splinters are only rendered more manifest by sweeping; mangled furniture, whose dents and scratches are only more hopelessly revealed by dusting; the dingy window, which, if cleaned, only shows a dingier alley; the faded and ragged calico dress for both morning and evening; little food to cook and less fire to cook it with; children chiefly thought of as creatures with appetites that can not be satisfied and bodies that can not be clothed; not a picture, book, or paper to furnish a story to read them or a fresh thought to talk over with them; the husband daily growing coarser, duller, and more purposeless; the certainty that to-morrow shall be as this day and much more disconsolate; that if business improves it will give only so much more to go into the maw of the remorseless saloon!

But Prohibition crystallizes faith into "the things needful for the body." It puts this oppressed woman into a comfort able home. It puts on the floor a bright carpet, pretty if cheap, curtains at the windows, simple furniture that is neat, trim, and strong, and some of the really beautiful pictures that modern art makes so inexpensive upon the walls. Now she will find a perfect joy in sweeping the last speck off that carpet, dusting the furniture till it shines, keeping the windows clear as a mountain stream. When she wishes to get dinner, there is a stove that will cook and fuel to put in it. In the pantry there is a sack of flour and her little jar of sugar, and all the spices and sundries that a good housewife needs. In her purse there's the money to make the market stall a promise and not a despair. How she will slave at that cooking because "John is fond of this," and "those will taste so good to the children!" She will not know that she is hot or tired. When she would sit down to her sewing, she can change the neat working dress of the morning for a pretty home dress for afternoon. She will take some pains to make herself a fair portion of the pretty home scene. When she goes to work on the children's clothes, there's something to make the little garments out of. She will hear songs of hope in the hum of her sewing-machine, and there will be a light in her eyes and a song on her own lips. How the children's eyes will brighten and their faces shine! How strong they will be for play and how ambitious for study! How dear their home will be to them! How the light of love and peace and joy will make their faces beautiful!

Then all around, among the people who were never intemperate, the wave of this prosperity will sweep. The stores and the mills, the railroads and the mines, the ships and the farms — all who produce or transport or deal in the goods which these rescued families are now able to buy — will share the blessing. With a city, a nation, of such homes, every business will boom, all our nation prospering and exulting through the two thousand million revenue of righteousness! Who would not help to bring the happy, glorious day? What true heart will not bid us God-speed as we toil to hasten its coming?

—*Rev. James C. Fernald.*

104. FLOWER MISSION.

A message rings from the quiet place
  Where a soul grows white under touch of pain;
And frail, fair hands with a tender grace

Are holding a loss that has turned to gain —
Turned into gain for the hearts that sigh,
  For feet which stumbled and went astray;
For lives that wrecked when the storm swept by,
  Are shut from the light of the common day.

The call rings softly from gentle lips
  That ready grow for the Angel's song,
Sweet as the note of the lark that dips
  Her wing at the brook, when the night grows long;
And souls that are loving, and hearts that pray,
  Shall heed the message that comes to-day.

      Go ye and gather
        The blossoms of June,
      Rare in their glory,
        And sweet with perfume;
      Gather the splendor
        Of summer's green bowers;
      Dawns with its mission
        The day of the flowers.

Stately or lowly, from garden or mead,
Lo, for your garlands the Master has need.
Not for the hall where the banquet is spread,
Not for the feast where the wine floweth red,
Not for the bridal of beauty and youth,
Not for the plighting of honor and truth,
Not for the brows of the children that play,
Not for the hands that are lifeless as clay,
Gathered to-day are the flowers that bloom,
Glowing with light, at the heart of June.

Their splendor shall shine on an altar place
  Where even at noon the shadows fall,
Where time creeps by with a leaden pace,
  And men make moans at a prison wall;
They come to hands that are touched with crime,
  To hearts grown weary with wrath and tears,
To lives shut in by a burning line
  That holds its judgment across the years.

The fragrance shall come with breath of love,
  To the homesick souls that went astray;

Shall cool the fever and lift above
　The thought of the watcher that longs for day.
O God! Wherever the shadows fall
　On any who suffer, or those that sin,
May rose and lily make plain to all,
　A path where the Christ may enter in.

— Mary T. Lathrap.

105. WHAT IS FAITH?

Men have strange ideas of God's dealings with us, and of faith in Him. What is faith? To walk right on to the edge of the precipice, and then stop? No, walk on! What, set my feet upon nothing? Yes, upon nothing, if it is in the path of duty; boldly set your feet on nothing, and a solid rock, firm as the everlasting hills, shall meet your feet at every step you take in the path of duty, only do it unwaveringly and in faith. What we have to do is to settle the point that we are right; and then onward.

You remember when the children of Israel went out of Egypt, when they were a band of escaped fugitives. Their ranks were encumbered with many women and children, and their mighty, but meek, leader was armed only with a rod. Here come the chariots and horsemen of Pharaoh, treading on their very shadow. A pillar of fire went before the Israelites by night, and a pillar of cloud by day; and they marched till they came to the shores of the Red Sea, and then — what? Read the magnificent narrative. And the Lord God said unto Moses from out of the cloud, "Speak to the children of Israel that they go forward." That was the only command. How can they go forward? There is no other command for them; but to Moses came these words: "Stretch forth thy rod," and the way opened. God never yet gave us a duty to do but he opened the way for us when we were ready to do it. He never yet gave an impossible command. So Moses stretched forth his rod and the water stood in heaps. Tramp, tramp, tramp went the three millions over the bed of the sea, and their enemies came in after them in the night-time. Now, what? "Forward!" "But our enemies are in the rear." "*Forward!*" "Yes, but before us is — we know not what — and the waters are on either side." "*Forward!*" "Yes, but we can feel the very breath of the horses upon our necks, and hear the chariot wheels grind in the shingle as they pursue us.' "*Forward!*" "Yes, but we must defend our wives and little ones." "*Forward!*" And the pillar that went before them passed over and stood in their rear. It was light unto them, it was darkness to their enemies; "and they came not near each other all the night." Those who had obeyed the command, "forward!" stood on the other side, and then the Lord God looked out from the pillar of fire, and troubled the Egyptians, and brake their chariot wheels. Those who had obeyed the command, "forward!" saw the wrecks of the chariots, and the carcasses of the horses, and the bodies of men strewing the strand. Let us settle the question, "Am I right?" And then, shoulder to shoulder, march on, our motto, "Excelsior"; our hope, that there is a better day coming; and our prayer, "God speed the right." —*John B. Gough.*

106. THE PATRIOT'S ALLY.*

Our fathers believed a government of the people possible, and thus the Republic was born, with all its great destinies anchored to the masses, with all its possibilities dependent upon the capacity of the individual citizens for self-government, and that capacity again dependent upon the enlightenment of the conscience and the understanding. Our fathers were far-seeing men. They did not leave this enlightenment of the conscience and understanding to the haphazard teaching of the street, of society, or even of the home or the church. Their underlying philosophy was the now accepted axiom, that "whatever we should have appear in the character of citizenship must be wrought into that character through the schools." As those times were simple, so were their schools.

But the curriculum of our schools has kept pace with the demand of our citizenship. When the war of 1861 burst upon us, it found a nation of civilians on both sides of the Potomac. That struggle was greatly prolonged, while "the boys in blue and in gray" were being transformed into soldiers. Taught by

---

*Extract from Address of Mrs. Mary H. Hunt, before the Committee on Education and Labor, United States Senate, in favor of the bill "Providing for the study of Physiology and Hygiene, and the effects of intoxicating, narcotic, and poisonous substances upon the life, health, and welfare, by the pupils in the public schools of the Territories and of the District of Columbia, and in the Military and Naval Academies."

that experience, many a State said, "This must never happen again," and added military drill for many schools.

But a greater evil is in all our land, to-day, than the one that temporarily estranged us in *ante-bellum* days. Uncle Tom could say, "This body is Massa Legree's slave, but this soul is God's free man." No slave of alcohol can say that. Enslaved soul and body are its victims, who are not an alien race, thus subjugated, but are our own sons and brothers, husbands and fathers, the best-beloved from the homes of an otherwise happy and prosperous people. A "first-born has been slain" by this destroyer, in all this fair land, between the oceans, the lakes, and the gulf. Never has any evil so undermined the character of our citizenship, and therefore proved so great an evil to our free institutions. Alarmed at the inroads of this enemy, the friends of this reform are knocking at the doors of the schools for relief. We come to ask for an enactment that shall result in the enlightenment of the consciences and understanding of the people, not as to the vice and evil of drunkenness, of which all are now assured, but as to the nature of alcohol, and of its effects upon the human system, that, thus forewarned, our youth may be forearmed.

I am here, gentlemen, not merely as a person, but in a representative capacity. There are two hundred thousand Christian women who are praying this morning for the results of this hour. They are in every city, in every town, all over this broad land, in every State and every Territory. They represent the homes, the Christian homes of America. If we save the children to-day, we shall have saved the nation to-morrow. In the name, then, of this womanhood, I stand here, to plead for the children who will be taught in the specified territory covered by this bill, and likewise for the influence of such legislation. Wherever our flag shall be unfurled over this and other lands throughout all Christendom, will be felt the blessed example, if this Congress of the United States shall thus provide for the temperance education of the children under its jurisdiction.

107. THE TEMPERANCE EDUCATION LAW.*

The old maxim says that "right wrongs no man." So I say that light wrongs no man. Truth wrongs no man. It controls

---

* From a speech in the House of Representatives, May 17, 1886.

no man, but it helps each man to control himself. There is and there can be no question of the terrible evil of intemperance. All thinking men are agreed that it is the greatest social evil of the age. It is an evil that most vitally concerns the State in many ways.

It degrades the individual citizen and unfits him for the duties and responsibilities of citizenship.

It is the most prolific cause of lawlessness, pauperism, and crime.

It is the great destroyer of national wealth.

It is the most common and the most dangerous agent for the corruption of the elective franchise.

There is no side of free government that it does not assail. It poisons the fountains of political power; it multiplies the burdens of taxation; it diminishes the wage-fund of labor below the line of decent living; it dwarfs the power of production to an alarming extent; it corrupts the franchise, and it threatens the future of the Republic by perverting and depraving the rising generation.

The great central root of intemperance is ignorance. The remedy must be more light.

This bill is the echo of God's primordial decree, "Let there be light!" It is the pleading of the millions of the children of our land, beseeching that they may not be sent naked, without shield or armor, into the battle of life to contend against odds not only with the open and disclosed enemy but also with those that lie in ambush and assail them in disguise. It is the appeal of hundreds of thousands of the noblest and purest women of the land in behalf of their homes, their offspring, their altars, and their firesides. It is the plea of the home, the church, and the school combined that if our tender ones and our helpless ones must run the gauntlet of the army of alcohol they may at least be forewarned and upon guard against the lurking danger.

In form this bill affects and applies only to the District of Columbia and the places under the exclusive jurisdiction of the United States; but in principle and in moral effect it is as broad as the nation.

Its passage will send a thrill of joy and a tide of blessing from ocean to ocean, from the great lakes to the Gulf, and from the Everglades of Florida to the waters of Puget Sound. It is a remedy peaceable, philosophical, radical, far-reaching. It trenches on no man's rights, proscribes no man's business, confiscates no man's property, dictates no man's habits, restricts no man's liberty. It appeals only to the power of truth upon man's free choice. It will be as silent and as beneficent in its operation as the dew and the sunshine of spring. It will come with bane for none, with blessing for all. We, who to-day record our votes for this bill, may not live to see its matured fruits. The world will move on much the same as before, but it will move upon a constantly ascending plane until it shall come at length, perhaps long after we are gone, into a clearer light, into a brighter hope, into a nobler, cleaner, and more beneficent mode of living.

We have it in our power here and now to confer untold blessings upon the future of our country, for which millions now unborn shall rise up and call us blessed. Can we neglect so grand an opportunity, so imperative a duty?

—Hon. Byron M. Cutcheon.

108. THE LOYAL TEMPERANCE LEGION.

We're a temperance legion
  Singing as we come,
Soldiers of an army
  Pledged to conquer rum.
    We're for home and mother,
      God and native land;
    Grown up friend and brother,
      Give us now your hand.

We're a gentle legion,
  In our sunny youth,
Bearing as our weapons
  Only love and truth.
    We're for home and mother,
      God and native land;
    Grown up friend and brother,
      Give us now your hand.

We're an earnest legion,
  For we surely know
What destroys the father
  Is the children's foe.

We're for home and mother,
  God and native land;
  Older friend and brother,
  Give us now your hand.

We're an honest legion,
  Wearing colors true,
Like our country's emblem,
  Red and white and blue.
    We're for home and mother,
      God and native land;
      Patriot friend and brother,
      Give *us* loyal hand.

We're a growing legion,
  By and by we'll stand
Citizens and rulers,
  Ballots in our hands;
    Then to home and country
      We will still be true.
      Vote for Prohibition,
      Grown up friends, will you?
          — *Mary T. Lathrap.*

109. THE TERRORS OF EVICTION.

Have you ever thought about a woman being turned out of her house — the little cottage that covers her and her children? Can you picture — you who live in comfortable homes filled with light and warmth and books and joy — can you think of these people — human beings, our brothers and sisters, the poor mother, brave though her heart is breaking, huddling her little children about her, and the father, weak but loving, and loving all the deeper because he knows his weakness has brought them to this want and degradation, and little children, those of whom our Saviour said: "Suffer them to come unto me and forbid them not," there asking, "Mamma, where will we sleep to-night?"— can you picture that and then their taking themselves up and the woman putting her hand with undying love and faith in the hand of the man she swore to follow through good and evil report, and marching up and down the street — this pitiable procession — through the unthinking streets, by laughing children and shining windows, looking for a hole where, like the foxes, they may hide their poor heads?

My friends, they talk to you about personal liberty, that a man should have the right to go into a grog-shop and see this pitiable procession — now stopped — parading up and down our streets again. They talk to you about the shades of Washington, Monroe, and Jefferson. I would not give one happy, rosy little woman, uplifted from that degradation — happy again in her home, with the cricket chirping on her hearthstone and her children about her knee, her husband redeemed from drink at her side — I would not give one of them for all the shades of all the men that ever contended since Cataline conspired and Cæsar fought! — *Henry W. Grady.*

110. A NEW SONG OF SIXPENCE.

Sing a song of ways and means,
  Nice good-natured man,
With an empty pocketbook,
  Hits upon a plan.
Gets a paper and a pen,
  Writes an application;
Gets it signed by twelve nice men
  Of decent grade and station!
When the paper's opened,
  'Tis clearly understood,
The whole thing is "conducive
  To the public good."

Fellow buys his license,
  Pays his money down;
Isn't that an easy way
  Of lighting up a town?
Make the sidewalks wider,
  Make 'em wide and straight;
Sometimes men come reeling
  Homeward rather late —
Once were babies cuddled tight,
  As though the love would smother;
Isn't this a pleasant sight
  To set before a mother?

Sing a song of broken hearts,
  Hearts that break for sorrow;

Eyes that look through blinding tears
   For a better morrow.
When the polls are opened,
   The votes and drink go down;
Isn't this a precious sight
   To set before a town?

Sing a song of ships afloat,
   Starry pennants wearing;
For a distant heathen port
   See them seaward bearing.
Tracts and whisky casks aboard,
   Rum and salvation;
'Tis a most consistent dish
   Before a Christian nation.

Sing a song of woman's work,
   Women's faith and prayers;
Four and twenty duties,
   Four and twenty cares.
Girls with sunny faces,
   Women with white hair;
Unions in the East and West,
   Unions everywhere,

Working for a Christian cause,
   Men that cause delaying,
Women with their ribbons white,
   Hoping, trusting, praying.
When the Book is opened,
   Where creed and act accord,
Won't *this* be a pleasant sight
   To set before the Lord?

                — *Mrs. N. S. Kitchel.*

111. THE POWER OF RIGHTEOUS LAW.

   I am aware that legal penalties can not kill appetite, or quench inward dispositions. But if this is an objection to a penal statute in one instance, it is an objection in all instances. The law against murder can not prevent the murderous disposition — the penalty for stealing, does not make one any less a thief at heart. Law is not a moral and regenerating force; it is restriction, and has reference to overt acts. And in this capacity it is legitimate and efficacious anywhere; it is so when it confiscates the implements of the gamester, or stops the traffic of the dealer in intoxicating drinks. It becomes every citizen to exert all his influence in erecting legal safeguards against those monstrous vices. It is a shameful inconsistency that the law should busy itself only with consequences, and neglect and even foster causes. It leaves uncared for the hotbeds of iniquity, and shuts up the vagrant and the thief. With one hand it licenses a dram-shop, and with the other builds a gallows. *Hearer, where are your influence and your vote in this matter?* — *Rev. Dr. E. H. Chapin.*

112. THE GREAT PROBLEM.

It was my great pleasure a few years ago to listen to an address by Bishop Thoburn from Calcutta, India, to the graduating class at Painesville, Ohio. In it he said:

"Life is full of problems, and education helps us to solve them. The scholar is accustomed to sit down to his example. The more difficult it is, the more time and thought he must consume in working it out. Does he give it up *because* it is difficult? Never! if he is the real scholar. Does he go to his class and say to the teacher, 'The easiest problems I have solved, but the more difficult and intricate I have left until my mind is prepared to grasp them, and I feel more like studying them out. I find my classmates also disposed to let them alone, so we have all concluded to do only what we are able easily and naturally to do.'"

Shall we be such scholars in the great school of life? One of the most intricate problems set before us is this of the temperance question. Shall we leave it alone, or shall we, in our quiet homes, study out the problem, and never rest until it is successfully solved?

You say it is intricate. Yes, there is the addition of woes, terrible beyond description. There is the subtraction of happiness beyond computation. There is the multiplication of sorrows and distresses, and there is the division of estates, of homes, of lives. There are questions of profit and loss — profit to the saloon-keeper, to be balanced by loss to the nation, the state, the church, the community, and the home.

There are questions of proportion; if a saloon-keeper pays $200, how many homes worth $2,000, $20,000, or $200,000 may be ruined? How many manly forms may he bring to drunkards' graves? How many mothers' hearts may he break? How many children may he keep barefoot and starving through the cold winter?

Ah, Christian women, is the problem beyond our solving? Shall we not join hands and hearts and brains to study out this stupendous question in its various relations?

Let us call to our aid clear minds that have given their best thought for years to its solution. Let us choose *their* words rather than our own in presenting these thoughts to others.

Let us sit low at the feet of these teachers and prove diligent and ready scholars.

Let us ask the blessing of the Divine Teacher on our every effort, and seek His presence and benediction first of all.

— *Mrs. Nettie B. Fernald.*

---

113. A PRAYER BY DR. DEEMS.

Look upon us, O God, our heavenly Father, in our helplessness before this great tyranny. Look upon us as they slaughter our children and our fathers, and look with pity upon the mothers and the fathers of the dead brave whom they have killed. Bring from out of the schools and colleges, the factories and the farms, those who are gifted to fight; and may all enter into this work with all their heart, brain, brawn, and life. Let not the sun of this generation go down in darkness. May the terrific rum traffic be crushed out. Let the powers of moral suasion, of preaching, of law, and of social influence be combined to beat down this Satan. Grant that this whole nation may be stirred increasingly over this greatest question that has stirred it since the continent was discovered. Break, we pray Thee, the power of every preacher, every editor, every poet, every reporter, every writer, who is engaged in giving countenance to the desolating curse of the centuries. And give strength to every feeble child, and to every weak woman, and every humble soldier fighting for Prohibition; and may the strongest amongst us be like David, and the Davids in this cause be powerful as angels of heaven.

—*Rev. Dr. Charles F. Deems, in Cooper Union, June 7,* 1887.

114. "THE MASTER CALLETH."

The golden test of character is in Colossians 3:17, "Whatsoever ye do in word or deed, do all in the name of the Lord Jesus." That is life's topmost round, its loftiest ideal, one that would carry with it happiness for others and for ourselves, and would bring out all the power there is in any one of us. If this is your ideal the forces of the universe are on your side; there is a momentum from the great Parental Spirit of the world. No harm can come to you on any planet if the supreme law that gives unity to your life is this one Master. It is a very practical thing to carry out this law, and if we are sincere it will make Christ master of our money, master of our time, master of our tongues, master of our influence; and if it does not, then what we claim concerning consecration is sounding brass and a tinkling cymbal, nothing more.

The Master calleth: He calls by joy, and I have thought when that suffices He does not call by grief. The sunshine, not the storm, is the preferred method of approach by Him who weareth light as a garment.

In my temperance work I often ask white-ribboners what enlisted them to fight this battle, and in nine cases out of ten I find it was the call of joy. Even as a lovely Southern woman said to me in a city of Virginia where I was forming a society, as she stepped forward to give me her name: "Just because my home has been so bright, because my husband and my sons never wish to spend an evening out, and have no habit that a woman might not cherish, I am glad to give my name and pledge my work. It is a token of my gratitude."

But if we will not be won by the sweet South wind, then comes the tempest, and He who loves us too well to give up calling, sends the call of grief. How many of us have sorrowfully proved that this is true! What scars upon the heart, known perhaps only to God, testify to the scourging of Him who doth not willingly afflict or grieve the children of men!

Jenny Lind was asked what she thought about when she was singing, and with a rapt gaze she answered, "Oh, I always sing to God!" The words were eloquent; they tell what every life should do — it should sing its noble psalm to God who gave it.

He calls by opportunity. The Foreign Missionary work — that blessed John the Baptist that prepares the way for women, and opens highways to the great causes of home philanthropy — the Woman's Home Missionary work, the Woman's Christian Temperance Union, with its beckoning hand and its stirring voice, "For God and Home and Native Land," the Christian Endeavor Societies, working so bravely "For Christ and the Church," the King's Daughters, with their glorious motto, "In His name " — He calls by opportunities like these, in a more winsome voice than Christian women ever heard before. Can any refuse to heed the call? — *Frances E. Willard.*

115. A WORD TO THE Y's.

A word to the Y's, and what word shall it be as sufficient? The answer arises in my own heart; the name of our organization covers the case entirely — "Young Woman's Christian Temperance Union" — the very first word of which suggests helpfulness, the second tactfulness, kindness, sympathy; the third, completeness; the fourth, the immediate necessity for the practical application of these attributes, and the fifth, the continued need of united labor. The air is full of the sound of organized effort, and titles and constitutions portray the objects for which the societies are formed, but none can mean more, or better meet the present social, moral, religious, educational, and, we might add, municipal, requirements of every town and hamlet, than the organization bearing the above name. Some will question, "Does it take the place of the Church?" No; but it comes forth from the Church and is an extension of church work, under a name, which, by its very sound, protests against the greatest enemy of the Church. The Crusade Spirit, a baptism which fell upon the women in 1873, largely eliminated the "fear of man" from the hearts of those who had been "called," and Christian courage and fortitude have long characterized the membership. Every God-inspired reform receives consideration and is practically set in motion by this organization; it not only passes resolutions on questions the most trying and difficult out on the frontier of moral warfare, but dares to stand by them; it plants its white banner, and then, clad in the "whole armor," "as good-natured as sunshine and as persistent as a Christian's faith," fights up to its colors. The name, "King's Daughters," is most beautiful and uplifting. The name, "Christian Endeavor," suggests aggressive Christianity. The name, "Young Woman's

Christian Temperance Union," means all this and more: it means striking at the root of the greatest evil of our times; it means personal self-denial; it means espousing an unpopular cause, and working for it; it means to be willing to march in the grand army of the W. C. T. U., which is fighting with peaceable weapons for the total prohibtion of the liquor traffic; for equal and an educated suffrage; for a living wage and proper working hours for men and women; for social purity; for the cause of peace and arbitration; for the maintenance of scientific temperance instruction in public schools. It stands for the protection of boyhood and girlhood in all stations of life, and if there is any other human need, however direful or unattractive, as a direct or indirect result of intemperance and sin, for it the Woman's Christian Temperance Union dares to raise its voice. Dear young women because there is "a shadow on the home and many hearts are sad to-day," we ask you to read over the forty departments of the National W. C. T. U., then look around you, and before God ask your conscience if there is not a need-be for each one, and question your hearts. "Have I come to the Kingdom for such a time as this; for such righteous demands as these?" and may you count it a privilege without delay to join our ranks, and to say: "Let my life be given me at my petition and my people at my regard." "Here am I, Lord: send me." — *Frances J. Barnes.*

116. WHAT WILL THE FARMER DO?

The assumption that the American farmer has reached the limit of his market for all the grain he raises not used in the drunkard-making industry is contradicted wherever there can be found a hungry, half-fed man, woman, or child. The limit has not been reached — and it is a crime to assert it — when there exists a half-starved human being within the range of the white sails and the smoking engines of American commerce. What is the farmer to do with his surplus grain? We commend to *The Gazette* the world of meaning in the answer of the Kansas farmer to a similar question propounded by an anti-Prohibition orator: "*We will raise more hogs and less hell!*"

Most emphatically, Prohibitionists do not propose to destroy the farming industry. On the contrary, they would give it a greater impetus. What tariff, high or low, would begin to benefit the American farmer like the existence about him of a community free from saloons and drunkards, with every member eating his three full meals a day, possessing his two or more good suits of clothes and sleeping under his sheets and blankets made from the products of the farm? Drink burdens the farmer by increasing his taxes. Drink narrows his markets just in proportion to the poverty and number of the drinkers. Banish saloons and saloon legislators and you open to the farmer the flood-gates of prosperity. — *The Voice.*

---

117. THE WHITE RIBBON ARMY.

Encircle the world with a ribbon!
   A beautiful ribbon of white,
The badge of the temperance women,
   The emblem of freedom and right;
Of freedom from bitterest bondage,
   The terrible bondage of drink,
That binds down the glory of manhood,
   And fastens a *heart* in each link.

Hear the pitiful wail of the children!
   And list to the mother's low moan.
Wives weep in the anguish of sorrow;
   Oh, what for such woes can atone?
Love, truth, and home life are shattered,
   And hope now lies crushed at the feet
Of the demon who tramples upon them —
   Every tie that made living so sweet.

Shall no standard be lifted against him,
   This foe that spreads ruin and shame,
And sullies our star-spangled banner
   By plying his trade in its name?
O yes! for while temperance women
   Have power to speak for the right,
We'll encircle the world with our ribbon,
   Our beautiful ribbon of white.
              — *Marian W. Hubbard.*

118. THE VOICE OF SCIENCE.

I am recording a matter of history — of personal history — on this question when I say that I, for one, had no thought of alcohol except as a food. I thought it warmed us. I thought it gave additional strength. I thought it enabled us to endure mental and bodily fatigue. I thought it cheered the heart, and lifted up the mind into greater activity. But it so happened that I was asked by the British Medical Association to study the action of alcohol along with a whole series of chemical bodies, and to investigate their bearing in relation to each other. And so I took alcohol from the shelf of my laboratory, as I might any other drug or chemical there, and I asked it, in the course of experiments extending over a long period, "What do you do?" I asked it, "Do you warm the animal body when you are taken into it?" The reply came invariably, "I do not, except as a mere flush of surface excitement. There is, in fact, no warming, but, on the contrary, an effect of cooling and chilling the body." Then I turned round to it in another direction, and asked it, "Do you give muscular strength?" I test it by the most rigid analysis and experiment I can adopt. I test muscular power under the influence of it in various forms and degrees, and its reply is, "I give no muscular strength." I turn to its effect upon the organs of the body, and find that while it expedites the heart's action it reduces tonicity ; and turning to the nervous system I find the same reply — that is to say, I find the nervous system more quickly worn out under the influence of this agent than if none of it is taken at all. I ask it, "Can you build up any of the tissues of the body?" The answer again is in the negative —"I can build nothing. If I do anything I add fatty matter to the body ; but that is a destructive agent, piercing the tissues, destroying their powers, and making them less active in their work." Finally, I sum it all up. I find it to be an agent that gives no strength, that reduces the tone of the blood-vessels and heart, that reduces the nervous power, that builds up no tissues, can be of no use to me or any other animal as a substance for food. On that side of the question my mind is made up — that this agent, in the most moderate quantity, is perfectly useless for any of the conditions of life to which men

119. "COMPULSORY MORALITY."

are subjected, except under the most exceptional conditions, which none but skilled observers need declare.

— *Benjamin Ward Richardson, M.D.**

119. "COMPULSORY MORALITY."

All men will not do right; that is, a great many will not — they are wrong-headed, black-hearted, an go in for securing to themselves the largest possible share of sensual gratification at the smallest cost of labor or exertion. Which then is to be preferred — that these men should continue to do wrong with impunity and seeming advantage at the cost of the general weal; or that the law should interpose to bar the path in which they choose to tread? Yet to do this latter is just what is stigmatized as "compulsory morality." We don't see how penal laws can enforce any other than "compulsory" morality, nor what they are required for if not for just this.

— *Horace Greeley.*

120. THE POLITICIAN'S WAIL.

Oh, I wish I could ride two horses
   Both going different ways;
I wish I could act on two stages
   Both running different plays!
I wish I could talk free silver
   To the wild and woolly West,
While I shriek in the East for the yellow dust
   That the Eastern man loves best!

I love to "smile" with the rummy
   Or walk with the dry Prohib.,
Or fix to please the Populist
   A neat little two per cent. fib.
I wish I could please all parties,
   I wish I could tickle all men,
So the points of the compass would all combine
   To run me for office again!

But they jam me into a corner
   And say I must do or die,
Must show my mettle, define my views,
   And let my banners fly!

---

* Ex-President of the Medical Society of London, Fellow of the Royal Society, Fellow of the Royal College of Physicians, etc.

Oh, where's my occupation
 If this country means to rise
And tear from our records and language books
 That good word, "temporize?"

I envy the little tree-toad
 Whose tough, elastic hide
Takes the hue of the stone or twiglet
 Where he doth, pro tem, abide.
Unblamed — oh, wasteful nature,
 Confer that gift on me,
For I am a patriot leader
 Who loves his salaree!   —*Edna C. Jackson.*

121. THE TEMPERANCE ARMY.
Recitation for Eight Boys.

FIRST BOY.

We've joined the Temperance Army, and the drink we mean
 to fight;
We've all enlisted early on the side of truth and right.
We're healthy, strong, and sturdy, and as time goes fleeting
 by,
If God doth spare our lives, we'll grow in stature tall and
 high;
And we'll go on as we've begun, and fight for freedom still.
We'll be loyal temperance soldiers — yes, that we will!

SECOND BOY.

Brave and obedient we must be, and prompt at Duty's word.
No fear must dwell within the hearts by love and pity stirred :
As soldiers here you find us, ready, every one, to fight
Until our foe, the tyrant Drink, is put to shameful flight;
As soldiers we *salute* you — and we wish that every one
Would join our Temperance Army, till our glorious work is
 done!

THIRD BOY.

We all believe in order, and we're proud of this our band —
We're trim and neat and steady, as we struggle heart and
 hand!
For shoulder unto shoulder, side by side, we boys remain,
We wheel to right, we wheel to left, and now we halt again!

We *shoulder arms* and *arms present;* and striving hard are we
To make the Temperance Army just as strong as strong can be!

FOURTH BOY.

Of course we have some music just to cheer us on our way,
So here we lift our bugles! Would you like to hear us play?
Or watch us as we sound the fifes, the cornet, and the drum?
With notes of triumph, and of peace, the Temperance soldiers come.
Roll, roll your drums, my comrades, till a mighty host we win —
And send the bugle-call to young and old, and bring them in!

FIFTH BOY.

Lift up the Temperance banner, let its folds shine out on high;
O children, lift it upward — upward to the smiling sky!
Hurrah for these our colors! all the world shall see them glow —
We'll wave our flag, our Temperance flag, in the face of Drink, our foe;
We'll plant our standard everywhere, and spread our fearless band
Till sober homes and happy hearts are known throughout the land!

SIXTH BOY.

With dauntless spirits, hero-like, forever may we go.
We're not afraid in freedom's cause to strike a steady blow;
We're not afraid of mocking, for we cry with a steadfast will:
" We will not touch nor taste the drink that worketh harm and ill!"
At every point we'll fight it, and we'll never, never yield:
We'll *charge* it all together, and we'll drive it from the field!

SEVENTH BOY.

This day we come recruiting for the army of the true!
Whate'er your name, whate'er your place, our ranks have need of you;
Please sign our pledge-book, join our band, come forward to our aid —
Now, now become a soldier in the Abstinence Brigade;

Our hands to you we'll all hold out, our welcome high shall
    sound;
Come, join our growing army that will help the weak around!

EIGHTH BOY.

Our strength is in *uniting*; if we muster one and all,
The powers of Drink that wrong our earth shall yet enfeebled
    fall;
The drunkard's chain shall be no more, the captive shall be
    free,
And vice and want and trembling fear before our ranks shall
    flee.
Come, gather, gather, one and all, until the strife be done;
By work and prayer we'll conquer yet and march victorious
    on!

ALL.

Come, Temperance soldiers, muster in life's morning glad and
    bright,
We'll gather, gather, side by side, and march to win the
    fight!
  (*They leave the platform in marching order, one by one.*)
— Mrs. Haycraft.

---

122. THE SAILOR LAD.

It was a sailor, brown and young,
    Whose ship had just sailed by;
Its fair white sails were proudly swelled,
Its great, dark hull was lightly held,
And, with the rippling waves did weld,
    As swept its prow around a curve,
    Without a single wavering swerve;
    And anchored safe did lie.

For many days the good ship had
    Battled with wind and main;
Storms had assailed, great winds did blow,
Calms had entangled in their slow
And weary currents, ice and snow
    Tried to enshroud her in their bands;
    Pirates attacked her in far lands;
    Yet here she was again.

Her captain was a stern, good man,
    Right worthy of his place;

His men were all brave, tried, and true,
Who loved their ship and ocean blue,
And little else of life they knew
  But that which centered round the life
  On ship, and mother, home, or wife,
    Or of the little face

That watched for him while far he sailed
    Along the boundless main;
Who counted hours, and weeks, and days,
And numbered all his little plays,
And all his small life's sunshine rays,
  By "When my father's ship comes back
  There's nothing pretty I shall lack —
    When he comes home again."

But now the proud ship was at home,
    At liberty the men,
Who, through the heat and through the cold,
Through dangers that were never told,
Had borne their trials, brave and bold,
  And faced grim death and gaunt despair,
  And now seemed walking in the air:
    "They were at home again!"

And all the men who'd wives and babes,
    Hastened blithe away,
And left this young brown sailor lad,
And who no wife nor infant had,
But whose old mother, blind and sad,
  Waited at home in her old chair,
  Waited with many a fervent prayer,
    For his return that day.

On shore he stood, so brown, so strong,
    A pleasant sight was he;
No brighter eyes were ever seen,
No face of nobler, sweeter mien,
No better boy was there, I ween;
  No heart was truer or more grand,
  In any mansion in the land,
    Than this lad from the sea.

He was a boy, no more than that,
    What wonder that he fell ;
When every street and rumshop door,
And every little bedecked store,
Persuasive sights, showed o'er and o'er,
    And begged him to go in —
    To drink, and steep himself in sin !
        They were the mouths of hell.

And he was robbed ; the little store
    That he had slowly won,
That for his mother he had brought,
That meant so much of love and thought,
Of comfort in her blindness sought —
    All now was gone; he saw the theft,
    And, like a beast of whelps bereft,
        He struck ! The deed was done !

Then, trembling in a vague alarm,
    He looked upon his hands ;
While round his feet a circling flood
Crept slowly, as he dumbly stood ;
And this dark circle — it was blood !
    Dark and sinister it lay,
    Circling about him every way,
        And forming linked bands.

The sight of that dark, awful stain,
    Was worse than of the dead,
Who lay there prone, with pallid face,
And form that matched the baneful place,
And from his breast that bubbling race,
    Of pouring blood that circled round,
    And wrought new figures on the ground,
        And filled him with sore dread.

A little while he trembling stood,
    As a baby tottering stands,
Bewildered by the horrid sight,
And then before him all grew night,
His gleaming knife the only light ;
    But when his senses came again,

And he could see a little plain,
    His hands were clasped in iron bands.

  *   *   *   *   *   *   *

A mother, pale, and bent, and blind,
    Knelt in a prison cell,
And kissed those brown and sturdy hands,
That now were clasped in iron bands,
That toiled so brave in many lands ;
    That never had an action done
    That was not right, except this one,
        In that red gate of hell !

The poor old, shrunken, sightless eyes
    Had not a tear to shed ;
Dry, labored sobs shook her old frame,
And through them burned the awful shame
That now had fallen on her name ;
    Yet, in all her sorrow, none
    Heard her blame that prisoned son,
        Who sat with bended head.

Too well she knew the pitfalls that
    The law allows to lie
Unchecked, unheeded, everywhere,
That catch unwary footsteps there,
Like some wild tiger in its lair ;
    That lay their toils to trap within
    The very ones least prone to sin,
        And gloating, see them die.

She had no hope ; red-handed he
    Was taken in the act ;
Tho he was drunk, that could not save,
And, tho he killed a thievish knave,
He now must fill a felon's grave ;
    No hope was there for this poor lad,
    Who, tho he sinned, was not all bad ;
        The law must go by fact.

'Twas done ! 'twas done ! that bonny lad
    Whose ship had just sailed in —
That handsome youth, his mother's pride,
Who, for one moment self-beside,

Had sinned when drunk, had shamed died;
  While those who were the guilty ones,
  Whose hearts are hard as nether stones,
    Cried, "We have punished sin."

*   *   *   *   *   *

And now a low and unmarked grave,
    Another close beside,
Shows where low lies the sailor lad,
The only one his mother had,
The boy whose heart was weak, not bad,
  Who had a dread and awful end,
    With none but one poor, weak, blind friend;
  While sin still lives in pride.

*   *   *   *   *   *

L'ENVOI.

Oh! friends, maybe to-morrow you
    A sailor boy may have,
Whose ship is sailing home again,
Whose heart is beating love's refrain,
Whose young life you would spare from pain;
  Then join, with prayerful hearts and true,
  And vote our Prohibition through,
    And thus your own boy save!

                — *Olive Harper.*

123. FOR GOD AND HOME.

Behind were rent hearts steeped in tears;
  Around, the day grown black with wo;
Before them lay the curse of years
  Feeding on all they loved below.
And what were they? A feeble band
  Of women weak, their loved ones gone!
They breathed a prayer, they heard a voice:
"Strike for thy loved! Press on, press on!"

For God they raised their standard high;
  For home they pressed against the foe:
The curse sent out its horrid cry,
  And raised its head as for a blow.
What could these fragile women then?
  The hope from them was well-nigh torn;

They knelt and prayed ; again the voice:
"Press on, press on, press on, and on !"

The world aloof — now here, now there,
   One joined with them for Native Land ;
The curse was troubled in its lair,
   And roused to swallow up this band ;
Like bold Goliath on Elah's plain
   It boasted loud at eve, at morn.
The women prayed : "Be Thou our strength !"
"I still am God ! Press on, and on !"

Their numbers grew ; brave leaders came,
   Sent by their Lord whose flag they bore.
The world is now their battle-field,
   Their courage ever more and more.
Adown the ranks, from file to file,
   Goes up the prayer, goes out the song —
God their commander, and His word :
" Fight on, fight on, and right this wrong !"
                            — *E. H. Chace.*

124. A TOWER OF SHAME.

Many of the designs and ingenious devices intended to outstrip the Eiffel Tower of Paris in our quadri-centennial celebration are stupendous and wonderful, yet lack the one idea to which such an object should tend ; namely, an exhibit to future generations of what has been accomplished since the formation of the Union. In doing this, I would suggest that a gigantic structure ought to be raised to show the principal business in which the country is engaged, and which, proving so lucrative, is commanding the admiration and capital of the Old World — a business in which we profess to lead the world, samples of which can be found in every clime where our flag is known, which has left its impress on both the civilized and uncivilized, and is to-day the ruling spirit of the land, controlling our politics, the schools and institutions, and, to a great extent, the homes of our vaunted "free America." This is the business which must be handed down to posterity, for which we have sacrificed so much, and of which we feel justly proud. The results of it have blest (?) every home in America so much that thousands of orphaned children and widowed mothers would subscribe their prayers and tears, and the Church in many cases, its blessing.

Then, to the honor of our country, let us erect on Capitol Hill, Washington, a monument to Bacchus, Beer, and Bourbon, that will reflect on her votaries and show to the world that we are advancing with rapid strides towards liberty to eat and drink what we please.

We would suggest that the structure be shaped like a demijohn, with an emblematic base, one side being built upon barrels, each representing the year and the amount spent from 1776 to 1891. The opposite side should represent the amount of crime, the crushed homes and souls ruined since its license by the Government, the wicker-work on the outside to be facsimilies of our silver-dollar bearing on its face "In God We Trust." The structure should be 1,100 feet high, each story ten feet high, representing the eleven decades through which we have passed; each story to have recorded on its walls the murders committed, victims executed, and homes ruined, and sons and daughters sacrificed during each decade. The two handles on its sides might represent the two great political parties who carry this mighty business on to success. At the apex we would place the Cork of Justice, blindfolded and appealing to Heaven for deliverance for a country of magnificent, God-given hopes, that has piled up such a collossal structure of misery and crime in a little over a century of existence. Here we would have a structure of which we might be justly proud, and could challenge the nations of the earth to watch it — a photograph of which we could proudly hang in every home in the land. It would be a true but thrilling picture. Let all contribute. Inscribed on tablets around its base we would also place on record the Christian churches who favor the liquor traffic. Oh, what a record! At its completion Satan himself would shudder. Congress would vote a grand appropriation, and the nation would respond and angels cry "Amen."

I tell you, my friends, that this liquor question is now really a great question of patriotism — a question how to save our country. I appeal to the men of all parties, to all patriots. Does it need that I should appeal to *Christian* men? We must not give up or lose this great battle. We must not let it be said that after only a hundred years of liberty we fell as Rome did, and lost our great birthright of Freedom in a mad revel of passion and appetite. Let no future Gibbon, in some distant land and under some other civilization, write the sad story of the downfall of the great Republic. Give us Prohibition. Strike down this great enemy, the liquor traffic, and our young and still mighty nation, shaking off this terrible load, will bound forward in a splendid and triumphant career of greatness and glory. — *W. A. Greenwood.*

125. THE ARSENAL AT SPRINGFIELD.*

This is the Arsenal. From floor to ceiling,
   Like a huge organ, rise the burnished arms;
But from their silent pipes no anthem pealing
   Startles the villages with strange alarms.

Ah! what a sound will rise, how wild and dreary,
   When the death-angel touches those swift keys!
What loud lament and dismal Miserere
   Will mingle with their awful symphonies!

I hear even now the infinite fierce chorus,
   The cries of agony, the endless groan,
Which, through the ages that have gone before us,
   In long reverberations reach our own.

On helm and harness rings the Saxon hammer,
   Through Cimbric forest roars the Norseman's song,
And loud, amid the universal clamor,
   O'er distant deserts sounds the Tartar gong.

I hear the Florentine, who from his palace
   Wheels out his battle-bell with dreadful din,
And Aztec priests upon their teocallis
   Beat the wild war-drums made of serpent's skin;

The tumult of each sacked and burning village;
   The shout that every prayer for mercy drowns;
The soldiers' revels in the midst of pillage;
   The wail of famine in beleaguered towns;

The bursting shell, the gateway wrenched asunder,
   The rattling musketry, the clashing blade;
And ever and anon, in tones of thunder,
   The diapason of the cannonade.

*By permission of Houghton, Mifflin & Co.

Is it, O man, with such discordant noises,
  With such accursed instruments as these,
Thou drownest Nature's sweet and kindly voices,
  And jarrest the celestial harmonies?

Were half the power, that fills the world with terror,
  Were half the wealth, bestowed on camps and courts,
Given to redeem the human mind from error,
  There were no need of arsenals or forts:

The warrior's name would be a name abhorred!
  And every nation, that should lift again
Its hand against a brother, on its forehead
  Would wear forevermore the curse of Cain!

Down the dark future, through long generations,
  The echoing sounds grow fainter and then cease;
And like a bell, with solemn, sweet vibrations
  I hear once more the voice of Christ say, "Peace!"

Peace! and no longer from its brazen portals
  The blast of War's great organ shakes the skies!
But beautiful as songs of the immortals,
  The holy melodies of love arise.

—H. W. Longfellow.

126. SHALL MOTHERS VOTE?

When at the fireside a question that has to do with the best interests of the home is discussed we say, "Mother, what is your opinion?" Mother speaks her opinion, and what has she done? She has voted. Her opinion thus expressed is an oral vote in the government of that home. An aggregation of homes constitute the general government, and all rightful governmental questions are home questions.

Now a day comes when the opinion of this home needs be aggregated with the opinion of a thousand other homes. Then mother writes yes or no on a slip of paper and drops it in the ballot-box. That constitutes the formula of a legal vote. Who assumes to say that mother shall not express her opinion? He who in childhood cried for mother, and would accept only her knowledge of his need. In the broader home of the world's activity does he need her opinion less? Blessed would be the nation if it were as safely counseled. *— Rollo K. Bryan.*

127. ON CERTAIN ADJECTIVES.

A "*generous*" liquor! Ah, if generous
Let it return, of what it steals from us,
At least one-tenth!—one soul for every ten
In mercy let it render back again;
One-tenth of all the homes, the land, the gold,
The peace, the joy, its close-mouthed coffers hold!
You sneer, you generous liquor. Well you know
All things to get and nothing to let go.
        "Generous," forsooth!

"A royal bumper!" "Royal?" Yes, a king
Whose reign means serfdom. There's no sacred thing
This "royal" liquor fails to override,
And whelm in fiendish lust and hateful pride.
His regnant scepter bends, and at the sign
Men yield themselves the crawling slaves of wine.
His throne is built of broken hearts, his crown
Gleams red with stars from heaven fallen down.
        "Royal," indeed!

"A sparkling goblet!" Yes, yes!—all ablaze
With horrid hell's most haggard, ghastly rays,
The light of happy eyes turned to despair,
The flash of hate, the eating flame of care,
The glitter of a madman's awful eyes,
The dying light that stabs one as it dies—
Hence does the "sparkling goblet" get the glow
And radiant glances that delight men so.
        "Sparkling," forsooth!

"Strong" drink, "strong" drink! Well may we call it strong
That drags so many myriad men headlong
Down wo's most awful path to dreadful death,
That shatters happy households at a breath,
And fastens with its hot and crooked hands
On temple roof and spire that loftiest stands,
While marts and studios and statesmen's halls
It levels to the slime wherein it crawls.
        "Strong" drink, indeed!

And "rare old spirits!" Ah, how many a prayer
Beseeches God that they become more rare!

Rare — till the widow's tears less common are ;
Rare — till dismantled homes are fewer far ;
Rare — till the children's sobs, the wives' despair,
The drunkard's dreadful anguish, grow more rare !
Brothers, to work ! to work with hand and will,
And make these "rare old spirits" rarer still !
  God for the right !
    — *Amos R. Wells, in "Golden Rule."*

128. MIDNIGHT SCENES OF A GREAT CITY.

Put on your wrap this dark night and come with me to some of the byways of the great city. But come not if you are timid and faint-hearted, for this is a time to be brave ; a time when you need courage.

The streets are dark, but blacker still the opium dens. Their darkness is penetrated by the dim light of a tallow candle, but there is a gloom brooding over them like a pestilence and surrounding them like an atmosphere — moral darkness that can never be dispelled only by the bright light of the rays of the Gospel.

In that City of Churches, of relief societies, of Christian Endeavor and moral enterprise, of well-conducted newspapers, religious editors and thousands of Christians, does it seem possible that the law has granted a right to open pitfalls into which feet, often shod only with the beauty of innocence, may fall? Snares alluring them to a ruin compared to which death would be an untold blessing !

If I could but unroof those houses at some midnight hour, and let the law-makers, from their pinnacle of self-righteousness, look upon the effects of their laws, they would call upon the rocks and the mountains to hide them. One day, when they have reached the border-line of time and pass into the great beyond, they will stand face to face with the result of their unrighteous legislation. Which of them, there, before the Judge of judges, will dare to ask, " Am I my brother's keeper?" Verily, each is his brother's keeper, and every wronged human being will then be avenged by the sentence of a just God.

  " Tho the mills of God grind slowly
   Yet they grind exceedingly small ;

>   Tho with patience he stands waiting
>   With exactness grinds he all."

Come with me into one of these dens!

A small room, destitute of comfort, without ventilation, furnished only with a rude bed — often boards across a sawhorse. What will you see, a number of Chinese only? Come nearer. There are women here, too. You are horrified to find they are white women. Come nearer still, and you will see traces of beauty. Yes, many of them have been beautiful girls. What can be more awful in any life than the star of hope sinking into the darkness of despair? This daughter of tenderest love had been taught at a mother's knee to lisp the prayer:

"Let who will be clever, but keep me pure, Oh, Lord!"

Yes, "Lord keep me pure and good," had been her girlhood prayer; but in an unfortunate moment she anchored her hopes to what so often fails a woman in this world, a man's changeful love. As a panacea for all heartaches she sought forgetfulness in the lulling, soothing effects of small doses of opium. Finding herself a victim to opium-eating, she thought it possible to give up the habit by taking an occasional smoke. Unknown to her friends, she resorted to the opium den with no other thought than to cure the habit of eating opium. But alas! the last form of taking the drug proved more irresistible than the first. It was impossible to longer conceal the habit from her family. The dull, heavy eye, the pallid complexion and sunken cheeks, the languor when the effects of the opium had passed off, all became matters of concern to her friends. On consulting a physician, the first question asked was:

"Do you ever eat opium?"

Confronted by this unexpected question, the girl was forced into a confession, and told she was a hopeless victim of the drug. The physician said to me:

"Her description of what she suffered, how she struggled, fought, and prayed to overcome the habit, were awful in the extreme." In vain did he try, by all devices known to medical skill, to cure her; to no purpose. When driven almost frantic by the pangs of the appetite, she would steal away for just another smoke, till even hearts of love turned from her, and she went to live with a Chinese; took up her abode among the filth, dirt, disorder, and fumes of an opium den, where she was so fully given up to debauchery that she was seldom found free from the intoxication.

Seven years finishes the story! Seven years! It is a short tale — pitiful and sinful — terrible in its losses ; unspeakable in its heartaches and disappointments!

One day some one came for me to go and see a dying girl. In company with a lady whose guest I was, we went into the Chinese quarters and reaching the abode of misery, entered. It was no time to pull aside our garments of purity lest this unknown woman should touch the hem. It was an awful hour! A sinful woman, *our sister*, stood where the cold waves of Jordan rolled at her feet. The mists and dews of eternity had already gathered about her brow and before long she must answer for a misspent life.

Photographed upon my memory, the scene must ever abide with me. In soiled garments, heavy with the odor of opium, on a miserable bed lay the dying woman. Her eyes were sunken and her body reduced to little more than a skeleton. She knew she was dying and had sent to her relatives, imploring their forgiveness, entreating them to come to her; but the hearts in that Christian home had no room for forgiveness. She had brought disgrace upon an old family name that for generations had stood unsullied. That the first stain came through a woman was too much for forgiveness! I doubt not had the boy been guilty of the same sin, at the first utterance of repentance he would have been received with open arms. But a woman — where in this cruel world is there forgiveness for her? Nowhere except where the sinful woman of old found it, at the feet of our Lord, who tried to teach the world a lesson when he turned to the *men* who accused her and said, "He that is without sin among you, let him first cast a stone." Then with that great spirit of love which every one of his followers should possess, he looked in pity upon her and bade her "go, and sin no more." This seems to be regarded, even by Christians, as a small thing for the Nazarine to have done ; but if the Son of God, in His matchless purity, whose life was spotless and free from sin, could look in compassion upon a penitent woman, why is it the world is so unforgiving?

I knew this woman's friends had refused to come to her. I knew she had nothing, simply nothing, to sustain her in this hour of death, an hour of such indescribable darkness.

If there is a sight in the world that will cause stout hearts to fail, it is to see a frail, wretched, miserable human wreck, trembling with fear and frantic with grief, afraid to die! Standing on the brink of Eternity about to launch out into the great unknown, with the Star of Hope, the last friend of man, forever set upon the horizon of life, with human strength gone, yet afraid to die!

Here was I with a fellow creature, a sister, who in her better days and perhaps even now, had like longings and yearnings with myself. Longings for a purer and better life; yearnings for home loves and the sight of dear ones; but forsaken by all save the Chinese with whom she had lived, she was left to "climb the midnight hill alone."

She passed

"Out of life's history
Into death's mystery."

This book of a young life, with many unwritten chapters, was closed and sealed with the stamp of death. The written chapters of that life, penned in sorrow and shame, and signed in human blood, should be read by all who helped to make it possible for such a fate to overtake even the weakest of our race. —*Jessie A. Ackerman.*

129. ONE BEAUTY OF CIVILIZATION.*

With all the means and appliances that progress has brought to aid the spread of the Gospel, it has surely raised up immense obstacles to that Gospel. Civilization has been so largely inspired and directed by physical needs and appetites that the physical man has waxed fat at the expense of the spiritual.

But civilization has done worse than this. In ministering to bodily appetites, it has debauched nature, creating unnatural cravings, adding, as it were, fuel to the flames; so that society to-day is menaced by an evil that has had no equal since the hordes of savage Huns swept down to the destruction of Roman civilization — an evil not external, but which feeds and grows upon the vital forces of society itself. If any other power under heaven wrought such havoc and ruin among us as is daily and hourly wrought by all the varied forms of intemperance — if any other power, I say, killed so many men

*From a sermon at Deems Memorial Chapel, Prohibition Park.

by such awful forms of death, wrecked so many homes, ruined so many lives, scattered so much disease. created so much poverty and squalor, made so many criminals. committed so many murderous crimes, destroyed such fabulous sums of national wealth ; that power would be hanged high as Haman if it took the national government to do it. If it were any other power, cities would call out their reserves, the States would call out the militia, the President would call out the national guard, and the people would rise as one man, and throttle the fiend, if it cost the last drop of blood to do it. But what do we see? The nation, the states, the cities, the villages, for the most part sitting complacently by, watching the bloody orgies of this Polyphemus of Intemperance without lifting a finger against him! We call ourselves a Christian people, and we stand this thing! We talk of the unspeakable Turk because once in a decade or so he feels plethoric, opens the national veins, and sheds a few thousand of Christian lives. It makes a difference where the killing is done, and who does it. If it is across the sea and by heathen Kurds, we rage; and the myriad tongues of the press cry out, "Why does not somebody stop it? England is a craven coward! Russia is brutish! Germany has no conscience! What is the world coming to, when such things can be, under the very eyes of Europe!" But as the horrible tale of death and ruin wrought by intemperance is served to us every morning with our cakes and coffee, we pass over the sickening story, growling against the public press that has become the news agency for crime and lust and blood. And we walk calmly along the streets by the very dens whence this stream of death is flowing, without a qualm, without a word, without a sign. This is one of the beauties of nineteenth century Christian civilization. — *Rev. Chas. R. Kingsley.*

130. A REMEDY WITHIN REACH.

Yes, the church *has* failed us. Thousands within its ranks are with us ; from pulpit and pew they have stretched forth to us the helping hand, have given us the kindly sympathetic word ; yet the fact remains, that the overwhelming majorities — the great masses of the church — men and women — are unmoved by, and indifferent to the great reforms *we* plead. To them the great temperance reform has as little personal interest as the double lines of canals on the planet of Mars ; and intelligent men and women often know as much of one as of the other.

If the great masses of the church knew of, and cared for the degradation and destruction — the misery and misrule — the wreck and wretchedness caused by the liquor traffic — if they knew, and *if they cared,* how long would that "sum of all villainies" be throned in power by votes of bishop, preacher, deacon, and Sunday-school superintendent — equally with the votes of brewer, distiller, and saloon-keeper? Not long, not long! So, too, woman reaching out for her just inheritance, withheld in the clear light of a knowledge that long ago scattered the darkness of barbarism — that long ago untwisted the stubborn perversions of Scripture always used against woman — that long ago tore into veriest shreds the unfair, illogical "Traditions of men, taught for the commandments of God," would every pulpit thunder forth its demands that simple, equal justice be done to her as to her brothers — how long would she be taxed without representation? How long be amenable to laws, unto which she had given no consent? How long bear the burdens and responsibilities of a partnership that yields returns to others, but none to her? How long face anguish and risk death at the will of another to give life to the child in whom she must hold but a secondary claim — the hope cherished beneath her heart, that through the conditions of society in which she has had no voice — may become the torture of that heart. Tendencies transmitted — temptations legalized by the fatherhood that deliberately dooms its own offspring to destruction.

Well does the liquor traffic understand the hostility of every true mother heart to the wily foe that would destroy her boy.

How natural than the utterance sent forth from the Brewers' Congress, "We are always and everywhere opposed to woman's political enfranchisement."

The old political parties know full well that they must not offend that arrogant oligarchy if they would ride into power with triumphant majorities; hence the silence of fair minded, intelligent politicians on this vital theme. But who will rise to explain to us the silence of the church on this question? Joseph Cook says, "As lightning to the oak, is woman's ballot to the rum traffic." The rum traffic is the deadly foe to morality and religion. The ballot in woman's hand would rend this traffic asunder as lightning rends the oak. Yet the masses of divines, officials, and members by inertia and opposition render this means to the end for which they pray, as yet impossible.

Here again has the church failed us; and failed the cause we love — and our sorrow and soreness of heart are commensurate with the tender memories of

> " Her sweet communion, solemn vows,
> Her hymns of love and praise."

But, dear comrades, there is one who has never failed! In the midst of smarting wounds received in the house of friends, how radiant and resplendent shines that character, tender, true, and just — ever woman's friend — the adorable — the beloved Christ — Son of Mary, and Son of God!

With this Tower of Strength into which we may flee; with this Shadow of a Great Rock in a weary land; with this "Present Help" in every hour of need; with this "Elder Brother" and Captain of our Salvation leading the way, why should we fear or falter — why cry or complain?

Shall we not rather take up Paul's ecstatic pæan "We are more than conquerors through Him that loved us. Neither death, nor life, nor angels, nor principalities, nor powers, nor things past, nor things to come, nor height, nor depth, nor any other creature shall be able to separate us from the love of God, which is in Christ Jesus our Lord."

— *Clara C. Hoffman.*

---

131. PEACE HYMN OF THE REPUBLIC.

There's a voice across the nation like a mighty ocean-hail,
Borne up from out the southward, as the seas before the gale;
Its breath is in the streaming flag and in the flying sail —
    As we go sailing on.

'Tis a voice that we remember — ere its summons soothed as now —
When it rang in battle-challenge, and we answered vow with vow;
With roar of gun, and hiss of sword, and crash of prow and prow —
    As we went sailing on.

Our hope sank, even as we saw the sun sink faint and far;

The Ship of State went groping through the blinding smoke
   of war ;
Through blackest midnight lurching, all uncheered of moon
   or star,
      Yet sailing, sailing on.
As One who spake the dead awake, with life-blood leaning
   warm,
Who walked the troubled waters, all unscathed, in mortal
   form,
We felt our Pilot's presence, with His hand upon the storm —
      As we went sailing on.

O voice of passion, lulled to peace, this dawning of to-day ;
O voices twain, now blent as one, ye sing all fears away,
Since foe and foe are friends, and lo ! the Lord, as glad as
   they —
      He sends us sailing on.
                        — *James Whitcomb Riley.*

132. AN APPEAL FOR THE HOME.

To-day the liquor traffic is destroying the home.

It is impossible to estimate the waste, the ruin, the utter desolation in the home and the nation by the liquor license system. The whole traffic is evil, evil only, and that continually.

Not only are many homes darkened by this wasting curse, but *every* home is imperiled. Lace curtains and satin tapestries can not keep out the demon of rum any more than can the cambric shades of the cottage. He drags his serpent length across velvet carpets, as well as over the bare earth of the hovel. He steals up the marble staircase and along gilded halls, as well as down dark passageways to underground dens of squalor and wretchedness.

Tamerlane, the Conqueror, asked for one hundred and sixty thousand skulls with which to build his monument. He got them and built a pyramid.

Suppose we gather the skulls of all the victims of rum ; it would build a pyramid so vast that Tamerlane's would be as a mole hill beside it, and its apex would pierce the clouds.

Oh the victims of rum ! They are found in our homes. In *our* homes did I say ? In the homes of the whole world. The mother-heart of the world cries out in anguish. Where is there help? Where is the strong arm that will crush this foe? Where is the power that will reinstate manhood, protect the weak, comfort the sorrowing, give back to the bereaved their hope in God and humanity?

It must come from the consecrated will of the people themselves. "God moves in a mysterious way his wonders to perform." And in the heart of the homes themselves there must be aroused a deeper, more enlightened spirit, a higher, purer morality, a more definite appreciation of man's relation to his brother man and his accountability to God.— *Mrs. Jessie Brown-Hilton, N. W. C. T. U. Secretary of Mothers' Meetings.*

133. THE WEAKNESS OF LOCAL OPTION.

Local option is a weak substitute for prohibition and is thoroughly unsatisfactory in practise. The enforcement of its provisions is nearly always left in the hands of officers who are either opposed to the law or indifferent to it. The consequence is that the land becomes infested with unlawful liquor dealers and no effort is made to drive them from their hidings. Agents are allowed to enter a town and openly sell their illicit wares while the Mayor and his brother officials look on quietly and smile approval without making the slightest effort to stop the influx. Young men hold high drinking carnivals, assaults are made and rioting indulged in, but an arrest is seldom made. All the while, the enemies of prohibition triumph and grow more defiant in their violations and insolence. All the while, so-called good men sit around inertly and discuss the deplorable condition of affairs, comfortably smoking their pipes or cigars or chewing their quids of tobacco, and lament the fact that Prohibition is a failure and weakly admit that the saloon might as well be running in full blast; not once thinking it necessary to raise their voices in denunciation or lift their hands to crush out the unholy thing. If I were a man I would be ashamed to occupy such a position ! If the men of this country are unable to protect our homes by the enforcement of law, in the name of justice, give the women the ballot and let them have a chance at it !

How sadly do the times need men ! not cigarette-poisoned, whisky-inflamed, morally-debauched specimens of the masculine gender made after the fashion of a man — but, men ! pure in mind, upright in heart, blameless in life! Men honest enough to live for truth; courageous enough to suffer for principle; unselfish enough to sink personal interest in the welfare of the community. Men who honor true citizenship! Men who are loyal to the church of Christ! Men who are willing to stand by word and deed, for righteous legislation, the purification of politics and the abolition of the liquor traffic!

— *Belle Kearney.*

134. GROUND OUT BY A CRANK.

I'd rather be dumb,
And always mum,
Than pray like some,
"Thy Kingdom come,"
Then vote for rum.

I'd rather be blind
And often maligned
And speak my mind
Than be behind
An age of this kind.

I'd rather be frank
And called a "crank,"
Not known at the bank,
Than stand on a plank
Both rotten and rank.

The cranks of to-day
Have come to stay;
To vote and pray
In the selfsame way
Till they turn the day.

The crank is bold
Like Daniel of old
When put in to hold
The lions, we're told,
Were badly sold.

No wonder, I own,
He was left alone,
Composed, as is known,
Like cranks, full-grown,
Of grit and backbone. — *C. M.*

135. THAT'S THE QUESTION.

In a lone house — a small house furnished bare — there sat a thin, pallid woman dressed in meager garments, through which the cold wind blew in fitful gusts. Around her were huddled three thin, pale, half-starved children. There was no food in the pantry, no fuel in the stove. Why was this the case? Ah! that's the question.

In a low grog shop in the neighboring hamlet, surrounded by a crowd of drunken men, there sat a being that had been a man. He was besotted with rum. His bloated face was buried in his red hands. He was asleep. He was a drunkard. Why was he a drunkard? Ah! that's the question.

"Mother, why doesn't father come home?" asked one of the three pale children of the pallid woman in the lonely house. Ah! that's the question.

"I will start out for him and bring him home, mother," exclaimed the child.

"Brave boy!" replied the parent, between her sobs. And so in the cold dark night the fearless child went out. But why was this midnight and perilous journey necessary? Ah! that's the question.

A tap at the door of the grog shop. A deep mutter among the men whose unlawful amusement it had interrupted. The door opened and the child walked in. "Father," he cried, as he leaned over the sleeping wretch, "will you come with me?" Ah! that's the question.

Father and child — drunken beast and pure, young innocence — hand in hand, pursued their lonely way over the dark and rocky road that led to the deserted home. By the side of the path was a steep precipice. Here the twain paused. The man sat down to think. What thoughts, think you, were passing through his rum-crazed brain? Ah! that's the question.

They were awful thoughts — thoughts of murder. He had been torn away from his haunts by the firm hand of his little child. His wife had set a spy on his track. The result should be wiped out. But how? Ah! that's the question.

Five minutes of silent but awful meditation suffice. Starting to his feet the enraged man grasped his little son by the waist and held him at arm's length over the steep precipice.

"Father," murmured the child, plaintively, "shall I ever see mother again?" Ah! that's the question.

"I don't see why little Johnny doesn't come home," exclaimed the pallid woman in the lonely house, as the first streaks of dawn lit up the empty pantry shelves. "Can any harm have befallen him?"

Dawn saw a pale man, trembling at every joint, gazing with bloodshot eyes over a deep precipice at a little heap of clothes lying on the cruel rocks below. The drunkard's brain reeled with horror. Had he murdered his child? Ah! that's the question.

In a solitary cell in the insane asylum there sits a pale, thin man, with long white hair and vacant eyes. All day long he moans aloud: "Why did I do it? Oh, why did I do it!" Oh! my friend, that's the question.

In the Judgment Day, murderers, saloon-keepers, law-makers, politicians and voters, distillers and doctors of divinity, rumsellers and religious citizens, sharers in the profits of legalized massacre, will stand before a just God. "What hast thou done? The voice of thy brother's blood crieth unto me from the ground. Where is thy brother?" Oh! *that's the question.*
— *The Constitution.*

136. WANTED — TRUE MEN.

To-day the pressing need of our country is *true men*. Great questions are before us for settlement. Stupendous problems are to be solved. Mighty issues present themselves for the profound thought and earnest consideration of statesmen.

Evils which threaten the existence of our free institutions are abroad in the land. Gigantic wrongs are holding triumphant sway and they must be righted and overthrown or this Republic, which is ours at so great a cost of blood and treasure, will go down amid greater ruins than followed the fall of Rome. O! for men who can get hold of this generation! When Greece was invaded by the armed million of Xerxes, to meet the awful emergency men of deathless bravery and patriotism sprang from mountain and valley to resist the foe.

When despotism sought to crush out English liberty Cromwell and his Ironsides with prayer and song valiantly took the field and overwhelmingly defeated the forces of tyranny.

When the homes and firesides of Scotland needed a courageous defense, Robert Bruce and his clans from Highland and Lowland gathered in battle array and beat back the enemies of their freedom.

In the days of the American Revolution when the fleets of England darkened our waters and the British armies landed upon our shores to strike down the spirit of independence, from every field and workshop, from city and country, from the hills of New England and the plains of Georgia, freemen buckled on their armor and drew their swords in the cause of human rights and won a victory that has blessed the race and placed our nation in the forefront of the world's progress and civilization.

To-day from the sun-bathed heights of duty and righteousness and truth, God is calling upon the American people, whom He has so greatly favored and blessed, to put down the infamous iniquity which is yearly, daily, hourly, blighting and cursing our fair land, filling jails and prisons and poorhouses, "cutting off the children from without and the young men from the street"; scattering wreck and ruin everywhere, and plunging lost souls, by the thousands, into eternal despair. O, that our countrymen would hear, and obey that voice! May our eyes soon behold the gathered millions of American voters in their sovereign power at the polls casting their ballots for home and God and against the most colossal evil of the 19th century.

We need men who have a true sense of life's sacredness and meaning and a proper appreciation of its golden opportunity.

We need men of intense patriotism — men who will stand for the best interests of their native land at whatever sacrifice.

We need men of unyielding moral courage — men, who knowing the right, will lose their lives, if necessary, to do the right. May God give us such men in this time of our country's great need. — *The Quest.*

---

137. THE MORAL WARFARE.*

When Freedom, on her natal day,
Within her war-rocked cradle lay,
An iron race around her stood,
Baptized her infant brow in blood;

---

* By permission of Houghton, Mifflin & Co.

And, through the storm which round her swept,
Their constant ward and watching kept.

Then, where our quiet herds repose,
The roar of baleful battle rose,
And brethren of a common tongue
To mortal strife as tigers sprung,
And every gift on Freedom's shrine
Was man for beast, and blood for wine !

Our fathers to their graves have gone ;
Their strife is past — their triumph won ;
But sterner trials wait the race
Which rises in their honored place —
A moral warfare with the crime
And folly of an evil time.

So let it be. In God's own might
We gird us for the coming fight,
And, strong in Him whose cause is ours
In conflict with unholy powers,
We grasp the weapons He has given —
The Light, and Truth, and Love of Heaven.
— *J. G. Whittier.*

138. RUN UP THE FLAG — NAIL IT TO THE STAFF !

The flag is the emblem of a nation's glory and a nation's power. There is a spirit of inspiration in its very folds, to the citizen and the subject, whose regal palace or humble hovel is protected by its stars and eagle, or its cross and lion. Are not the stars and stripes to us Americans "a thing of beauty and a joy forever?"

Our fathers loved the brilliant folds, but do not we love them even more since they came back through the dense death smoke — rent and torn, to be sure, and leaving many a brave standard bearer behind on the field dead — but victory-crowned and showing to our gladdened eyes not one star plucked from its glorious constellation? Oh, yes, that grand old flag is a magnetic battery sending thrilling power and enthusiasm through and through every hand that touches the pole of its standard.

The late war has filled the world with the romantic stories — stories whose truth is stranger than fiction — of valiant deeds done under the inspiration of our nation's flag and for its protection. What's a nation without a flag? What's an army without a banner? In the holy wars of the Jews the peculiar people of God carried their ensign, and every tribe knew and followed its own banner. And we must have a flag, an ensign, for the tribes of that "peculiar people" that the Lord God has raised up among us, the imperial army of Prohibition Crusaders. There is already a mighty host, mighty in numbers, but mightier by far in the strength of their invincible cause, the cause of God, and outraged humanity. And this army is reinforced with the millions of prayers and pleadings, the sighs and moans, the craving hunger and burning thirst of millions of unwilling victims of the dread power of that curse and tyrant of civilized lands — *the traffic in bottled poisons with the State seal on every cork!*

This huge national army of rum is more than "a thousand thousand, and three hundred chariots of iron." But the Lord God raised up a standard against them, and they that are with us are more than they that are with them. This imperial Prohibition army must rally under a common standard, with one motto and one heart. It must not fight in independent divisions without unity of purpose, but in whatever part of the field a corps or a brigade may be engaged its blows must fall upon the foe at that point, where it can push through the enemy's thinned ranks, to the Capitol of the Rebellion — the legalized saloon.

So, then, we must have a flag, and run it up, and nail it to the staff. Let that flag be *a field of pure white*, emblematic of the stainless sincerity of our soldiers' *total abstinence;* let its border be of *blue*, betokening the imperial power of the omnipotent God, which surrounds our cause, and hedges us in from danger on every side; and let its folds be covered with *golden stars*, the bright and precious *promises* of God's Holy Book; words that have cheered discouraged souls, and won victories for the weak and the timid in many an unequal strife. And let there be a motto written on that ensign, not in a dead language, but in plain mother tongue, so every child can read and know its full sense and meaning, and let it be:

PERPETUAL PROHIBITION:
"IN GOD WE TRUST."

By this we shall conquer; with this we shall gather to the support of our cause every *true* man and woman, every uncompromising friend of temperance and humanity. By this we shall be able to "discern between the wicked and the righteous, between him that serveth God and him that serveth him not." Then run up the flag — nail it to the staff! No compromise, no surrender. This army leaves not the field until the last redoubt of the enemy is carried.

— *Rev. Dr. Wm. H. Boole.*

139. FOUR MILLION "CHRISTIAN" MURDERERS.

Times change, and we change with them. The pagans of old Rome used to pit man against man in the gladiatorial arena and bid them fight each other to the death, that the popular love for exciting sport might be gratified. For fifteen centuries Christians have been boasting that that sort of brutality was stopped by Christianity. It is about time that these boastings were laid on the table indefinitely.

In the days of Luther a great revolt was instituted against the sale of indulgences as carried on by Tetzel. For four centuries Protestants have been censuring the Roman Catholic Church for having sold indulgences to sin, for a price, and the Catholics have been protesting against the charge as false and unjust. It is about time that the dispute be laid on the table indefinitely.

There never was, in the brutal gladiatorial combats of Rome, anything to compare, in atrocity and cruelty, with the black record that lies to-day upon our four million "Christian" voters of America; and the most sweeping charges brought against Tetzel and his times pale into insignificance beside the dark shame in which Catholics and Protestants are alike participating to-day. Where is the sense in Christians boasting about the cessation of the gladiatorial combats when in their place we have 200,000 men commissioned to employ all the arts that money can command in pauperizing, crazing, and poisoning their fellow men? Where is the sense in Protestants and Catholics disputing over the responsibility for a few indulgences six centuries ago when year after year they are jointly issuing for much smaller sums indulgences infinitely more villainous?

When the gladiators fought, each man had something like an equal chance; to-day art is pitted against ignorance. Then it was a sword against sword, trained skill against trained skill; now it is slow poison against unsuspecting and uninformed victims. Then it was a duel; now it is assassination.

Then the public gazed upon slaves and barbarians fighting each other; to-day men are commissioned by Christian voters to weave nets about their own sons and daughters and drag them down to a living death. Then the responsibility rested upon an autocratic ruler and the pagan public merely cheered the contest; to-day the people are the rulers and four million church members are responsible for the infamy. Then the sport was continued to gratify the love for an exhibition of personal skill and courage; to-day our modern crime is perpetuated because 4,000,000 church members want a certain set of wily and scheming politicians to win. Then, at the most, a few hundreds perished in a year; now thousands perish every month. Then it was pagan darkness; now it is Christian enlightenment. Then the fatherhood of God and the brotherhood of man had not dawned upon the world; now the phrase is in nearly everybody's mouth.

Four million "Christian" murderers! Is the phrase the result of a heated imagination? Who then is responsible for these thousands that stagger into drunkards' graves each month? Are they responsible for their own deaths? In a measure, yes; but how many thousands of them went along the road to ruin utterly ignorant of the physiological effects of liquor, believing to the last that beer is nourishing and whisky is stimulating, and never knowing their danger until their system was diseased and minds enslaved past all hope? Who is responsible — the men who enticed them to drink and sold them the poison? In a measure, yes; but how many of these have never had reason to question the propriety of the business, that is legalized and protected by the great mass of respectable citizens? Who is responsible — those who issued the licenses? In a measure, yes; but these men were carrying out the functions for which they had been elected to office and for which they received their salaries. Who is responsible — the legislators? In a measure, yes; but the legislator, in a representative form of government, is but an agent, a representer, of others whose purposes he is carrying out. Who is responsible — those who constitute the government, in whom reside all the authority and power, the voters of America, by whom are empowered all who make or administer laws? Yes; above all others are these responsible for these thousands of murders, and among all men the voter has the least pretext of excuse for his guilt.

The drunkard has in most cases, at least among the lower classes, the excuse of ignorance; the saloon-keeper wants to support his family, and this is a lawful method of doing it; the administrator of law and the legislator can claim to be but agents acting under instructions; thousands and perhaps millions of voters can for their share of the guilt plead an excusable ignorance; but for these four million church members, or at least the overwhelming majority of them, what excuse is there? Can they plead ignorance? If so, ignorance of what? Ignorance that the saloon is sending men and women to death and disgrace? Ignorance that the saloons are licensed by law? Ignorance that those who make the laws are elected by the people? There was some show of excuse for the voter when the curse of slavery overshadowed the land, for the power of the voters, under the Constitution, was in dispute; but to-day there are four million church members in this land who are directly responsible for these murders of men, women, and children, and not a shadow of excuse is there for their unutterable crime. It is the greatest outrage upon humanity that has ever been recorded in history, and an infinitely blacker crime than African slavery ever was. — *E. J. Wheeler.*

140. THE BIG FOUR AND THE LITTLE MAN.

There was a man — a mighty man —
  Who wrote a mighty grammar,
To be beat into children's heads,
  And knocked in with a hammer.
And if you wish for grammar-lore
  His book's the place to seek it,
It tells us how to speak our tongue
  The way we ought to speak it,
A learned book filled up with rules,
  With rules of all conceptions,
Ten thousand rules from all the schools,
  Ten million more exceptions.

There was a man — a mighty man —
  Who had a mighty "projick"
To write a great Compendium
  Of Universal Logic.
He told us how to range our facts
  In proper collocation,

To analyze and synthesize
   And keep from obfuscation.
By his advice the target truth
   By hot shot could be shot full —
He told us how to think our thoughts
   And make our thinking thoughtful.

There was a man — a mighty man —
   A mighty rhetorician —
Who made a rhetoric that ran
   Into the twelfth edition;
He taught us not to write like clowns,
   Or any coarse clodhopper,
But how to write with elegance
   Preeminently proper.
He told us how to write our thoughts
   In true concatenation,
And fix and rig 'em up in style
   By rule and regulation.

There was a man — a mighty man —
   Who made a contribution
To wisdom's great totality —
   A work on elocution.
He told us how to throw our arms
   To make our words emphatic,
And told us how to twist our mouths
   To make our speech dramatic;
He told us how to coo like doves
   Or roar like any bison;
And told us how to throw our voice
   All over the horizon.

There was a man — a little man —
   A very little fellow,
Who used to stand upon the stand,
   Just stand right up and bellow.
He mauled and murdered rhetoric,
   Threw logic in confusion,
And broke all the commandments of
   The Book of Elocution.
He filled the palpitating air
   With universal clamor,

With cracked debris of rhetoric
    And ragged shreds of grammar.

One day the great grammarian
    And the great rhetorician
And the great elocution man,
    Likewise the great logician,
Went down to hear this little man,
    This very little fellow,
To see him mount upon the stand
    And then to hear him bellow.
Loud sneered the great grammarian,
    Pooh-poohed the rhetorician,
The elocution man was shocked
    And shocked the great logician.

But while they sneered, these learned men,
    The ignorant congregation
Showed its tumultuous delight
    In thunderous acclamation.
For, oh! this man — this little man —
    This Prohibition fellow,
Just played upon men's heart-strings as
    Upon a violoncello.
For tho he was a little man,
    He had a mighty message
Which found its way to people's hearts,
    Nor stopped to pay expressage.

The people cried and clapped and wept,
    And soon the rhetorician,
Grammarian, elocution man,
    Likewise the great logician,
Were laughing just like common men,
    Or crying just like the women,
While through his sea of eloquence
    The little man was swimmin'.
And loud haw-hawed and loud boohooed
    These deep and learned fellows —
His hands were on their heart-strings and
    He played his violoncellos!

Now grammar's good and logic's good
    And rhetoric's good and proper,

And elocution's excellent
   To train the coarse clodhopper;
But this my little fable shows,
   My little fable teaches,
The man inspired with zeal for truth
   All formulas o'erreaches.
He breaks the rules of scribes and schools
   As fast as they can make 'em,
And grammar men and logic men
   All go to hear him break 'em.
—*Adapted from Sam Walter Foss, in "Golden Rule."*

141. A SHORT STORY.*

The Newman M. E. Church is the largest in the city of Bloomsbarre, having over 800 members.

The official Board is in session.

A very animated discussion is going on over the withdrawal of twenty-seven of the members of the church.

Dr. Williamson, the eloquent pastor, is speaking:

"I admit that in point of numbers, twenty-seven out of over eight hundred would make but very little difference, but see who the twenty-seven are— the very ones who carry on our prayer-meetings and attend to the spiritual affairs of the church. It is true that they are not the wealthy part of our church, but a church can not be run with money alone."

"Brother Williamson," spoke up the Hon. Chas. Smith, a member of the Legislature, "I say let them go; we will get along much better without them. They have grown crazy over the Prohibition party, and right here in our prayer-meeting some of them have grown so bold as to declare that any man who did not vote their ticket was supporting the liquor traffic. Now, I claim to be as good a Prohibitionist as any man in the Prohibition party, and indeed, a better Prohibitionist, for the reason that I had the honor of voting for the enactment of our present license law, which has done more for temperance than the Prohibition party will ever accomplish."

Then Judge Grant, one of the county Judges, spoke up:

"Gentlemen, this recent discussion about the church being the bulwark of the liquor traffic is nothing short of blasphemy in calling the faithful followers of the Lord Jesus Christ, the

---

* Copyrighted by the author.

upholders of the rum traffic, the greatest curse the world has ever seen. I agree with Brother Smith, let those Prohibition cranks go, and our church will then go on in peace." (Applause from the other members of the Board.)

"Of course," said Dr. Williamson, "we will have to give them their letters, for we can find no fault with their Christian character. But we have none to take their places in the public prayer service. This is one of the evils of bringing politics into religion; they won't mix. The Grand Old Republican party is a good enough temperance party for me, and while it is not up to the standard on the temperance question that I would like to see it, yet I am not going to throw away my vote on a party that hasn't a ghost of a chance of electing its candidates."

(Applause.)

"I don't understand what these fanatical Prohibitionists want," said the Hon. Mr. Smith. "Our church, as a church, has declared that the 'liquor traffic can not be legalized without sin,' and nothing stronger than that could be uttered. The man who sells liquor for a living is worse than a ——"

Just then there was a sharp knock on the door.

"Come in," responded the double-bass voice of Dr. Williamson.

The door opened and the portly form of the saloon-keeper across the street appeared in the doorway. He was the first to break the oppressive silence:

"Gentlemen, knowing this to be your regular meeting night, I decided to come over and inform you that I and my family have made up our minds to join your church and help along the good work you are doing."

This speech was greeted with dumb astonishment by the members of the Board. Dr. Williamson was the first to speak:

"Have you given up the saloon business?"

"No, sir," replied the saloon-keeper.

"Are you going to?"

"No, sir; I am conducting a respectable place and see no reason why I should."

"W-e-ll," slowly replied the Doctor, "our church rules prohibit us from taking in dealers in liquors, and for that reason we must refuse you."

"Oh," said the saloon-keeper, a flush of anger coming into his already florid face, "I was not aware of that. On what ground does your church refuse to admit saloon-keepers?"

"On the ground that they are engaged in a business that sends souls to hell," replied Dr. Williamson. "The Bible says that no drunkard shall inherit the kingdom of God and therefore no drunkard-maker can. More than that, our Board of Bishops has declared that the liquor traffic can not be legalized without sin."

The saloon-keeper was thoroughly aroused by this time, and in a suppressed, angry tone, he asked:

"Do you know that a great many of your members are regular customers of mine?"

"I have heard that some were," said Dr. Williamson.

"Do you know that two of this official Board, now in this room, are among my regular customers?"

No reply, but two very red faces showed who had been hit.

"Do you know that I got my license from Judge Grant, who sits right here, for which I paid the regular license fee?"

"Hold on," said Judge Grant, "you are going too fast, my friend; I do not make the laws, and I am compelled by the license law to grant licenses; therefore I am not responsible."

"Well, the law was enacted by Mr. Smith there, and other Republicans."

"You can't place the responsibility on me," said Mr. Smith. "I carried out the wishes of those who elected me. Had I been elected on a Prohibition platform I would have voted for a prohibitory law. My party stands for license and I voted for the law."

"I understand that fully," said the saloon-keeper, "but I voted for you; so did Judge Grant; so did Dr. Williamson; the rest of this Board and the great majority of the voters in your church. I took it for granted that all who voted for you believed in license. Now, I am politely told that I can not join this heaven-bound band and that I shall go to hell. Dr. Williamson here voted for you, Smith, to pass a license law which *compels* Judge Grant to give *me* a license — *to go to hell!* I am the *fourth* party to the agreement and without the consent of you three I *could not* engage in the whisky business. You three are bound for heaven, where you will wear crowns and play on golden harps, while I am to suffer the torments of the damned! Gentlemen, if your Bible is true, and I go to hell for selling whisky, *you will go with me to hell for voting to give me the legal right of doing so.* Goodnight."

With that he vanished, closing the door behind him with a vigorous slam.

The members of the official Board looked steadfastly on the floor, each one seemingly afraid of breaking the silence. They were Christian men; believed they were doing their Christian duty. But the saloon-keeper, in his fierce arraignment of those present, had placed a tremendous responsibility on their shoulders. Each one was doing some pretty serious thinking when Dr. Williamson ended the silence by saying slowly :

"Brethren, that saloon-keeper told us some terrible truths. Brethren, our hands are not clean nor our skirts unspotted. Let us go home and pray for light." — *Tallie Morgan.*

142. JUST THE SAME.

Yes, you hate to be bought and you hate to be sold,
And you hate to be forced to pay Shylock in gold,
You hate the hard times, but you're bound to die game,
You hate 'em — but you vote for 'em just the same!

You hate politicians that swagger and rant,
You hate a good deal of the old party cant,
And you hate a large share of the ticket you name —
You hate it, but vote for it just the same!

You hate to be cramped in a financial way,
And you hate giant fraud going on day by day,
You curse in your soul the corruption you blame —
You curse it — and you vote for it just the same !

You long for good laws and prosperous times,
And you want to see boodlers sent up for their crimes,
You want more reforms than we've space here to name,
But — you never vote for them just the same!

You hope for a change, and you pray for relief,
And you swear you'll bring partisan schemers to grief,
Then you march to the polls to put blockheads to shame
But — vote the old ticket again just the same.

—*The Every-Day Church.*

143. A WOMAN'S ANSWER.

Do you know you have asked for the costliest thing
   Ever made by the hand above —
A woman's heart and a woman's life
   And a woman's wonderful love?

Do you know you have asked for this priceless thing
   As a child might ask for a toy,
Demanding what others have died to win,
   With the reckless dash of a boy?

You have written my lesson of duty out,
   Man-like you have questioned me;
Now stand at the bar of my woman's soul
   Until I shall question thee.

You require your mutton shall always be hot,
   Your socks and your shirts shall be whole;
I require your heart to be true as God's stars,
   And as pure as heaven your soul.

You require a cook for your mutton and beef;
   I require a far better thing:
A seamstress you're wanting for stockings and shirts;
   I look for a man and a king.

A king for a beautiful realm called home,
   And a man that the maker, God,
Shall look upon as He did the first,
   And say, " It is very good."

I am fair and young, but the rose will fade
   From my soft, young cheek one day,
Will you love me then 'mid the falling leaves,
   As you did 'mid the bloom of May?

Is your heart an ocean so strong and deep
   I may launch my all on its tide?
A loving woman finds Heaven or hell
   On the day she is made a bride.

I require all things that are grand and true,
   All things that a man should be;
If you give all this, I would stake my life
   To be all you demand of me.

If you can not do this — a laundress and cook
  You can hire, with little to pay,
But a woman's heart and a woman's life
  Are not to be won that way.
                    — *Mary T. Lathrap.*

144. DECORATION DAY — 1882.

Brightly bloom the fairy flowers
  At the call of lovely May —
Can we better use their beauty
  Than for Decoration Day?
Twining them with memories tearful
  For the brave we ne'er shall view,
Strew them with a hand impartial
  Over graves of "Gray and Blue."

Not a day of glad rejoicing,
  Not a day for jubilee,
But to call back saddest memory
  Of a dear-bought victory,
'Tis a day to warn our children
  Of the wrong and blinded pride
Which brought on those bloody battles,
  Where our brave young soldiers died,
Tell them of that dreadful war-time —
  Tell them *why* the soldiers died!

Tracing back this saddest story
  Of our Nation's rugged life —
Past the victory, past the glory —
  Past the fratricidal strife —
History evermore shall linger
  Picturing Slavery's dark stains,
When a people God created
  Languished, manacled in chains!

Dreadful came the retribution
  Over all our country wide,
Slavery fell in bloody carnage —
  And 'twas thus the soldiers died!
Freedom came with death and weeping,
  And the thousand nameless graves
Hide our long-remembered brothers.

Where no rose or willow waves,
Thousands lie 'neath wild-wood blossom,
　Wet by tears of Heaven's sweet rain,
Some we strew with rosy garlands,
　But for others seek in vain!

Forward looking toward the future
　Down the vista grand, of years,
Still in power and greatness growing,
　Shall our country dry her tears,
Other conquests are before us,
　Other tyranny to match —
Other long and weary marches,
　Forts to hold, and beacons watch,
We have fields for moral warfare
　Calling forth the brave and bold,
Can we sleep while giant errors
　Half our liberties withhold?
Ignorance sways among the millions;
　Ruins intrenched, our homes around!
And opinions false and cruel,
　Chain so many to the ground!

Ye who bear the name of Christian,
　Ye whose lips His name invoke,
Be not lulled by martial music,
　Look behind ambition's cloak;
Gospels teach, and truth is dawning —
　Peace some day shall surely reign,
When shall grim war's awful visage
　Cease to gloat o'er thousands slain?

Haste the day when ceases carnage,
　When our flag's red stripes shall fade,
Swords for plowshares, tears for gladness,
　Man, one brotherhood be made!
Haste the day which Seer and Poet
　See in visions sweet afar —
When the Church shall dig and cover
　The red grave of the monster War!

When the Nations, all enlightened,
　Arbitrate their rights and wrongs,
When all peoples, tribes, and races,

Celebrate the day with songs,
Work then ever brave and faithful,
Pray — our prayers are full of power ;
God but waits for men to waken
To bring forth that happy hour.
— *Thos. H. Burgess.*

145. LIBERTY.

Strange, there should be so many opinions about a subject that has but *one side*.

Strange, there should be so many ideas as to *what* constitutes *personal liberty*.

"O, Liberty!" cried the French martyr, Madame Roland, as she was being dragged to the guillotine by the drunken mob, "O, Liberty! what crimes are committed in thy sacred name!"

It is in this sacred, but profaned name, and for such carnivals of crime as those that deluged Paris with the blood of its citizens, that the dram shops of America are fitting the minds and the hearts of the people of to-day. O, sacred name of Liberty! What tho our fathers wrote it in martyr graves all over this land and plucked down the stars of Heaven to emblazon it upon their banners ; what tho our eagles cry it from every mountain peak, and bear it on their rushing wings through all the boundless skies, these lands with lips of blood, those skies with tongues of fire, proclaim our perfidy ; they upbraid our national hypocrisy and guilt.

Here in the midst of our *boasted* civilization, beneath our flag of stars and stripes, a million poor inebriates, slaves of intemperance, clank their chains of fire, in hopeless, awful servitude.

And yet, this million of enslaved inebriates wield the freeman's ballot, control the elections, and rule this nation. They are bought and sold like slaves in the market. Corrruption runs riot at the ballot-box, in the halls of legislation, and invades even the sanctuary of Justice.

The dram shop to-day is the supreme political power ; and before it rulers and people, parties and politicians, bow the knee of homage, and base subserviency. The heavens are tired of weeping over the crimes and miseries caused by the liquor traffic ; O! if we still fold our arms, and linger, and pause, and hesitate, and wait — it would seem that the very dead themselves, the buried and the martyred victims of the liquor traffic, would rend their sepulchers, and do this work for us.

But there *are* those who are trying to do this work; they constitute the *Salvation Army* of the temperance cause. And because others are shirking their duties so is the work of these brave soldiers all the harder to accomplish. And you would sometimes think, by the obstacles that are placed in our way, by foes from without and within, that we were trying to bring about some great evil, instead of the work of love and reform, for " God and home and native land."

Our cause is a noble one; it is a worthy one, and it is *bound to win.*

The principles for which we are contending are laid deep in the hearts of its defenders. A noble structure is being raised, its architect is philanthropy, its foundation walls rest in the hearts and souls of *the people.* Day by day its walls rise higher and higher — the good, the noble, and the true, each contribute alike, their share of material for its completion.

From the North to the South, from the East to the West, a great enthusiasm is being created. Soon the keystone will be set in the arch, and it will tower above us complete in its majestic beauty.

Down deep in its vaults shall be buried forever, *not treasures*, O, no! but the tears, the sighs, the heartaches of broken-hearted wives and sorrowing mothers, with the wail of suffering orphaned children.

Its doors shall be broad enough and high enough to admit all temperance reformers who desire to enter therein.

Its windows shall be as beacon-lights to guide the weak and erring past the rocks and shoals of danger.

From its high tower shall chime forth a song of jubilee, and from the pinnacle of its spire shall float *our banner*, upon which shall be inscribed, as in letters of flame, these words: " *America freed from the curse of rum.*"

Do you, my brothers, and do you, my sisters, wish to do *your share* in this great work? If so, lend us a helping hand; labor and toil for this good cause; and *you*, my brothers, must not only labor and toil, but on *every election day vote for Prohibition*, and future generation will rise up and call you blessed. You will not only earn blessings upon this earth, but a rich reward in the eternity which is to come.

— *Mrs. L. E. Bailey.*

146. SIMON GRUB'S DREAM.

The text was this: "Inasmuch as ye
Have done it to these, ye have done it to me."
Soon Simon slept, for 'twas sultry weather,
And the dream and the sermon went on together.

He dreamed that he died, and stood at the gate
Of the outer court, where the angels wait
For those who hear the glad "Well done,"
And can enter the realms of the Holy One.

While Simon waited, and wondered if he
Had forgotten the password, or lost the key,
A voice above him said, loud and clear,
"Do you know you must bring your witnesses here?"

"Of witnesses there are many," said he,
"My brethren and neighbors will all speak for me,"
But the brethren and neighbors came not near,
And he heard only a whinny, familiar and clear.

And old Gray Foot, the horse, stood just at his right,
While around on the other side, just coming in sight,
Was a crowd of dumb creatures so forlorn and so poor
That the angel wept as he opened the door.
Then Simon grew pale, and, trembling with fear,
Said, "Oh! why are not some of the brethren here?
Pray wait, pray wait, they'll surely come."
'Twas Gray Foot that spoke then, and Simon was dumb:

"On wintry nights I've stood in my stall,
When the cold winds blew through the cracks in the wall,
Till every joint and sinew and bone
Seemed frozen and dead as the coldest stone.

"I've shivered the dreary time away,
With only some of the poorest hay,
Then put to work with shout and blow,
So hungry and faint I could scarcely go."

Then old Brindle came, and with soft brown eyes
Fixed on her master in sad surprise,

Told a pitiful tale of starvation and cold,
And how he had sold her food for gold.

The poor sheep told their story, too,
Of bitter wrongs their whole life through;
Turned out in cold and stormy weather,
To starve and freeze and cry together.

They were lowly cries, but they turned to prayers,
And, floating upward, had rested there,
Close by the ear of Him who says,
"I will hear the cries of my poor always."

The old house-dog, tho treated ill,
Came near, and fawned on his master still,
Because the love those dumb things know
Is more than human, more faithful, more true.

Then conscience woke like some torpid thing
That is brought to life by the sun in spring,
And lashed and stung him like poisoned thongs,
As memory brought him his train of wrongs.
Forgetting nothing of word or deed,
Of cruel blows or selfish greed.

His cruelly-treated friends that were dumb,
Would they follow him on through the ages to come?
Must he see them forever, gaunt, hungry, and cold?
For "Time and eternity never grow old."

How oft in dumb pleading they'd ask a caress
From hands that had beaten them! Ah! yes,
He remembered it all, and it stung him to know
That their pleading had ever been met with a blow.

Oh! could he live over the life that was past,
And leave out its sins, to stand here at last
With a soul that was white, for a happier fate,
Was it conscience that whispered, "Too late, too late!"

He'd cruelly passed o'er life's narrowing track,
Till remorse claimed its own — for that never turns back;
And sins scarce remembered, remembered too late,
Grew black as he saw them from heaven's barred gate.

'Twas in vain that he strove to speak, to say
Those sweet old words, "Forgive, I pray."

Sin's last sad cry ; he was silent there ;
He was dumb with such woful need of prayer.

Then voices seemed floating on every breeze :
" Ye did it to these.   Ye did it to these.
Go hence, be homeless, go starve and freeze ;
Ye did it to these.   Ye did it to these.

" And when you are faint and weary with wo,
You will still hear the shout, you will still feel the blow,
While a voice from which you shall ne'er be free
Will whisper beside you, ' Ye did it to me.' "

But hark ! What melody over him rolls?
Do the angels sing requiems over lost souls?
His last hope had fled.   In an agony new
He awoke — to find himself safe in his pew.

What his dumb friends thought, none ever knew
When food was plenty and blows were few ;
But the teacher who follows us ever, it seems,
Gives his strongest lessons, sometimes, in dreams,

Remember, dear friends, that the lips that are dumb,
May be those that will speak when our time shall come
To stand at the entrance and watch and wait
For the angel to open or close the gate.
   — *Western Humane Journal.*

147.   "ABOU BEN ADHEM."

(A CONTINUATION OF LEIGH HUNT'S POEM.)

Abou Ben Adhem, wise with life's increase,
Awoke one night — not from a dream of peace,
For sorely on his faithful spirit weighed
The pangs of all the creatures God had made ;
And worst, man's power abused, man's charge betrayed.
He listened, till it seemed the very stone
To shame man's cruel hardness, made its moan.
But vain the speechless, agonized appeal,
While sage and saint seek only *human* weal.

Then to the watcher, sad for human blame,
The Angel with the Record, tempting, came ;
Who stood and said : " Dost thou not envy, then,
These, who have loved and served their fellow-men ? "

Ben Adhem saw a long and shining roll;
Heroes and Martyrs, Prophets of the soul,
Great Preachers, Statesmen molding freedom's laws,
And grand Reformers, brave in duty's cause.

"All these," said Adhem, "these have wrought and planned
For man already rich in brain and hand.
Who pleads for those whom few can understand —
Our dear dumb brothers, piteous-eyed and meek?
O, that I were the tongue for them to speak!
Nay, not for me let Fame her laurels bind,
Nor faith her palms; but, if thou wilt be kind,
Write me as one who fain would choose his lot
With those whom man despised and Heaven forgot;
Who found in fields and woods his friendly teachers,
And ever loved his lowliest fellow creatures."

The Angel wrote and vanished. The next night
He came and showed, high on his roll of light,
The names of those who served their own race best;
And lo! Ben Adhem's name led all the rest.
— *Caroline Spencer.*

148. A LETTER EXERCISE.
[*In Concert.*]

We've a story to tell you to-night, dear friends,
    A story so strange and sad.
We shall spell you the name of a well-known thing
    That is dangerous, cruel, and bad.

We wish we might tell you of pleasanter things,
    Or say that this curse is not here,
But such ruin and sorrow, such danger and pain,
    Oh how can we silently bear.

[*Separately.*]

S is for Sorrow, Shame, and Sin
    That come with the use of strong drink —
Or it stands for Sober, Safe, and Sound —
    Now, which is the best, do you think?

A is the aching of mothers' hearts
    As they see their boys destroyed.

Or A is the Appetite binding the slave
   Ere he learns strong drink to avoid.

L is for Lives by Liquor Laid Low —
   By thousands and thousands they fall,
Or L is the License to do this foul wrong,
   To murder, to rob, to despoil.

O is for Orphans whose fathers have died
   Because they drank legalized rum.
O is Oppression in this our fair land,
   Destroying our friends and our home.

O is Opinion about this thing —
   But what is it worth, tell me, pray,
Unless we are earnest to act as we think
   And try to put evil away?

N is the Nation, a partner to-day
   In this worst of all evils we know,
Accepting the bribe of a share of the gold
   That is made by this business so low.

N means for Noble men Now to say No!
   To say No! to the poisonous slop.
To say No! to the man who permission would ask
   To open an alcohol shop.

[*In Concert.*]

S-A-L-O-O-N is the hateful word,
   We have read it upon the street,
'Tis a business place, like a dry goods store,
   With its sign all painted neat.

But our mothers have taught us truly and well
   'Tis a business of wrong and death —
Tho protected by law like any good thing,
   There's a gulf of dark ruin beneath.

We've learned, too, that votes are what keep the saloons—
   We wish that the children could vote.
We'll show where saloons then would speedily go,
   Right where they belong, underfoot.

We can stamp out this miserable business
   If we want to and try to, we know;

That is, *you can*, dear friends —
  We will pray while you vote ;
Won't you say, " *The saloon must go ?* "

— *Eva Jones.*

149. A LITTLE GIRL'S ADVICE.

I am but a little girl,
  Very small and weak ;
But I'm going now to try
  One small piece to speak.

Just a little tiny verse,
  Maybe they are two —
Anyway I promise this :
  I won't tire you.

This is what I have to say,
  Do the thing that's right ;
That which you believe to be
  Pleasing in God's sight.

Leave results to Him, He knows
  What is wise and best ;
Do your duty, do it now,
  Trust Him for the rest.   — *Union Signal.*

150. GETTING AT THE ROOT.

It has gone out of fashion to abuse saloon-keepers, to rail against the iniquity of the liquor traffic and tell blood-curdling stories of the brutal acts of drunken men. There is no philosophy in it. Temperance workers have grown weary of lopping off the branches and cutting away the leaves of the upas tree of strong drink, and are beginning to dig for its roots. These are found creeping in every direction. Part have wound themselves around the national capitol at Washington and the legislative halls of every state ; part have run back to the home and into society, and part, alas ! have coiled themselves tightly about the pillars of the church.

While riding over Toronto once with a party of friends, our driver, who was a witty Irishman, stopped the carriage at a certain point and said : " Here are four corners. On the first is a college, on the second is a church, on the third is the Parliament building, and on the last is a saloon. They are called respectively: Education, Salvation, Legislation, and Damnation." These four corners are near neighbors in more places than Toronto, and the saloon corner is the most popular and powerful of all. Without doubt, the liquor traffic is the most potent factor in modern civilization. How has it gained its strength? Through the license system. It has been legalized and made a legitimate institution. The clink of gold has deadened the consciences, blinded the eyes, silenced the tongues, and palsied the hands of the sons of men. By such treacherous logic it deceives the best of citizens and makes them enter into a compromise that kills their principle and transforms them into slaves. A great deal is said about Prohibition failing to prohibit. We have never had a full prohibitory law yet, and never shall have until congress unites with the people to secure one. Instead of license checking the consumption of liquor, it increases its volume many fold by the cloak of respectability that it gives the traffic, by establishing its position in business life, and by drawing the liquor dealers of the state and nation into a mighty combination that constitutes the leading moneyed and political power of the land, rendering it almost invincible. Prohibition for the states is made null and void by the protection that the National Government gives the liquor traffic; by the shipment of liquor from state to state, the issuance of permits, and the importation of liquor from foreign countries.

Away with such a system of license. Its folly and wickedness should be our shame, as they already are our ruin. Let us stand for a rational, clean-cut, patriotic policy of destruction for the destroyer and protection for the home.

— *Belle Kearney.*

---

151. MOTHERS WHO WEAR THE RIBBON WHITE.

Mothers who wear the ribbon white,
Longing to keep the hearthstone bright,
Yearning to make the home so fair
That nothing evil can enter there —
Dearer, oh, dearer than life to you
Is the beautiful boy with eyes so true.
Oh, could you only keep him so —
Sweet as violets — pure as snow!

Mothers who wear the ribbon white,
A dainty daughter is yours to-night,
A wee, little, soft-eyed, clinging girl,
Pure and fair as the rarest pearl,
Innocent-hearted, free from guile —
But oh, she is yours such a little while !
Could you but keep her as she is now,
With the innocent eyes and the truthful brow !

Mothers who wear the ribbon white
Are we in earnest in this great fight?
Are we believing that good will come
If only *our* part of the work be done?
Oh, are we striving as strive we should
With all the power of womanhood,
Pleading in prayer, and laboring, too,
That the world may grow honest and good and true?

He who has promised His blessing will give —
He who suffered that we might live —
He who took to His pitying breast,
Those long-ago children so wondrously blest —
Ask it in faith and only believe
And strength for the burden the soul shall receive !
Oh, mothers who cherish the ribbon so white,
'Tis coming ! 'tis coming ! the triumph of right.
— *Harriet Francene Crocker.*

152. LEAD THE BOY.

Of a loving household band
  He's the joy ;
Father, may thy guiding hand
  Lead the boy.
He's the child of hope and prayer ;
From the wily tempter's snare,
From the depth of dark despair,
  Lead the boy.

Of a loving mother's heart
  He's the pride ;
Father, may no cruel dart
  Hope deride ;
Let no evil enter in

To defile his heart with sin,
Keep him pure and white within,
   Lead the boy.

May the memory of home
   Ne'er depart,
Round the fireside altar cling
   Loving heart.
In the future years to come
As he wanders far from home
Guard him through life's journey lone,
   Lead the boy.

From the wine-cup's ruddy glow —
   Fleeting joy,
Where the poison lurks within,
   To destroy ;
From the shrouded path of gloom,
From the drunkard's fearful doom,
From the shadows of the tomb
   Lead the boy.

And when life is ended here
   Safe at last,
Free from earthly strife and sin
   May he pass ;
To the higher realms above,
Where, redeemed by thy dear love,
Saved at last our prayers will prove —
   Lead the boy.

153. CONSCIENCE CRYSTALLIZED.*

There is a medium of exchange that is more important to a country than its money.

It is light, precious, untarnishable, and indestructible. It may be lost but not spent, stolen, sweated, hoarded, cornered, or counterfeited. It is uninflatable, it was never known to be at a premium, it is incapable of discount — inexorably par. It is always equal to the volume of trade. It is adapted equally

---

* From address at the Prohibition National Convention in Pittsburg, Pa., May 27, 1896.

to great and small transactions. It is the highest security for a bank's issue or a laborer's wage. It appertains alike to business, society, government, and religion. If it be used by a double standard of unequal intrinsic measuring power, the baser token drives out the nobler and makes itself the exclusive measure-unit of the local market, whatever fiat may forbid the usurpation. Nevertheless, the nobler thing, albeit unminted or in exile, remains the arbiter and autocrat of values for all nations, for both worlds, for time, and for eternity.

It is conscience, the one possession of humanity that can not be degraded to a commodity, the one unshrinkable asset of the universe.

But conscience can be crystallized only about a fact, it is never visible in a mere theory, and so we have to have "an issue" from the start, it must be an undebatable fact. We found the liquor traffic ready to our hand. The church had denounced it the enemy of God and man. The law had branded it a public enemy. The courts had declared it a nuisance. Ethics, economics, sociology, criminology, physiology all agreed. No voice defended it.

What shall our issue be?

There is but one possible.

Read it on the banners yonder.

Read it in the faces of these women.

Read it in the resolutions of the church.

Read it in the statutes.

Read it in the Supreme Court reports.

Read it in the hospitals.

Read it in the madhouses.

Read it in the prison bars whence bleared and hopeless eyes look out to haunt you.

Read it in the potter's field.

Read it everywhere.

Oh, friends! I see in your eyes a look that never came of thinking of gold or silver or tariff or party. Your own faces confess my argument. Your own hearts are saying that we ought to march into this campaign, no ragged battalions of theorists with a dozen flags, but all together, close order, quick time, forward to the glory of God the Father!

—*John G. Woolley.*

154. A PEOPLE'S VOICE.*

Men of Columbia! where's the manly spirit
   Of the true-hearted and the unshackled gone?
Sons of old freemen, do we but inherit
      Their names alone?

Is the old Pilgrim spirit quenched within us,
   Stoops the strong manhood of our souls so low,
That Mammon's lure or Party's wile can win us
      To silence now?

What! shall the statesman forge his unseen fetters,
   Shall the false jurist righteous laws deny,
And in the church, their proud and skilled abettors
      Make truth a lie?

Torture the pages of the hallowed Bible,
   To sanction crime and robbery and blood,
And in the Rum King's hateful service, libel
      Both man and God?

Shall fair Columbia stand erect no longer,
   But stoop in chains upon her downward way,
Thicker to gather on her limbs and stronger
      Day after day?

O no; methinks from all her wild green mountains,
   From valleys where her slumbering fathers lie,
From stately cities, broad streams, welling fountains,
      And clear blue sky —

From each and all, if God hath not forsaken
   Our land, and left us to an evil choice,
Loud as the summer thunderbolt shall waken
      A People's voice.

O, let that voice go forth! The bondman sighing
   For long-lost freedom from Drink's galling chain,
Shall feel the hope, within his bosom dying,
      Revive again.

Let it go forth! The millions who are gazing
   Sadly upon us from afar, shall smile,
And unto God devout thanksgiving raising,
      Bless us the while.

---

*By permission of Houghton, Mifflin & Co.

O, for your ancient freedom, pure and holy,
  For the deliverance of a groaning earth,
For Liquor's victims, bleeding, crushed, and lowly;
  Let it go forth!

Sons of the best of fathers! will you falter
  With all they left you periled and at stake?
Ho! once again on Freedom's holy altar
  The fire awake!

Prayer-strengthened for the trial, come together,
  Put on the harness for the temperance fight,
And with the blessing of your Heavenly Father,
  Maintain the Right!
    — *Adapted from J. G. Whittier.*

155. A FATHER'S WOE — HIS RESPONSIBILITY.

A father recently called upon me to labor with his drunken son, and, if possible, to persuade him into a sober life. The head of this father, and that of his good wife, have rapidly whitened under the grief and disappointment caused by the fact that their eldest born is a confirmed and, apparently, hopeless drunkard.

I know of no more delightful or Christian home than that of this friend. A devoted and domestic mother has spent her best years for her sons, but, alas, this sorrow. Everything that persuasion and medical skill could do has been tried to reform this loved one, but to no avail. After the hope of the Keeley cure, which was the last effort made, was shattered, the father appealed to me.

My reply was, "No, sir, I can do nothing for your boy. I prefer laboring with *you*, the responsible party." The father looked with amazement, and said: "Labor with me! you know I am a strict teetotaler and not a drop of intoxicants has ever been permitted in our household; the boy never learned to drink at home. It has been the saloon, with its open door, that has ruined James." "Certainly," I replied, "it is the open saloon that has done this deadly work. But are you not responsible for these open doors, so far as you have the power to be? The saloon exists because of license laws, and you have voted for men to make these laws. Of course, where there are saloons, there must be drunken boys. Have we not had three sets of candidates nominated for the Legislature, the body that legally controls this business, before the voters of this county, for many, many elections? Yes, one was a Democrat, who publicly declared that he would legislate for the open saloon. No one could be deceived as to what he would do if elected. Another was a Republican, who as loudly proclaimed that he would permit the saloons to run, with open doors, if each would pay into the city treasury $250. No one was necessarily deceived by him. Another was a Prohibitionist, who fearlessly announced that if he gained a seat in this law-making body, he would make it a crime with ample punishment, to sell this poison, indiscriminately, in any community. This candidate is always selected with reference to his sobriety, ability, and Christian character. He is always recognized as an able man for the position. Did you, good father, vote for the man (or the party) who promised to protect your boy instead of the saloon, the man who would have made it easy for your boy to have escaped temptation, to have done right, to have grown into a sober manhood?"

The father looked steadily upon the floor, in deep meditation for a moment, and said: "No, I have believed that the Republican theory of high license was the best solution of the saloon question, and I have always voted that ticket."

I replied, "Very well, than do not complain now that you have a drunken son. You have sown a high license ballot, you have reaped a high license boy. I know of no man in our county better situated to have a drunken son than you are. You have home and wealth, a spirit of patience and charity; you can and will shelter and care for him and his little family. It is far better that your son should be a drunkard than that the son of some poor widow or of aged parents dependent upon such a boy should fall by the way. It is indeed selfish in you to vote for the high license saloon and wish that other sons than your own should be drunken, and yours should escape. The city treasury has the $250, you have the boy. You are the more responsible because you are a regular attendant upon prayer meeting and church service and an officer in a Christian church. You have not sinned without the light, for you have heard the appeals of nearly all our best advocates of Prohibition; you have had an abundance of literature placed in your hands, but apparently to no avail. You have made an idol of party and your party legislation has ruined your son. If your sorrow scourges your conscience, remember it is God's way to punish those who violate his law, at the ballot-box, as elsewhere, for "Whosoever plougheth iniquity and soweth unrighteousness, reapeth the same."

With pale face and a sense of deep humiliation, the father said, "I never saw it in that light before. I will ask God to forgive me for my blindness and hereafter vote to protect the boys instead of the saloons."

Fathers before me, look into the cradles, into the innocent faces of the rising generation, and the boys of larger growth, and answer, at the ballot-box, every election day, whether it is more or less t-a-r-i-f-f, or more or less whisky that needs legislative attention, at your hands, until this saloon problem is fully settled, and settled right. — *Helen M. Gougar.*

156. THE WHITE RIBBON STAR SPANGLED BANNER.

Fling it out to the breeze ; let it tell to the world
   That the faith which has raised it will never surrender ;
Let it tell that the love which our banner unfurled,
   Is the guard of the home and the nation's defender ;
Let it gleam as a star, for the shipwrecked afar,
Like a beacon that warns of the treacherous bar ;
Let that banner of freedom and purity wave,
As a signal of hope 'midst the perils we brave.

Hold that banner aloft ; let our colors be seen
   From Siberian snowfields to African valleys,
Lift it up for the truth ; let the rays of its sheen
   Drive the shadows of night from the byways and alleys.
Let it tell to the lost that we count not the cost,
That our bridges are burned and our Rubicon crossed ;
That the banner of motherlove ever shall wave,
Till the paths are made straight for the sin-burdened slave.

Let it fly at the front ; it is washed in our tears,
   And the smoke of the battle increases its whiteness,
Tho our hearts may be pierced by the enemy's spears,
   Yet the flow from our wounds shall but add to its brightness,
And this ensign of light, it shall float o'er the fight.

Till our wrongs are avenged by the triumph of right;
And a radiant victory at last it shall wave
O'er the ramparts we've stormed, o'er King Alcohol's grave.

Swing it out from the staff, let it shadow the ground
  Where the fathers of liberty sleep 'neath the mosses;
Run it up o'er the homes where the mothers are found
  Who through watches of anguish are counting their losses.
In the tear-moistened sod, which our martyrs have trod,
We are planting it deep for our land and our God.
And this banner of world-circling love e'er shall wave
In the name of our Christ, who is mighty to save.
— Kate Lunden.

157. ON A LEHIGH VALLEY TRAIN.*

It was the morning after election.

The Lehigh Valley day coach between New York and Buffalo was pretty well crowded, and naturally the general discussion was the election.

The attention of the passengers was attracted to a clerical-looking individual who sat about the center of the car and who was talking in a rather excitedly loud tone of voice to a man in the seat just ahead.

The reverend gentleman was saying:

"No, sir; I did not throw away my vote, but you and every other man that voted the Prohibition ticket did. I believe in Prohibition, preach for Prohibltion, and pray for Prohibition——"

"But vote for whisky," quietly interrupted the man in the front seat.

"You insult me, sir!" replied the preacher in a voice that startled everybody in the car, and at once all the passengers ceased their conversation and gave their attention to the preacher. "No man shall tell me in my face without being rebuked that I vote for whisky. I have preached for twenty years, and my voice has always been for Prohibition, but I do not believe in bringing the matter into politics. I have voted with my party for over twenty years and don't propose to throw away my vote on a party that never can elect its candidates."

Just then a man sitting in a rear seat, who had been an interested listener to the discussion, came forward, and fastening

* Copyrighted by the Author.

two bright black eyes, which looked out through a pair of gold eyeglasses, on the preacher, said:

"Pardon me, sir; did I understand you to say you are a preacher?"

"Yes, sir."

"That you believe in Prohibition?"

"Yes, sir. I have preached it for twenty years, and I believe the liquor traffic to be the curse of this nation, and that every rumseller ought to be behind prison bars."

"You also said you voted yesterday for the candidates of one of the old parties?"

"Yes, sir; the party I have always supported."

"Is your party in favor of license or prohibition."

"I don't think the question has anything to do with political parties."

"Probably not, but did any rumseller vote the same ticket as you?"

"Oh, yes; probably many thousands of them."

"Do you think that a single rumseller in the United States voted the prohibition ticket yesterday?"

"Certainly not."

"Why?"

"Why? Why, because they would be fools to support a political party that would, if it got into power, sweep away their business into everlasting oblivion."

"Oh, I thought you said the question of Prohibition was not a political one. The rumsellers evidently think it is. Now, sir, if a liquor man who believes in license, defends license, spends money for it, talks it and votes it, would be a fool to vote the Prohibition ticket, I would like to know what you are, who believe in Prohibition, preach it and pray for it, but vote the same ticket as the rumseller?"

There was a pause. The sharp, black eyes of the questioner were fixed on the reverend gentleman, who evidently was not prepared for such a direct thrust.

Finally he managed to say: "I refuse to answer such an insulting question, sir. I vote according to the dictates of my conscience and ——"

"I beg your pardon, sir, but you do nothing of the kind. Every time you cast your ballot for your rum-ruled liquor law party you vote in direct opposition to your conscience and you know it. You also know that the liquor business of this nation is licensed every year by law. You know that political parties make and maintain the law. You know that your political party could not, if it would, pass or enforce prohibitory laws. You know that fully one-half of the saloonists and brewers and distillers of this land vote the same ticket as you do.

"You know that your vote yesterday will be counted as being in favor of the saloon. You know that the only way you can inform the government that you believe in Prohibition is through a Prohibition ballot. You know that there are 4,000,000 Christian voters in this nation who profess, like yourself, to favor Prohibition, but the most of whom vote every year with you for whisky. You know that the angel Gabriel could not pick out your vote from that of a rumseller as it lay in the box yesterday.

"You know all this, I say, and yet you raise your hands in a holy protest when this gentleman here ventured to remark that you voted for whisky. Let me tell you, sir, that the rumseller who votes with his license party for the protection and perpetuation of his business is a thousand times more deserving of respect for honesty and consistency than you, who profess to favor Prohibition, but voting directly for whisky. Your professions in that line, sir, are a lie, your preaching a farce, your prayers a mockery, and your vote a protest against your own conscience, your church and your God!"

Just then a brakeman opened the door and in a slow, distinct and sonorous voice cried out:

"Allentown! Change here for Reading and Harrisburg! Do not overlook your baggage!"

The preacher made a dive for his coat and valise and darted out of the car, saying as he went: "Sorry I can't stay with you longer. I'll think over what you have said."

— Tallie Morgan.

158. THE CALF PATH.

One day through the primeval wood
A calf walked home, as good calves should,

But made a trail all bent askew,
A crooked trail, as all calves do.

Since then two hundred years have fled,
And, I infer, the calf is dead.

But still he left behind his trail,
And thereby hangs my moral tale.

The trail was taken up next day
By a lone dog that passed that way;

And then a wise bell-wether sheep
Pursued the trail o'er vale and steep,

And drew the flock behind him, too,
As good bell-wethers always do.

And from that day o'er hill and glade
Through those old woods a path was made,

And many men wound in and out,
And dodged, and turned, and bent about.

And uttered words of righteous wrath,
Because 'twas such a crooked path;

But still they followed — do not laugh —
The first migrations of that calf;

And through this winding wood-way stalked,
Because he wobbled when he walked.

This forest path became a lane,
That bent and turned and turned again;

This crooked lane became a road,
Where many a poor horse with his load

Toiled on beneath the burning sun,
And traveled some three miles in one.

And thus a century and a half
They trod the footsteps of that calf.

The years passed on in swiftness fleet;
The road became a village street,

And this, before men were aware,
A city's crowded thoroughfare,

And soon the central street was this
Of a renowned metropolis;

And men two centuries and a half
Trod in the footsteps of that calf;

Each day a hundred thousand rout
Followed the zigzag calf about,

And o'er his crooked journey went
The traffic of a continent;

A hundred thousand men were led
By one calf near three centuries dead;

They followed still his crooked way,
And lost one hundred years a day,

For thus such reverence is lent
To well-established precedent.

A moral lesson this might teach,
Were I ordained and called to preach.

For men are prone to go it blind
Along the calf-paths of the mind,

And work away from sun to sun
To do what other men have done.

Enacting " wise," evasive laws
Pertaining to the temperance cause.

They follow in the beaten track,
And out and in, and forth and back,

And still their devious course pursue,
To keep the path the others do.

But how the wise old wood-gods laugh,
Who saw the first primeval calf!

Ah! many things this tale might teach.
But I am not ordained to preach.
— *Adapted from Sam Walter Foss, in "Golden Rule."*

159. WANTED — A BOY!

Mr. A——, the rector, is dying to-day,
  With the hope of heaven on his face;
He'll be missed in the pulpit and home, when we pray.
  Wanted — a boy for his place.

Mr. B——, the judge, is dying to-day,
  With the lines of true life on his face ;
He'll be missed on the bench for many a day.
  Wanted — a boy for his place.

Mr. C——, the doctor, is dying to-day,
  And a sympathy beams on his face ;
He'll be missed in the homes, when disease comes to stay.
  Wanted — a boy for his place.

Mr. D——, the saloon-keeper, is dying to-day,
  With a look of dread on his face ;
He'll be missed where the path leads downward alway.
  Wanted — a boy for his place.

Mr. E.——, the drunkard, is dying to-day ;
  Oh, the marks of sin on his face !
He'll be missed at the club, in saloon, in the fray.
  Wanted — a boy for his place.   — *Indiana Phalanx.*

160. THE RECORD OF NON-PARTISANSHIP.

For twelve long years, "non-partisanship" has controlled the great mass of the nominal friends of temperance. What has it accomplished?

In many ways it has kept the standard low. Instead of sounding the bugle call to high endeavor, it has weakly "petitioned" and made futile attempts to run caucuses, and tried to help elect a "good man" in this or that license party (usually "this"); it has sustained a law which involves an option to sin ; it has brought about a vote on a prohibitory amendment, after the great liquor parties have organized its defeat ; it has left Prohibition, wherever enacted, a helpless orphan ; it has magnified the supposed blessings of such compromise measures as the screen law, the civil damage act, the 200 feet law, the Sunday closing law, and many petty changes in that four-hundred-year failure, the license system, and it has seen to it that each of these pet features was also an orphan.

It has diverted attention from the main work, by organizing the "Voters Union" in Ohio in 1883, the State Temperance Assembly in New York in 1884, the National Non-Partisan League in 1884, the "Union Prohibitory League" in Pennsylvania in 1889, and numerous other like failures whose graves are green.

"Non-partisanship" has afflicted us with "High License" and "State Control," which give a tremendous "revenue" club to our opponents.

Even now, "non-partisanship" is trying to mislead the young students of Christian citizenship into these same swamps and bogs where their elders have so long floundered.

In 1884 the aggressive temperance sentiment of America, was fast crystallizing into the National Prohibition party. The vote leaped from 10,000 to 150,000. Angels held their breath, for the mightiest moral revolution since Pentecost was impending. But "non-partisanship" blocked the way, and shrewdly deployed the forces of timidity, conservatism, and party spirit to check the rapid unification of moral power, and to delay the triumph of right. In this, while "powerless for good it was powerful for evil." It has ever interposed the lower issue. It has done its work. It has made its record. It has granted liquordom time to create the most oppressive monopoly and the greatest political power which this land ever saw. It has divided our friends and compacted our foes.

For twelve years "non-partisanship" has wrought its will upon our land. Figure for yourself the dreadful total. Twenty-five thousands of millions of dollars, lost by American homes and American labor, because of toying with this pitiful "fad."

More than one million of human lives, sacrificed during these twelve years of temporizing with crime. A nation of compromises. Heroism a memory. "Revenue" regnant. Sobs and wails in millions of homes. "Non-partisanship" in full fruitage.

Men and brethren, we can not pay this terrible cost. Let us abandon this weakness. Let us be men — and not eunuchs. Let us have convictions which are strong enough to dominate our votes. Let us be manly "partisans" in behalf of right. Let us lift a party banner around which alone the church and our Christian citizenship can consistently rally. Let us proudly and steadily and devotedly stand for that "partisanship" which is both wise and strong. Then we can strike telling blows for our God, our country, and our homes. — *A. R. Heath.*

161. A PUZZLED SANTA CLAUS.

Oh, say, it's the funniest story !
I've just heard all about it, you see !

And I hurried right over to tell you,
  'Cause a part of it means you and me.

In Christmas-land (you know where that is,
  Tho ne'er a geography tells,
Away, far away toward the sunlight,
  Is where Santa — old Santa Claus, dwells)—

In Christmas-land, whispers of trouble
  Were afloat in the air. "It's so queer!"
Said Santa's chief clerk, "for we always
  Have sunshine and gladness up here.

"But surely there's something the matter,
  For never in all of my life
Have I seen Father Santa so worried,
  Nor so bothered, Dame Goody, his wife."

And just then a bugle rang clearly,
  And fairies and elfins and all—
Yes, all of the Santa Claus helpers,
  Went hurrying off to the hall.

To the great, bright hall of the palace,
  And Santa awaited them there,
His eyes all aglow in the sunlight,
  And gold-crowned his snowy-white hair.

"It's all right!" they said one to another,
  "Father Santa's discovered a cure
For the trouble that worried and vexed him,
  And he'll tell us about it, be sure."

And old Santa did tell them the story,
  And he told it so well that they cried,
And then laughed and hurrahed till the echoes
  Went ringing through Christmas-land wide.

Of course I can't tell it as he did,
  But I'll do just the best that I may
To explain why dear Santa looked troubled
  When he thought of the glad Christmas-day.

You see he had planned all his presents,
  And his people were working by night
And by day, so they'd surely be ready
  With the Christmas-time's store of delight.

But just as he rubbed his hands gaily,
    And chuckled to think there would be
No delay in the filling of stockings,
    No lack in each Christmas-tide tree,

Lo! a telegraph-boy with a message,
    And it read, "*Mr. Dear Santa Claus,
There are boys and girls, ever so many,
    Who can't have any Christmas, because*

"*Their papas have lost all their money —
    And the rumsellers stole it, we b'lieve —
We big ones can stand it, but babies —
    Say, Santa, you know how they grieve.*

"*Now can't you just help us a little?
    Just enough so the babies will think
That Christmas means loving and kissing,
    And something to eat and to drink?*"

Poor Santa! Sure never and never
    Was he half so much troubled and vexed,
"Some children — and nothing to give them,"
    No wonder the saint was perplexed.

His gifts were all promised. The orders
    Had been in for a twelvemonth or more,
Dame Goody assured him the helpers
    Were working as never before;

No time and no stock for the making,
    Not even a dolly to spare,
Nor so much as a bagful of candy,
    No wonder he groaned in despair.

But Santa's not worked for the children
    Without learning to know them, you see —
And soon he untangled the tangle,
    And laughed out again in his glee.

"I have it! That Temperance Legion
    Will be only to happy to lend
Their help to a puzzled old fellow
    Who's sorely in need of a friend.

"I'll tell to the Legion the story —
    Indeed, I will tell them the whole —

Of the brave little laddies and lassies,
   And the Christmas the rumsellers stole.

"About the dear babies I'll tell them,
   I know how their hearts will be stirred,
I know how they'll rally to help me
   As quick as I send them the word."

So saying, old Santa touched quickly
   A curious kind of a spring,
And the telephone bells on the Earth-land
   'Gan to merrily jingle and ring.

And this is the way that I heard it,
   And why I have hurried to you —
And now there is only one question.
   "*Just what can you and I do?*"
                        —*Alice M. Guernsey.*

162. A SONG OF HOPE.

Children of yesterday,
   Heirs of to-morrow,
What are you weaving —
   Labor and sorrow?
Look to your looms again;
   Faster and faster
Fly the great shuttles
   Prepared by the Master.
Life's in the loom,
   Room for it — room!

Children of yesterday,
   Heirs of to-morrow,
Lighten the labor
   And sweeten the sorrow,
Now — while the shuttles fly
   Faster and faster.
Up and be at it —
   At work with the Master
He stands at your loom,
   Room for Him — room!

Children of yesterday,
   Heirs of to-morrow,
Look at your fabric

>   Of labor and sorrow,
>   Seamy and dark
>   With despair and disaster,
>   Turn it — and lo,
>   The design of the Master!
>   The Lord's at the loom,
>   Room for Him — room!
>   — *Mary A. Lathbury.*

163. THE FARMER AND HIS GUN.*

CHAPTER I.

"Great Scott, Maria, I do wish you would quit your talking to me about Prohibition. If men want drink they are going to have it, and all your Prohibition laws in the world ain't agoing to stop them from getting it."

"But see here, Joshua, don't you know ——?"

"Yes, I do know considerable more about it than you women do. Why, only yesterday, that lightning rod man told me that he could get all the liquor he wanted to in Prohibition States. I am in favor of repealing all prohibitory laws so long as they are violated in that manner. Maria, the only way to deal with this question is to persuade the drinkers to quit — sign the pledge. Moral suasion will do more good in one day than prohibition that does not prohibit will do in a year. Then make the rum-sellers pay a high license. That's what I call practical temperance."

CHAPTER II.

"Maria, this 'ere stealing from my orchard has got to stop or by ginger there will be a few dead thieves around here pretty soon. I won't stand it any longer!"

"Joshua, isn't there a pretty strong prohibitory law against stealing in this State?"

"Yes, sir, there is, and by George I am going to see it enforced. I will get a first-class gun and hire some man to watch the thieves and shoot them on the spot!"

"Say, Joshua, what's the use of trying to enforce that law? It is violated every day, and wouldn't it be better to repeal all laws against stealing until public sentiment was ready to enforce them?"

---

* Copyrighted by the author.

"Public sentiment be hanged! That shows how much you women know about practical matters."

"But, Joshua, you can't make men honest by law, you know, and the only way you can settle this thieving question is to persuade the thieves not to steal — get them to sign the pledge, you know, and——"

"Maria, are you going crazy?"

"No, Joshua, I'm getting to be a little 'practical,' don't you see. As I was saying, get the thieves to sign the pledge never to steal again, and make those who refuse, pay high license for stealing. That's what I call practical work."

"Great Scott, Maria, what a dandy legislator you would make! Under the magnificent schemes of your fertile brain, all great problems would be solved in two weeks. Now, I propose to show you that the law against stealing can be enforced."

CHAPTER III.

"Well, Maria, I have been to town, bought a gun, have hired Bill Sykes to handle it and keep a sharp lookout for the thieves and bang away at the first one that shows his head over the fence."

"Well, Joshua, you know that prohibition doesn't prohibit, and here you have gone and spent $20 or $30 for a gun that will do no good. If men want to steal they are going to, and all your prohibition laws in the world won't stop them."

"For Heaven's sake, Maria, stop your confounded nonsense. Wait for a few weeks and we'll see if the thieves can be squelched or not."

CHAPTER IV.

"Well, Joshua, six weeks have gone by and the thieving goes on just the same. Now, what are you going to do about it?"

"You just wait and see."

"That's exactly what I have been doing. Prohibition doesn't prohibit, does it?"

"Not yet, but just you wait."

"Is the gun all right?"

"Yes, the gun is first-class."

"Gun loaded?"

"Yes, the gun has been properly loaded all the time."

"And the stealing has been going right along?"

"Maria, you are enough to drive any man crazy, and if you let up for a few minutes I will tell you why the thieving has not stopped. *I have just discovered that Bill Sykes is one of the thieves.*"

"Oh! that's it, is it! Well, now, since you are one of these non-partisan temperance men, your next move will be to get up a petition addressed to Bill Sykes, begging him to do the work he was hired to do. Or, perhaps, you will organize a law and order league to force Bill Sykes to enforce the law?"

"Maria, I am not a natural born fool, and I want you to understand it once for all. *I have discharged Bill Sykes and hired a man in his place who has no sympathy with thieving or thieves.* Now, I expect that prohibition *will* prohibit."

"Joshua, if you had the sense of a fresh water clam you would learn a lesson from this. You complain that prohibition of the liquor traffic does not prohibit and that the liquor men violate every law passed for the protection of society. Yet you and the rest of your party vote men into office like Bill Sykes, who are a part of a gang of law breakers. Instead of voting to discharge these men and put Prohibitionists into office, you reelect the same old crowd and then whine that 'prohibition does not prohibit,' and 'you can not make men good by law,' and such cowardly nonsense. Joshua, vote to discharge forever all the Bill Sykes's and place the prohibition guns in the hands of Prohibitionists, who have no sympathy with rum-selling or rum-sellers."

"Oh Lord, these women! these women!"

— Tallie Morgan.

164. A FUNERAL TO-DAY.

As I write a funeral procession is passing my door. It is the burial of a neighbor who has died of alcoholism, our national disease. He returned but a few weeks ago from the Keeley cure, strong in faith that he would never yield to the appetite again. He is the second man in this community to die of a debauch after this treatment and another of our citizens is "on a spree" now, who has received this so-called cure. The father of this last one is heart-broken. "For," says he, "I thought my boy was redeemed, but now there is no hope."

As I see the man carried to his grave, a man who has occupied seats high in the councils of the nation, I can but exclaim:

"What a costly revenue we derive from the 'poison traffic!'" and ask, "O Lord, how long, how long will we continue to collect it?" A friend sitting by me says: "He deserves no sympathy; he had every help to make life a success and he would not do it."

Ah, stop! The Word says: "No drunkard can inherit the kingdom of heaven!" Do you say "no sympathy is due?" Remember, he was poisoned in early manhood by the social glass, as I have heard him say. The chains of appetite have bound him tighter and tighter, and in the days of his ripest usefulness he is a victim of a traffic sustained by the votes of Christian men. The victim deserves the deepest sympathy; let us condemn the system that creates him thus helpless in the clutches of disease.

He will be laid to-day by the side of his Christian mother, whose greatest sorrow was that this "most brilliant of all my sons" was a drunkard. She went to her grave uttering a prayer for his salvation. And this is the way this man government helps answer the prayers of Christian mothers. God hasten the day when mothers can vote as well as pray.

By his side stand Christian brothers who have been devoted to his reformation, but when asked to vote a ticket that would send men to the Legislature who would prohibit the poison dens that beset this weaker brother's pathway will idly answer, "O there's no use; liquor will be sold anyway and I think it best to vote my party ticket once more." Ministers speak by the side of his coffin to-day who read the sad history in the fate of the dead, men who know the vast number falling all around them but who refuse to open their churches to voices that would sound the alarm in the presence of 103 saloons in this city of 15,000 souls. No gospel temperance meetings are held in the 27 churches that set on our thoroughfares, locked six days out of seven, given over to dust, must, and cobwebs. O no, somebody might tell the members of these churches, who are at ease in Zion, that they ought to carry their religion with their ballot on election day, and thus wound the Christian in his pew, who is the greatest sinner at the ballot-box. So as this one falls into a drunkard's grave others fall into the procession on the other end, to fill up the ceaseless gap and give these preachers "something to do."

By the side of this coffin to-day business men march who

think they "can drink or let it alone," men whose faces show the "danger signal," who call me a "crank, a regular John Brown born before my time," when I ask them kindly, "Won't you read on this subject if I give you the books and papers?" In the strength of their present will they smile and — go on a steady march to fill a drunkard's grave, believing as they say, "O I know when I have enough. I am not such a weakling as to over-drink."

Beside this coffin to-day are the editors of our papers who write pathetically of this "ruined life," but who will not allow a line of prohibition sentiment to find its way into their columns lest it offend the liquor sellers who patronize their sheets. One of these editors, a brother in the church, writes tenderly of this man's death and publishes in one issue of his paper thirty-one notices of application to sell liquor! So the work goes on upheld by press, pulpit, and people.

The wife sits clothed in the habiliments of mourning by the side of his coffin. In her youth and beauty she gave her life and happiness into the keeping of this brilliant young man; they were just out of college, thoroughly equipped to build a Christian home. She saw the tempter at work; all that love, gentleness, and devotion could do she had done. Her patience, persistence, and endurance were remarked by all, but when all hope had fled she was obliged to let him drift and die, away from her ministrations of tenderness and love. It was an unequal contest. The whole legal power of State and Nation was pitted against her, for this government of males stays the hand of the outraged wife, takes no pity on her, but upholds the saloon-keeper in his deadly work. She is a widow to-day, the husband and home have been destroyed by the will and power of the government, for the sake of "revenue."

Women flock to this funeral and drop tears of sympathy with this sister beside the bier, but they have no time to join the W. C. T. U., to read our papers, to fill themselves with knowledge; they have no time to educate their children in the physical effects of alcohol that they may go out in the face of the ever-present tempter forewarned and forearmed. O no, these women are too busy hunting "favors for progressive euchre" or "cinch" parties, to carry the gospel of teetotalism into palace and hovel alike, so their sons, a little later on, will go the same way; some are well started now.

Beautiful daughters weep for the absence and protecting care of a loving father. They are forced into the industrial world to compete with men bread-winners. In this way the industrial problem is made most serious. Women and children compete with and cut down the income of male wage-earners and the labor problem comes uppermost, only to be solved when we solve the liquor question.

The train of evils following in the wake of this funeral, one of 125,000 each year, shows how the government protects (?) the home, the wife and children, and the best interests of the society.

The saloon can not be legalized and the home protected under the same flag.

Men-voters, what are you going to do about it, and when are you going to do it? Will you begin next time you vote? Your answer will be in the size of the next Prohibition party vote. *— Helen M. Gougar.*

165. THE WAR GOD.

"Who art thou, mighty one, hastening down the vista of the years, thou of such brilliant apparel, such clarion voice, such stately tread?"

"I am the War God," replies the gallant specter, "the king of all the kings of the earth."

"How didst thou come into possession of so high a throne?"

"Because of my power. Since the birth of man, the reins of all the governments of the world have been placed in my hand. An absolute monarch have I ever been, my word the law of all nations. How oft, to indulge my fancy, have I ordered my subjects to turn some majestic city into a gigantic bonfire, or to butcher a thousand children that their cries of anguish might add a new strain to the songs raised for my diversion."

"Dost thou flatter thyself that thy subjects all serve thee from pure love?"

"If praise be a sign of love, the affection all bear for me must indeed be intense. Poets have dedicated to me their noblest efforts. My achievements have inspired artists to create their masterpieces. Inventors have devised martial toys innumerable for my amusement. Philosophers have used their sagest arguments to prove me worthy of all the honor I receive. Kings without number have thrown their crowns at my feet and unmurmuring have surrendered to me their domains, while my special followers love me more than home or comfort, wife or child, mother or God, forsaking all to abide with me."

"What recompense do thy faithful adherents receive?"

"A soldier's name," returns the War God with a complacent look, "a soldier's renown, coveted by all. Man forsakes every vocation that he may become a bearer of arms. He leaves the carpenter's bench that he may destroy beautiful buildings, the mill and the store that he may turn their fruitage to a mighty conflagration. The physician hurries away from the dying that he may carry death into the ranks of the enemy. The lawyer closes his office, deaf to the appeals of the down-trodden, that within the army he may break every law of nature and of God.

"Thus, eager for the conflict, man marches forth to the most inspiring music genius can produce, his path strewn with flowers by the loyal hands of mother, wife, and child.

"But highest fame is his, no matter what his private life may have been — after he has fallen in death upon the field of strife. His name is ever after held in the most sacred reverence. Thus do I share my honors with my disciples!"

"Pray, what hast thou done to deserve such homage?"

"I keep thousands of men in compulsory idleness, which leads to every dissipation. I keep children from their schools and mothers from their families to toil in the fields and factories. I take food from the mouths of half starving peasants and clothes from their backs that the cost may be expended in constructing arsenals and forts for my amusement.

"And what an impressive past has been mine! I have unfurled my gory banner in every clime. I have turned peace to strife, plenty to famine, righteousness to unbridled crime, temperance to base revellings of King Alcohol, the heaven of civil prosperity to the hell of the battle-field, where every evil appeared in its most hideous form.

"Because of petty misunderstandings among sovereigns, I have flooded earth with blood, I have sent millions in inexpressible agony to untimely deaths, I have left them unburied in alien lands, I have reared asylums for those who have become crazed by dwelling on the horrors of my career. I have filled the sky with wails of widows and orphans, I have given the torch to myriads of once happy homes, I have destroyed countless works of art which no genius can ever reproduce, I have given to the flames great libraries—treasuries of the garnered wisdom of ages, now gone for aye—I have levelled cities as does the spring the hillocks of snow. I have bequeathed to the sea unnumbered fleets with their human cargoes. And with one breath have I annihilated whole races."

"O thou terrible one, how is it thy reign has been so long?"

"Because mortals have desired my rule."

"Must this fair earth always be marred by thy bloody footsteps? Wilt thou never surrender thy kingdom to another?"

"Aye, there is one more powerful than am I who waits to ascend my throne, whenever men decree. Peace is this sovereign. She comes from the olive plains that surround the throne of God. Her advent was announced by the angels who carolled the birthsong of the Prince of Peace. Her kingdom shall be an everlasting kingdom, while mine shall vanish for aye." — *Alice May Douglas.*

166. GREAT ADVANCE.

The Prohibition Party has been for years a stubborn, righteous minority. Said De Tocqueville: "Stubborn minorities are the hope of republics." Especially true is this when a minority stands for conscience, for a truer, better manhood, for a nobler nationhood. President Seelye, some time before his death, declared that the Prohibition Party was the most hopeful sign above the political horizon. Charles Sumner was profoundly right when he said: "If you would save the nation you must sanctify it as well as fortify it." The Prohibition Party stands for political sanctification, a quickened and a quickening conscience in politics.

What does the balance sheet of the Prohibition Party reveal? If we have done nothing for the present generation or for posterity we should step aside. Posterity? "Why," said Patrick when urged to do something for posterity, "why should I do anything for posterity? What has it done for me, I should like to know?" We differ with our Emerald friend.

A ship heavily laden, sailing in the Gulf Stream, was caught in the doldrums. Day after day the surface current was moving against the ship's course, but not a breath of **air** stirred the sails. The hearts of the sailors were failing them. It seemed useless to raise or shift a sail, or move the rudder. The vessel lay in a dead calm and the drift was contrary; but after a time a reckoning was taken, and lo! the ship had gained hundreds of miles. All the time the sailors were complaining and discouraged, while all the surface indications were that the ship was moving backward, the strong undercurrent of that wonderful river in the ocean with its thousand hands had gripped hold of the bottom of the vessel and was pulling it toward the desired haven.

In 1888 the Fisk campaign seemed to have left the Prohibition Party in the political doldrums. No pulling, no tugging of sails has appeared to help. There has been a world of lamentations and croakings. The surface indications have been against us; here and there a hand has dropped discouraged, and several of our best-known leaders have gone beyond the vale and the shadow. Some say that we have made no progress; some, that we have drifted backward. Let us take a reckoning and see how true it is that the great undercurrent that sets toward righteousness throughout the universe has all these years been carrying the party onward toward final victory. To change the figure, we have been as one walking westward on an eastern-bound lightning express. While he is taking one step westward he is carried by the train a hundred steps eastward. Our party has been carried by a power that encompassed us, and is greater than we, onward and upward.

Let us look at the credit side of the Prohibition Party balance sheet.

Note first the fact: The party has been a leading factor in getting conscience into politics. It is to-day, and has been for years, the grandest and most potent educational force, moral and political, in our nation. Its steadfastness for the right, its unflinching courage, its clearness of vision along moral political lines, its cheerful self-abnegation, and its endless sacrifices for conscientious convictions, are a leaven that is working irresistibly in the American meal-tub.

Some one croaks, "But the Prohibition Party is not large." A bit of leaven is not large, and yet it has in it that which leavens all the meal. But another exclaims, "The party has not grown." The Golden Rule and the Ten Commandments are not a particle larger than when first uttered, and yet all through the ages they have been lifting the world higher and higher, and never so effectively as to-day. The test is not size, but what that size contains. God chooses the apparently little things, weak things of the world, to work His wonders and confound the mighty.

Ten years ago politics stood for greed. "To the victors belong the spoils," "All is fair in politics," "Politics is politics," were common maxims that ruled; and the name politician was a synonym for trickster from Maine to the Golden Gate and from the Lakes to the Gulf. To the old party politicians the Ten Commandments and the Golden Rule were iridescent dreams. Against all this the Prohibition Party has been an organized, untiring, immovable protest. Every year the county and state Prohibition Party platforms and nominations were the voice of conscience, of a higher, truer political ideal; "a still small voice" they may have been, but they were a voice that has been heard from one end of the country to the other, heard and at last somewhat heeded. The day-dawn of cleaner, truer politics in America is beginning to be recognized everywhere.

Nor will our party have done its perfect work until the most sacred spot to the people in all this land will be the ballot-box; until a dishonest act there, corruption there, will be recognized as the greatest possible crime against the Republic. To fool, to cheat at the ballot-box is treason, and such treason must be made unspeakably odious. During the past decade the political conscience of the American people has grown visibly many a cubit.

Prior to ten years ago you will look in vain in the records of the Presbyterian General Assembly for an utterance like the following:

> "No political party has the right to expect the support of Christian men so long as that party stands committed to the license policy, or refuses to put itself on record against the saloon."

Prior to 1884, find, if you can, anything like the following in the minutes of the Methodist General Conference:

> "We do record our deliberate judgment that no political party has a right to expect, nor ought it to receive, the support of Christian men so long as it stands committed to the license policy, or refuses to put itself on record in an attitude of open hostility to the saloon."

These are but typical of the recent utterances of about all

of the churches. And the great Christian Endeavor Association, under the guidance of that master leader, John G. Woolley, is not far in the rear. By and by it will lead.

But, does some one say, what do these resolutions and sayings amount to if they do not take the form of action?

Get intelligent, conscientious men to think right and keep them at it, and they are bound by the irresistible laws of the mind and heart eventually to act right. The Prohibitionists have gained a stupendous victory in compelling the churches to think right.

The church is slowly but surely leading its membership up to the high level of its resolutions. This is one point we must insist upon : the ending of the inconsistency between church resolutions and membership action. There must be harmony between the head, heart, feet, and hands of the church. A captain in the old-fashioned militia once offered this toast: "Here is to the militia, invincible in peace, invisible in war." That has been the church in its fight with the liquor traffic "invincible in synods and in conferences; invisible on election days." That must end. It is our business to so plan and so fight that it will be impossible for this inconsistency to continue.

Again, what changes are being wrought in almost every direction by a recognition on the part of many business men of the facts Prohibitionists have been gathering and publishing. To-day, it is not safe anywhere for a young man to seek employment with the smell of liquor on his breath. I have gone through large restaurants in Chicago, and Boston, and New York at lunch time, and have not seen a bottle at one plate in twenty. Ten years ago, in these same restaurants, the bottle on an average was at every other plate. Last December the Chicago and Alton Railroad published Rule 75, which reads:

> "Any conductor, trainsman, engineer, fireman, switchman, or other employee who is known to use intoxicating liquors will be promptly and permanently discharged."

Orders have been issued by almost all of the leading railroads of the country forbidding the sale of liquors at railroad restaurants and forbidding their employees to go inside of a saloon, many of them, with the Chicago and Alton Railroad, insisting upon absolute abstinence. The significance of these weighty facts is that over a million men are employed on the railroads, and that this recognition is a commercial one. The enlightened pocket-book has become a factor in our reform in America in the closing decade of the nineteenth century. When fully enlisted it will become irresistible.

He who can not see in such triumphs as these great encouragement must be fatally blind. The Prohibition Party, beyond any other educational agency, beyond all others combined, is to be credited with these changes. It forced agitation, and agitation is a tremendous educational power.

— *Rev. Dr. I. K. Funk.*

167. SAINT MONACELLA'S LAMBS.

Within the ancient Powysland they call
The timid hares that swiftly run for life
Wyn Melangell, "Monacella's lambs,"
And tell of that fair Saint this legend strange.

When Christ the Lord, six centuries was dead,
Brochwel, the Prince, aroused himself one morn
While yet the sun was early in the sky,
And rolling mists hung o'er the mountain side.
"This day," he cried, "with merry horn and hounds,
We'll hunt the hare in blythesome Powysland."
And with the Prince rode chieftains stern and true,
And lovely ladies, with dark glancing eyes —
Eyes that for pity should be moist to tears,
But now were swift to look on pain and death.

And as the morning grew apace, the sun
Shone in bright splendor, and burned up the mist,
And bathed the hills and vales in radiant light.
The joyful baying of the deep-mouthed hounds
Proclaimed that they at last had found the hare.
But swiftly as they ran, still faster ran
The panting creature flying for its life.
Across the plain it fled, and close behind
The eager dogs, the courtiers, and the Prince,
Who far outstripped his gallant retinue,
And felt the inspiration of the chase
Thrill through his being to its inmost core.
But the swift hare, thus doomed to cruel death,
Found refuge in a small and thorny wood,
Scarce larger than a thicket in its size.

No horseman e'er could find a path therein,
And Brochwel leapt from off his gallant steed
And forced a passage through the branching trees
Until he reached an open space, wherein
A lovely lady, clothed all in white,
Knelt on the green sward, and with clasped hands,
Prayed Heaven for mercy on a wicked world.
The hare had found a harbor of defense,
And, nestled 'neath the white fold of her robe,
Turned to the dogs an aspect undismayed.

The Prince was startled by this vision fair,
Emblem of pity in a ruthless world ;
But soon the master passion took its way.
With angry voice, and gesture fierce, he urged
The dogs to seize the hare — which peaceful lay
Half-covered by the white robe's falling fold.
The hounds, more reverent than the angry Prince,
Shrank ever further from the kneeling maid.
Nor could the huntsman, who had joined the Prince,
Blow on his horn a single forward note,
But spellbound, gazed upon the white-robed form.
Then heavenly awe fell on the Prince's heart,
And sweet compassion entered in his soul ;
No more he sought the timid hare to slay,
But bowed his head before the Saint who thus
Could tame the fierceness both of man and brute,
And begged to know the secret of her power.
Strange was the story the white lady told
To listening Brochwel, Prince of Powysland ;
For she, whom we Saint Monacella call,
The hermit fair, Melangell then was named —
Melangell, daughter of an Irish King.
She fled her father's court that she might 'scape
A loveless union with a noble fierce,
And in this lonely place her spotless life
To Chastity and Pity she had given.
Here fed but by the kindly fruits of earth,
Her thirst assuaged by the water brooks,
Her home a welcome refuge had become
For the bright creatures thoughtless man destroys.
The birds sang sweetly round her lonely bower

Their hymns to Mercy, and to Mercy's God.
The wild hares gambolled tamely round her knee,
And every dumb thing here lived out its day,
Nor dreamed of torture or the deadly knife.

Brochwel, the Prince, came of a warrior tribe,
His days to battle and to chase had given;
Yet here he saw a vision beautiful
Of a white world where slaughter had no place,
Where Holiness and Mercy fair had met,
Where Contemplation had not scorned to throw
A shield protecting e'en the humblest things
To which the heavens had given the gift of life.
So, tho his hands were red with human blood —
A warrior and a hunter from his birth —
Brochwel a gift unto Melangell made,
A tract of land to be for her and God;
A Place of Holiness, where hunted things,
Whether of human kind, or of the brute,
Should find their safety and might rest secure.
Nor fear the hunter's horn nor butcher's knife,
Nor the wild vengeance that man wreaks on man.

There Monacella lived her lonely life,
And succor gave to all that fled to her.
Yea, from her girlhood to her dying day,
When old and feeble she gave up her breath —
Through those long years her hermitage became
A picture of the Paradise of God —
A place of peace from war and bloodshed free.
A symbol of the future, when the world
Shall learn the Message of the Carpenter,
And Love shall rule in Earth and Heaven alike.
— *William C. A. Axon.*

168 THE VOICE OF A STAR.

Dark night her tent once more unfurled, on Power's first-century home,
Upon the marble heart of the world — the great, grand city of Rome.
And hushed at last were the chariot-tires, and still the sandalled feet,
And dimmed the palace window-fires, on many a noble street;

And to a roof a maiden came, with eyes as angels love,
And looked up at the spheres of flame that softly gleamed
    above.

She gazed at them with a misty eye, and spoke, in accents sad:
"O tell me, gold-birds of the sky! if ever a voice you had,
Is Justice dull from a palsy-stroke, and deaf, as well as blind?
Else why must e'er the heaviest yoke be placed on woman
    kind?
Why should the solace of man's heart be oft his meanest slave?
Why is her life e'er torn apart, by those she has toiled to save?

"Why should the mold of the human race be crushed and
    thrown away,
Whenever it lacks the outward grace that woos the stronger
    clay?
Why must the mothers of men be bought and sold like beasts
    that die?
Why are they scourged for little or nought, and barred of all
    reply?
Why are we women of Rome e'er told that we should happy
    be,
Because not kept like flocks in fold, as those across the sea?

"Have we no heart? Have we no mind? Must not our con-
    science speak?
Say, must our souls be dumb or blind, because our hands are
    weak?
Must we be ever the laughing-stock of man's fond, fickle heart?
Were we but born for Fate to mock — to play a menial part?
Must all our triumphs be a lie — our joys in fetters clad?
O tell me, gold-birds of the sky — if ever a voice you had!"

Then from the East, a new, bright star flashed to her flashing
    eye,
And seemed to speak to her from afar, with soft and kind reply:
"Why weep, fair maid, upon the eve of victory's coming morn?
It is o'er strange, for one to grieve, whose champion's to be
    born!
To-morrow, a new king appears, with dimpled, mighty hand,
And He shall rule a million years, o'er many a kingly land.

"His mother a queen the world will see, whose reign doth e'er
    endure;

All women shall his sisters be, whose ways are just and pure;
A woman's fault shall not be her death, by men or angels seen;
Repentance, and His God-strewn breath, shall grandly step
 between.
A woman's fame, by merit won, shall add to her queenly grace,
And higher, as the years march on, shall be her destined place.

"And four great words the world shall see, enwoven with
 man's life:
Mother and sister two shall be — and two be daughter and wife.
It shall be felt that she whose care the lamp of thrift makes
 burn,
Can take with him an equal share of all their lives may earn;
That she whose soft and healing hand can soothe, with blessing
 bright,
Is no less great, and true, and grand, than he who leads the
 fight."

Like one who through the woods may grope till light comes to
 his eyes,
The maiden thrilled with new-born hope, and seized the glad
 surprise;
The voice of the star she understood; its glorious meaning
 knew;
And all her dreams of woman's good, seemed likely to come
 true.
And when against the twilight gray was brightened by the
 morn,
Within a manger far away, the infant Christ was born.
 — *Will Carleton, in Ladies' Home Journal.*

169. A WHITE HEAT.

Not long since we heard a very disappointing sermon on an important theme. It contained much religious truth, but it was fearfully cold. It was the Gospel frozen, and fed out with a teaspoon.

Much of the "temperance" talk of the day is like that sermon. The speaker, or the writer, is really "opposed to intemperance"— of course. He is sorry for the drunkard, and would like to help him. He sees that the saloon-keeper is very wicked, and the saloon very dreadful. He wishes there were no saloons — at least not so many. If he had his way, the saloons would be abolished. But as he can not have his way, he will "do the next best thing"—let them stay. He will not go to extremes. He will not be violent or excitable. He will do what everybody will agree to, and he hopes that in "the long result of time" this foul blot will be removed from our civilization. He can not see why any one should object to such a proper and discreet utterance, and asks, "What would you have more?"

Good sir, we would have fire. You will never do anything by handling the cold iron of public opinion in that style. Put it in the fire of intense conviction, burning pity for the tempted and the broken-hearted, and hot indignation at the destroyer! Then when you strike, the sparks will fly, and you can shape that public opinion into a sword that will smite the accursed saloon, hip and thigh, with unsparing slaughter. The lack of fire is what we object to.

A man walking across a bridge sees a boy struggling in the water. "Ah," he exclaims, "I pity that boy! It's a dreadful thing to be drowned. It will be very sad for that boy's father and mother. I should sympathize with all wise and well-directed efforts to save that boy." Now, where is the fault in these excellent remarks? Another man rushes up in hot haste and prepares to plunge in, with blazing eyes fixed on the struggling boy. The first man says, severely: "Sir, this is very undignified and impolite behavior. You almost knocked me down; and you have flung your coat and boots into that dirty pool. Sir, I felt great sympathy for that boy before you appeared, but your violent measures have destroyed all my interest, and now I don't care what becomes of him."

If the rescuer gives a hot answer, can you blame him very much? At least, when he struggles ashore with the rescued boy in his arms, you will forgive him.

That has been the way with reformers in all ages. Garrison's *Liberator* used to make Beacon street gentlemen mad to the lynching point. Wendell Phillips's polished sarcasm and invective cut so deep that many a time the police had to see him home. Doubtless these men were sometimes too severe, yet the world does not now remember that they hurt the feelings of some people, but only that they shook slavery down. How did Sheridan turn the tide of battle at Cedar Creek just thirty years ago? In his own story of the victory he speaks over and over of the worth of enthusiasm. He says:

> "I already knew that even in the ordinary condition of mind, *enthusiasm* is a potent element with soldiers; but what I saw that day convinced me that if it can be excited from a state of despondency, its power is almost irresistible."

Flashing past the crowd of fugitives, waving his hat, shouting, "Face the other way, boys, face the other way!" one man all ablaze set an army on fire.

Oh, for that sacred fire of enthusiasm in the temperance cause now! Oh, that the leaders of thought would but give utterance in ringing tones to the feeling burning in the hearts of millions, instead of laboriously hushing it down! Away with "critical coldness" at such a time!

During the late war, at evening roll-call, a captain said to his company: "Soldiers, I am ordered to detail ten men to a very dangerous service, but of the greatest importance to the army in the coming battle. I have not the heart to pick the men, for the chances are against their ever coming back. But if there are ten men in the company who will volunteer for this service, they may step two paces to the front." As the captain ceased speaking, that whole line stepped two paces forward, and stood there with every man in place, and ranks as even as before. The captain's eyes were dim, and his voice faltered as he said: "Soldiers, I thank you; I am proud to be captain of such a company." That is what we want now, brave hearts and even ranks, moving forward all together for the right.

Let every man who believes Prohibition to be the duty of the hour, act with prompt decision for himself, and he will be astonished to find how many will step forward with him. Every man who decides helps some other to decide. Let all who believe in Prohibition be alive, awake, and speak, act, and vote with high resolve and burning enthusiasm for the New Emancipation of Humanity! Then it will come!

— *Rev. James C. Fernald.*

170. WOMAN'S HOUR.

Between the past and the future hangs
  A gate that so lightly clings,
It seems a breath might put it ajar,
  Yet it never stirs, or swings;

But under the arches in silence waits
A coming hand with a touch of fate.

Beyond the gate in the distance glows
   A splendor serene and high,
A fairer glory than touches yet
   Our vision of sea and sky ;
And mellow and clear it softly clings
To the gateway's edge like a golden fringe.

Over the arches a perfume falls
   Like breath from the hills of balm,
And melody sweeps to a world in pain,
   As notes from an angel psalm ;
The song rings out, like a prophet's cry,
And tells of a day that is drawing nigh.

Beyond the portal that never swings
   Is waiting the age of gold,
The dawn of peace on the day of God,
   By poet and seer foretold ;
Who holds the key to the lofty gate?
Where lingers the hand with the touch of fate?

'Tis centuries now since the holy star
   Was aflame over Bethlehem,
And centuries old is the mighty song
   Of "Peace and good-will to men,"
The wise men came when Christ was born,
   And wise men came when he died,
And wise men wandered from Olivet
   To preach of the Crucified.

But darkly the shadows are lying yet
On the world where the cross of Christ was set.
Why lingers the hope of the world so long
After the sweep of the angel song?
Why waits the dawn that shall surely bring
The reign of glory, when Christ is king?
      While pitiful cry
      And wrathful sigh
Yet enter the ear of the Lord on high.

Ah ! wise men ruling in church and state,
   Where did you miss it — the Master's will?

His glory is waiting to flood the earth,
　His love is ready all hearts to thrill.
　　　Well may you question
　　　　Your souls in fear,
　　　What hinders the day
　　　　That should be here?
Who holds the key, since the wise men stand
Before the portals with empty hand?

Behold a strong and gentle host!
They gather from every clime and coast,
With steady faith and a purpose high,
And hearts united by holy tie;
Who runneth may read — 'tis woman's hour.
The lips, long silent, are clothed with power!
　　　The heart of the world
　　　　Has come abroad,
　　　　Its cry has entered
　　　　The ear of God,
The age of might grows old and late,
When woman stands at the mystic gate.

The wise men, toiling the world to win,
　Have sought the prisoner and set him free;
Have drenched the valleys of earth with blood,
　In giving to slaves their liberty.
They have lifted the serf to a noble place,
And wrought for half of the human race.
　　　But the golden day
　　　　For which they pray
Shall never dawn upon slave or throne,
'Till woman cometh unto her own.

She has given the world the dew of tears,
　The nations are born in her cry of pain —
The nations, that after the weary years
　Lie at her feet, the strong ones slain.
'Twas here they missed it — the Master's will —
And hindered the promise he shall fulfill,
But lo! at the arch of the mystic gate
Is woman's hand with the touch of fate.
　　　　　　　　— *Mary T. Lathrap.*

171. SILENCE IN THE CHURCHES.*

They say we must keep party politics out of the pulpit. It is too late; it is there.

The double-headed party treason by which the saloon wins as a Democrat and "holds over" as a Republican, year after year, and that works its alternating shift, debauching the public service, deflowering the public virtue, degrading the public justice, debasing the ballot, defeating the church, has formed a kind of a pulpit "trust," and regulates the output of the pulpit and the religious press according to its own damnable will, shuts one, opens another on half time, and has well-nigh buried fearless, independent patriotism in the very ministry and put a gravestone over it with the scoffer's epitaph, "The Rest is Silence."

And when some brave man holds out against it, refusing to be bought or scared or sold, it slits his ears, breaks his joints, nails him to the cross of failure, and starves his wife and children before his eyes. Do not be angry with me. What I say is of no importance, unless it is true. But I tell you that the American pulpit is well-nigh swamped with subservient, salaried, Simonaical silence — which is the most virulent and deadly form of party politics.

The spoils treason of the old parties is but the other bank of the dumb treason of the pulpit and, by means of their parallel and interoperative disloyalty to church and state alike, between them flows the putrid river of American politics, and one bank of a stream can not rebuke the other for causing the channel to deepen and hold on its way.

Peter no more denied Jesus when he swore he did not know Him, than when he warmed himself in craven acquiescence at the fires of the insulters of his Lord.

We can not, if we would, exclude politics from the pulpit, but the Prohibition Party offers it a kind of politics that will honor it and help on the kingdom. — *John G. Woolley.*

---

172. A NATION EXALTED.†

Tell me, O Voice of the Ages, what power exalteth a nation?
Is it the conquest of arms — the force of victorious battle?

---

*From an address at National Prohibition Park, N. Y., July 4, 1896.

†Read by the author at the ratification banquet, Prohibition Park, N. Y., July 4, 1896.

Swift comes the answer, "Not so; such victory ever debaseth;
France was but wayward and weak with all of Napoleon's
    triumphs.
Ruins of Rome still proclaim, 'All martial success is a shadow,
Degrading the soul of the nation;' and Wisdom hath said that
    greater
Is he who ruleth his spirit than he who taketh a city.
Never was nation exalted by prowess in carnage and warfare."

Tell me, since war so degrades, is it Wealth that exalteth a
    nation?
Answering come the words:. "Neither gold nor silver ennobles;
Know that in every land with lofty and pure aspirations
The treasure of all the Orient would not suffice for content-
    ment."

Voice of the Ages, once more: is the honor and glory of
    nations
In lineage, pedigree, rank, such as lords of the old time boasted,
Ancestry, in whose veins the bluest of blood is mingled?
"Seldom from stately mansion has come the song that up-
    lifteth,
The music that stirs the soul — the painting whose magical
    colors
Seem blended with Heaven's rare light, interwoven with heart-
    felt meaning.
From the peasant's cottage, more oft than from palace or
    throne comes the message
Waking the world to gladness,— the glory and pride of a
    nation."

Then, O Voice of the Ages, declare you that Genius exalteth?
That culture is more to be sought than riches or social distinc-
    tion?
"More to be sought; yet culture, like that of Greece, may be
    soulless,
Intellect void of God is intellect wasted, belittled."

What then, O Voice of the Ages, is Creed the hope of the na-
    tions?
Dogma against unbelief,— devotion to churchly professions?
"Not by its creed alone can a nation be truly exalted,

The greater devotion to form, the less to the substance within it.
Bigotry hath not fled since the horrors of Spain's Inquisition,
Never can faith be increased by narrow and rigid coercion.

Surely it must be Liberty, then, that exalteth a nation.
Have I not guessed it at last, O puzzling Voice of the Ages?
Can we in Freedom's land find a nation truly exalted?
Answering come reluctant the words, "Thou art still unsuccesful.
Lighted is Liberty's torch, but if not from the stars heaven-lustrous,
The light is a will o' the wisp, that leadeth astray the pilgrim.
So is it in this land where the Goddess of Liberty dwelleth.
Surely could she but know of the death and destruction about her,
Caused by the traffic in rum, where 'personal liberty' triumphs,
Liberty, casting away her torch in despair and horror,
Would vanish forevermore and leave the land to its darkness.
— Listen, O questioning one : There is naught that exalteth a nation
Save Righteousness ; this alone bringeth glory and honor eternal."

Hushed is the Voice of the Past ; but I see in the Future's horizon
Dawning the day of hope; and approaching, are three fair spirits,
Faces aglow with light, and these words on their garb interwoven, —
"For God, Home, and Country ;" "For Christ and the Church ;" "God's word and works for the many."

Already their presence illumines the ground that before was o'ershadowed :
All welcome the Ribbon of White, with Chautauqua and Christian Endeavor !
List : 'tis the Voice of the Future, the words of these Spirits of Progress :
"Prohibitionists, would you share in the glorious time that is coming ?

Quit you like men; be strong; for so shall you join in the
   triumph.
Sternly excluding forever all jealousy, strife, and injustice,
We pledge our faith and our friendship alone to the manly and
   noble."

Fades from my sight the vision. Around me are those who
   are worthy—
Worthy the proffered aid of these loftiest Spirits of Progress.
Grieve not for these who desert; we shall find them retracing
   their footsteps,—
Else 'tis the purging away of the dross that the gold can well
   banish.

Onward, then, men of the grandest reform that the world has
   yet witnessed!
Righteousness ever your watchword, and faith in the mandate
   eternal;
Faith — and the knowledge that through this standard, up-
   borne 'mid the conflict
By hands like those you have chosen, the nation will be exalted.

—Lilian M. Heath.

TOPICAL INDEX.

BALLOT.
	No.
Back to his Chrysalis	23
Brand of Cain	26
Coming Era	27
Exactly of a Size	35
First Reform	83
Ground out by a Crank	134
House that Sam Built	7
"I've Got It!"	65
Just the Same	142
Level of Civilization	101
Not a Mushroom Party	52
On Certain Adjectives	127
Prohibition's Bugle Call	78
Question for Patriots	12
Quest Magnificent	21
Red Niagara	32
Reformer, The	43
Sermon in a Saw-Mill	38
Shall Mothers Vote?	126
Song of the Hour	2
Three Views of a Whisky Bottle	34
Unfortunate Trellis	44
Voting vs. Resolving	47

CHRISTIAN ENDEAVOR.
Christian Endeavorer's Position	60
Dreaming and Waking	51
"Feed My Sheep"	49
Flower Mission	104
Great Advance	166
Master Calleth, The	114
Unfortunate Trellis	44
Vessel in Danger	36
Victor, The	19

CHURCH VOTER.
American Desert	16
Brand of Cain	26
Christian Endeavorer's Position	60
Conscience Crystallized	153
Deacon Beery's Protest	72
Exactly of a Size	35
Four Million "Christian" Murderers	139
Funeral To-day	164
Great Advance	166
Greatest Missionary Need	102
Ground out by a Crank	134
House that Sam Built	7
Midnight Scenes of a Great City	128
On a Lehigh Valley Train	157
One Beauty of Civilization	129
Our Beneficent License Laws	41
Practise vs. Professions	91
Remedy Within Reach	130
Sermon in a Saw-Mill	38
Short Story	141

	No.
Silence in the Churches	171
Three Views of a Whisky Bottle	34
Tramp's Views, A	31
Twisting and Turning	46
Unfortunate Trellis	44
Voting vs. Resolving	47
What do You Care?	71
Which are You?	92
Whisky Deacon	84

COMPROMISE.
Back to His Chrysalis	23
Conscience Crystallized	153
Deacon's Match	56
Don't Sell Your Conscience	10
"Dorlesky's Errents"	74
Forces of Battle	42
Mainspring of Triumph	8
On a Lehigh Valley Train	157
Our Beneficent License Laws	41
Politician's Wail	120
Present Crisis	81
Sense vs. License	18
Twisting and Turning	46

COWARDICE.
Don't Sell your Conscience	10
"Dorlesky's Errents"	74
Effect of Moral Cowardice	90
Farmer and His Gun	163
Indictment	39
Mainspring of Triumph	8
Present Crisis	81
Reformer, The	43
Shovel Out	33
Weakness of Local Option	133

EDUCATION.
Anti-Suffragist's Lament	25
Certainty of Progress	20
Mainspring of Triumph	8
Patriot's Ally	106
Self-Government	85
Temperance Education Law	107
Voice of Science	118
Wanted—a Boy	
Worried about Katherine	

ENTHUSIASM.
Big Four	140
Gen. Neal Dow	87
Land of Prohibition	66
Mainspring of Triumph	8
Prohibition's Bugle Call	78
Puzzled Santa Claus	161
Quest Magnificent	21
Run up the Flag	138
Song of Hope	162
Song of the Hour	2

TOPICAL INDEX.

	No
Vessel in Danger	36
White Heat	59

FINANCE.

Conscience Crystallized	153
Does it Pay?	94
Great Problem	112
Liquor and Wages	96
Queer, Isn't It	55
Red Niagara	32
What will the Farmer Do?	116

HOME.

Appeal for the Home	132
Baby Shoes	15
Case of "Personal Liberty"	28
Cost of a License	13
Difference, The	103
"Dorlesky's Errents"	74
Drink	63
Funeral To-day	164
Glorious Monument	62
Lead the Boy	152
Shall Mothers Vote?	126
Stamp it Out	4
Supreme Curse	69
Terrors of Eviction	109
Wanted — a Boy	159
What do You Care?	71
Worried About Katherine	59

INTEMPERANCE.

American Desert	16
Baby Shoes	15
Boundary Post	57
Case of "Personal Liberty"	28
Coming Era	27
Cost of a License	13
Drink	63
Glorious Monument	62
Jug an' Me an' Jim, The	17
Letter Exercise	148
Moaning of the Bar	9
On Certain Adjectives	127
Quest Magnificent	21
Six Boys	48
Song of the Sot	11
That's the Question	135
Three Views of a Whisky Bottle	34
Tramp's Views, A	31

JUSTICE.

Give them Justice	88

LABOR.

Does it Pay?	94
First Reform	83
Liquor and Wages	91
What will the Farmer Do?	166

LIBERTY.

Back to His Chrysalis	23
Case of "Personal Liberty."	28
Compulsory Morality	119
Faith and Liberty	37
First Duty of Citizens	40
Liberty	145
Mainspring of Triumph	8
"Personal Liberty" Cry	80

	No.
Question for Patriots	12
Red Niagara	32
Song of the Hour	2
Temperance Revolution	30
Unfortunate Trellis	44
White Ribbon Banner	

LICENSE.

American Desert	16
Cost of a License	13
Deacon Beery's Protest	72
Deacon's Match	56
Getting at the Root	150
Glorious Monument	62
Letter Exercise	148
Mussulman's View	6
Our Beneficent License Laws	41
Red Niagara	32
Run up the Flag	138
Sense vs. License	18
Sermon in a Saw-mill	38
Stamp it Out	4

LOCAL OPTION.

New Song of Sixpence	110
Tramp's Views, A	31
Weakness of Local Option	133

MANHOOD.

Back to His Chrysalis	23
Battle Rally	53
Calf Path	158
Christian Endeavorer's Position	60
Curtain Lecture	82
Cut Down the Tree	77
Don't Sell Your Conscience	10
"Dorlesky's Errents"	74
Effect of Moral Cowardice	90
Fanatic, A	61
Farmer and His Gun	163
Gen. Neal Dow	87
Glorious Monument	62
Ground Out by a Crank	134
"I've Got It!"	65
Mainspring of Triumph	8
Moral Warfare	137
On a Lehigh Valley Train	157
One Beauty of Civilization	129
Present Crisis	81
Prohibition's Bugle Call	78
Quest Magnificent	21
Red Niagara	32
Reformer, The	43
Run up the Flag	138
Self-Government	85
Shovel Out	83
Song of Martyrdom	76
Song of the Hour	2
Stand Firm	64
Unfortunate Trellis	44
Wanted — True Men	136
Weakness of Local Option	133
What Do You Care?	71
Which are You?	92
Woman's Answer, A	143

MORAL SUASION.

Compulsory Morality	119
Moral Suasion Not Sufficient	58

TOPICAL INDEX. 243

	No.
Only Conclusion	22
Vessel in Danger	36

NON-PARTISANSHIP.

Politician's Wail	120
Record of Non-Partisanship	160
Supreme Curse	69

ORATORY.

Big Four	140
Expression	1

PATRIOTISM.

Columbia	29
Cut Down the Tree	77
Gen. Neal Dow	87
Moral Warfare	
Our Watchword — Union!	14
People's Voice, A	154
Question for Patriots	12
Run Up the Flag	138
Self-Government	85
Song of the Hour	2
Temperance Revolution	30
Tower of Shame	124
Unfortunate Trellis	44
Wanted — True Men	136
Warning	89
White-Ribbon Banner	156

PROGRESS.

Anti-Suffragist's Lament	25
Back to His Chrysalis	23
Calf Path	158
Certainty of Progress	20
Columbia	29
Coming Era	27
Forces of Battle	42
Fundamental Reform	98
Great Advance	166
Land of Prohibition	66
Nation Exalted, A	172
Only Conclusion	22
Our Watchword—Union!	14
Present Crisis	81
Prohibition's Bugle Call	78
Reformer, The	43
Self-Government	85
Song of Hope	162
Song of the Hour	2
Temperance Revolution	30
To-morrow	95
Vessel in Danger	36
Vot der Voomans Haf Ton	24
Wanted—a Boy	159
Warning	89
What is Faith?	105
White-Ribbon Banner	156

TOTAL ABSTINENCE.

Cut Down the Tree	77
Glorious Monument	62
Gold of Right Habits	5
If	75
Liquor and Wages	96
Moaning of the Bar	9
Not from My Bottle	3
Only Conclusion	22

	No.
Run up the Flag	138
Six Boys	48
Temperance Army	121
Temperance Revolution	30

VOTER'S RESPONSIBILITY.

Brand of Cain	26
Case of "Personal Liberty"	28
Columbia	29
Core of the Rum Question	86
Cost of a License	13
Father's Woe, A	155
First Duty of Citizens	40
Funeral To-day	164
House that Sam Built	7
Letter Exercise	148
Midnight Scenes	128
Mussulman's View	6
Not from My Bottle	3
Power of Righteous Law	111
Prohibition's Bugle Call	78
Question for Patriots	12
Responsibility of Voters	45
Sailor Lad	122
Sermon in a Saw-Mill	38
Temperance Revolution	30
That's the Question	135
Three Views of a Whisky Bottle	34
Tramp's Views, A	31
Whisky Deacon	84

WATER.

Nectar of the Hills	67

WOMAN.

All the Rights She Wants	93
Anti-Suffragist's Lament	25
"Dorlesky's Errents"	74
Eve's Recompense	73
Funeral To-day, A	164
Level of Civilization	101
Remedy Within Reach	130
Shall Mothers Vote?	126
Voice of a Star	168
Vot der Voomans Haf Ton	24
What J. M. B. Thinks	50
Why?	68
Woman's Answer, A	143
Woman's Hour	170
Worried About Katherine	59

WOMAN'S CHRISTIAN TEMPERANCE UNION.

Evangelistic Dep't.

Prayer by Dr. Deems	113
Vessel in Danger	36

Dep't of Flower Mission.

Flower Mission	104

Dep't of Franchise.

All the Rights She Wants	93
Anti-Suffragist's Lament	25
"Dorlesky's Errents"	74
Eve's Recompense	73
Level of Civilization	101
Remedy Within Reach	130
Shall Mothers Vote?	126

	No.
Why ?	68
Woman's Hour	170

Dep't of Loyal Temperance Legion.

	No.
Loyal Temperance Legion	108
Puzzled Santa Claus	161
Temperance Army	121

Dep't of Mercy.

	No.
"About Ben Adhem"	147
Dawn of Mercy	100
Place in Heaven	79
Saint Monacella's Lambs	167
Simon Grub's Dream	146
Speechless, The	70

Dept't of Mothers' Meetings.

	No.
Appeal for the Home	132
Baby Shoes	15
Case of "Personal Liberty"	28, 39
Cost of a License	13
Difference, The	103
Glorious Monument	62
Lead the Boy	152
Mothers Who Wear the Ribbon White	151
New Song of Sixpence	110
Shall Mothers Vote ?	126
Terrors of Eviction	109
Wanted — a Boy	159
What Do You Care ?	71
Worried About Katherine	59

Dep't of Narcotics.

	No.
Case for Charity	90
Midnight Scenes of a Great City	28

Dep't of Peace and Arbitration.

	No.
Arsenal at Springfield	125
Decoration Day — 1882	144
Peace Hymn of the Republic	131
War God, The	131

Dep't of Prison and Jail Work.

	No.
Flower Mission	104
Sailor Lad	122

Dep't of Rescue Work for Girls.

	No.
Midnight Scenes of a Great City	128

Dep't of Scientific Temperance Instruction.

	No.
Patriot's Ally	106
Temperance Education Law	107

Dep't of Soldiers and Sailors.

	No.
Sailor Lad	122

Dep't of Temperance and Labor.

	No.
Does it Pay ?	94
Liquor and Wages	96

Dep't. of Y. W. C. T. U.

	No.
Word to the Y's	116

W. C. T. U.—General.

	No.
For God and Home	123
Great Problem	112
Master Calleth, The	114
Unfortunate Trellis	44
White-Ribbon Army	117
White-Ribbon Banner	156

www.ingramcontent.com/pod-product-compliance
Lightning Source LLC
Chambersburg PA
CBHW021409230426
43666CB00006B/679